Integrated Reporting and Performance Measurement Systems

Despite the development of innovative approaches to strengthen accountability and the quality of integrated reporting disclosures, stakeholders are increasingly demanding more objective and unambiguous data. Therefore, the use of non-financial performance measures that assist in collecting comparable information and the verification thereof by independent experts can help to establish trust in a firm's communication with its stakeholders. Certainly, non-financial information should complement mandatory financial reporting to go beyond traditional financial ratios and link them to non-financial risks and achievements. This book examines the possibility of using information provided by performance measurement systems in the process of preparing integrated reports.

It presents an overview of the integrated report from the supply side, which undoubtedly affects the quality and usefulness of the information presented as well as enhances the manner in which the data and analyses are suitable for independent assessment. The book looks at the ways in which various groups of stakeholders – management; those who prepare non-financial reports; investors – influence the scope of the key performance indicators (KPIs) used for integrated reporting purposes, and what categories of KPIs are the most significant. Further, it analyzes which performance measurement systems provide information for the different components of integrated reports.

The book is interdisciplinary, its thematic scope is at the intersection of accounting, business reporting, and business management, and thus it provides an important source of knowledge for students, scholars, and researchers of economics, finance, and management. It will also be a valuable guide for those preparing integrated reports or other forms of non-financial reporting.

Bogusława Bek-Gaik is an Associate Professor at the Faculty of Management, AGH University of Krakow, Poland.

Anna Surowiec is an Associate Professor at the Faculty of Management, AGH University of Krakow, Poland.

Routledge Studies in Accounting

44. **Artificial Intelligence in Accounting**
    Organisational and Ethical Implications
    Othmar Lehner and Carina Knoll

45. **The Financial Reporting Quality of Public Companies**
    The Cultural Dimension
    Katarzyna Mokrzycka-Kogut

46. **Strategic Pricing and Management Accounting**
    David Dugdale

47. **Statutory Audits in Europe**
    Latest Reforms and Future Challenges
    Michael Kend, Giulia Leoni, Cristina Florio and Silvia Gaia

48. **The Privatisation of British Rail**
    How Not to Run a Railway
    Sean McCartney and John Stittle

49. **The UK Accounting Standards Board, 1990–2000**
    Restoring Honesty and Trust in Accounting
    David Tweedie, Allan Cook and Geoffrey Whittington

50. **Auditing Transformation**
    Regulation, Digitalisation and Sustainability
    Edited by Jan Marton, Fredrik Nilsson and Peter Öhman

51. **Integrated Reporting and Performance Measurement Systems**
    Bogusława Bek-Gaik and Anna Surowiec

For more information about this series, please visit www.routledge.com/Routledge-Studies-in-Accounting/book-series/SE0715

Integrated Reporting and Performance Measurement Systems

Bogusława Bek-Gaik and Anna Surowiec

Routledge
Taylor & Francis Group
LONDON AND NEW YORK

First published 2024
by Routledge
4 Park Square, Milton Park, Abingdon, Oxon OX14 4RN

and by Routledge
605 Third Avenue, New York, NY 10158

Routledge is an imprint of the Taylor & Francis Group, an informa business

British Library Cataloguing-in-Publication Data
A catalogue record for this book is available from the British Library

ISBN: 978-1-032-37257-0 (hbk)
ISBN: 978-1-032-37259-4 (pbk)
ISBN: 978-1-003-33606-8 (ebk)

DOI: 10.4324/9781003336068

Typeset in Sabon LT Pro
by KnowledgeWorks Global Ltd.

Reviewers:

Prof. Ewa Walińska, Lodz University

Prof. Juan José Juste Carrión, University of Valladolid

Contents

Tables

Figures

Acknowledgment

I want to thank Prof Ewa Walińska from Lodz University and Prof. Juan José Juste Carrión from University of Valladolid their detailed review.

Introduction

Recent years have seen intensive development in financial and non-financial information reporting. The non-financial information development trend in organizational reporting and the significant increase in its importance are undoubtedly related to the transition to a knowledge-based economy, globalization, increased competition, and the harsh criticism of the informational content of financial reports (Eccles et al., 2010). Moreover, non-financial reporting responds to modern market conditions, which induce new challenges for organizations and make stakeholders expect more transparent reports, presenting the organization's value-creation process (White, 2005; Eccles et al., 2010).

New forms of corporate reporting, particularly non-financial reports, seem to help organizations provide information on value creation and business models. Moreover, they can help all stakeholders understand the overall condition of the organization and enable them to make more informed and rational business decisions. Certainly, non-financial information should complement mandatory financial reporting beyond traditional financial ratios and link them to non-financial risks and opportunities. Currently, the integrated report, though considerably controversial, is considered the most ideal form of reporting non-financial information. According to Eccles and Krzus (2010b), organizations see integrated reporting as an opportunity to communicate and implement a sustainable development strategy that creates value for shareholders in the long term while contributing to a sustainable society. Integrated reporting primarily aims to present a more holistic image of the organization by integrating economic, social, and environmental issues, risks, and impacts in a single report (e.g., Eccles et al., 2010; Maroun and Solomon, 2012).

Over the past 20 years, many proposals have aimed to improve non-financial reporting, almost all of which focus on disclosing more non-financial information and improving its quality and comparability. Since 2008, many organizations have published frameworks and guidelines for reporting non-financial information (Eccles et al., 2011). Various bodies such as the American Institute of Chartered Accountants (AICPA), the Financial Accounting Standards Board (FASB), the Global Reporting Initiative (GRI), the UN Global Compact (GC), and the Institute of Chartered Accountants in England and

DOI: 10.4324/9781003336068-1

Wales (ICAEW) have developed reporting models that formulate recommendations for the presentation of non-financial indicators (Orens and Lybaert, 2013). In 2013, the International Integrated Reporting Council (IIRC) published the integrated reporting framework (<IR> Framework), which provides guidelines for the preparation of integrated reports.

The practice of non-financial reporting is diverse. Its key form is undoubtedly integrated reporting, which integrates financial and non-financial information in one document (i.e., the integrated report). Apparently, it responds to the limitations of traditional financial reporting, which is strongly criticized, primarily for focusing on the past, omitting intangible assets, lacking information on the value-creation process and all value-creation sources, information overload, lacking a description of interrelationships between sustainable development and financial performance, lacking information on an organization's business model, and presenting unrelated information (cf. Eccles et al., 2010; Black Sun, 2012).

Integrated reporting merges two trends in corporate reporting in recent years (sustainability and corporate social responsibility [CSR] reporting) into one report.[1] Integrated reporting, based on the <IR> Framework, aims to provide a clearer, more concise, and comparable presentation of a firm's performance. It develops a single-source document that captures a holistic story about the activities of an organization, confirmed by financial and non-financial data. Integrated reporting is also a tangible result of the debate on and gradual expansion of the guidelines and frameworks for non-financial reporting, which in recent years has increasingly evolved amid a search for a solution comparable to highly regulated and generally accepted financial reporting standards.

The dynamic development of integrated reporting resulted in the need for appropriate means to facilitate its preparation. Notably, the <IR> Framework does not propose any information sources that should be used in preparing integrated reporting, nor does the international framework provide any specific measurement methods or performance indicators. It seems the requirements set by integrated reporting can be met via an information base by performance measurement systems (PMSs). Many years of developing the concept of performance measurement have induced the creation of an extensive catalog of tools, methods, and systems for performance measurement. The most important concepts of performance measurement in the literature and economic practice include the balanced scorecard (BSC), total performance scorecard (TPS), Tableau de Bord, performance pyramid, business management window, performance prism, and value-creation index. Numerous performance measurement tools developed for the internal management of an enterprise can provide strong support for the preparation of an integrated report. Therefore, PMSs are undeniable information bases for integrated reporting. They are used to formulate and implement an organization's strategies, thereby constituting significant support in the preparation of integrated reports, the purpose of which is a more coherent and effective approach to corporate reporting to "improve the quality of information available to providers of financial capital to enable a more efficient and productive allocation of capital" (IIRC, 2013d).

Over the past 20 years, many proposals have aimed to improve non-financial reporting, almost all of which focus on disclosing more non-financial information and improving its quality and comparability. Indeed, since 2008, many organizations have published frameworks and guidelines for reporting non-financial information. However, the literature is silent on the Polish context regarding the current state of integrated reporting and the preparation of integrated reports. In Poland, there is a lack of research on the perception of non-financial reporting by management, and no consensus has been reached on the main objective and purpose of non-financial reporting. Accordingly, this study explores the current state of integrated reporting in Poland, its quality, and the scope of using the information provided by PMSs in the preparation of integrated reports. It answers the following five main questions:

1 What is the quality[2] of integrated reporting in Poland and how has this quality changed over time?
2 What are the mandatory norms concerning integrated and non-financial information reporting applicable to EU companies?
3 Do various groups of stakeholders (management, preparers of non-financial reports, investors) influence the scope of key performance indicators (KPIs) used for integrated reporting purposes?
4 Which PMSs can provide information for different components of integrated reports?
5 What categories of KPIs are the most significant for integrated reporting?
6 Which lessons can be learned to further develop integrated reporting and, particularly, improve the quality of the information provided and the reliability and comparability thereof?

Chapter 1 discusses the issues regarding the development of the non-financial information trend in accounting, starting with a criticism of the traditional reporting model. It also discusses definitions of non-financial information, emphasizing their ambiguity. The chapter presents non-financial reporting's voluntary and legal standards and requirements and a systematic review of the published research results on integrated reporting.

Chapter 2 focuses on the key form of reporting non-financial information: an integrated report. It presents the concepts of integrated reporting, its genesis, fundamental concepts, and content elements. The chapter discusses the informative and transformational function of the integrated report and the internal determinants of integrated reporting preparation in the organization.

Chapter 3 discusses the importance of PMSs for integration, which, according to the authors, can provide strong support in the preparation of an integrated report. The PMS is a source of information disclosed in an integrated report to provide a more coherent and effective approach to corporate reporting and improve the quality of information available to providers of financial capital for a more efficient and productive allocation of capital. The selected PMSs are also discussed.

Chapters 4 and 5 present the results of the authors' research on the practice of disclosures in integrated reporting (2013–2020) in Poland and the use of information provided by different PMSs for integrated reporting.

The empirical research regards the qualitative assessment of integrated reporting of Polish companies (2013–2020). The study also indicates the possibility of improving the process of preparing an integrated report in the organization by using the information provided by different PMSs. Using information provided by different PMSs for integrated reporting was analyzed using case studies of integrated reports prepared by selected capital groups. Moreover, it presents the results from questionnaire surveys on the assessment of the level of knowledge about integrated reporting, factors determining the implementation of this type of reporting, and the scope and possibility of supporting the preparation of integrated reports by different PMSs.

Notes

1 The predecessors of integrated reporting include reports on sustainable development and corporate social responsibility and the BSC and triple bottom line. J. Elkington, an expert in social responsibility and sustainable development, coined the term "People, Planet and Profit," which has become popular in literature as the triple bottom line.

2 The quality of integrated reporting is defined per the purpose of the research conducted by Pistoni et al. (2018).

1 Non-financial information in accounting

1.1 Criticism of the financial statement model and its evolution

Recently, significant changes have occurred in all spheres of the economy, including accounting as an information system. In the era of globalization, stakeholder expectations have changed significantly, and accounting has become a source of reliable, transparent, and comparable information about the business activity of the company and sources of value creation in the organization intended for all groups of stakeholders. Notably, accounting must respond to the needs of users, and when the needs change, it must adapt and offer information in a form that meets these needs.

The financial statement, as the final product of the accounting system and the basic element of the company's information policy, has recently been severely criticized, particularly after subsequent economic crises, which proves the weaknesses of the current reporting model.[1] Questions often asked include the following: what will be the target reporting model? What role will the financial statement play in it?

Shortcomings mentioned by stakeholders regarding the financial statements concern the following:

- Historical nature of the information contained in the financial statements
- Financial statements' high degree of complexity and, thus, challenges in their interpretation
- Ambiguity of the financial statement structure
- Incomplete presentation of all company resources (e.g., lack of information on intellectual and relational capital)
- Lack of information on the company's business model in the financial statements

Currently, prospective information on the company's strategy and plans and all sources of risk and uncertainty are of particular importance to investors and other stakeholders. Hence, the main drawback of financial reporting is the historical nature of the information in financial statements. Undoubtedly, the most important information stakeholders expect from the organizations'

DOI: 10.4324/9781003336068-2

reports is information on value, which, according to Walińska et al. (2016, p. 18), induced a change in purpose and measurement rules in management and financial accounting, given the transition from the measurement of profit to measuring value. Moreover, traditional reporting has been criticized for focusing on short-term performance and a retrospective approach. Further, financial reporting provides information regarding the past, whereas users need information about the future. Financial reports also lack disclosure regarding risks and uncertainty. Issues on the lack of information about the organization's business were also raised. Given the shortcomings of traditional financial statements and research on stakeholder expectations, a good report should

- Be the result of an integrated accounting system (financial and management) (cf. Sobańska, 2003, p. 248)
- Be a tool for implementing a company strategy
- Reflect the business model of the company
- Show the current financial condition of the company
- Consider the conditions of the organization's environment
- Contain warning signals for the future
- Show the organization's sustainability performance
- Inform on the value of the organization
- Provide a clear and detailed explanation of the relationship between financial and non-financial performance

Another challenge for financial statements in the global environment is to extend the scope of the use of modern technologies such as eXtensible Business Reporting Language (Samelak, 2013, p. 111). Identifying the needs of stakeholders has become a challenge in searching for a new reporting model for the organization (Walińska, 2014, 2015).

Researchers argue that financial information alone is insufficient to ensure an accurate picture of the current and future performance of an organization. In response to these imperfections in corporate reporting, great interest has been gained in reporting non-financial information for transparency, accountability, and the link between organizations and stakeholders. While traditional financial information is relevant to the presentation of performance, non-financial information is fundamental for understanding the presented results. Non-financial reporting goes beyond the traditional financial dimension and covers other dimensions, such as social and ecological, which are extremely important to assess the performance of the organization.

According to Lev and Zarowin (1999), a decrease in the importance of financial information to explain organizational value induces the recognition that the information contained in financial statements is insufficient to meet the information needs of stakeholders to assess the organization's performance.

Currently, there is a need to extend the scope of information reporting and improve transparency. This need results from modern management theories, such as the theories of social responsibility, stakeholders, and legitimacy (Borys, 2005, p. 353), which emphasize the organization's responsibility toward all stakeholders and thus better transparency of financial statements.

Criticism of financial report content has induced many restructuring actions to improve it (Walińska et al., 2016, p. 18). Such activities comprise two basic groups: the change in the structure and form of the reporting model and the increase in the information content of financial reports (Bek-Gaik, 2015). The first group comprises the proposal of the business concept of financial statements, such as the Staff Draft of Exposure Draft, International Financial Reporting Standards (IFRS) X, Financial Statement Presentation (IFRS, 2010),[2] and the introduction of the concept of comprehensive income. The second group comprises an improvement of financial reporting, focusing mainly on supplementing traditional financial data with non-financial information, which increased the information content of the management commentary and, above all, the idea of integrated reporting.

An attempt to modify the financial statements was extremely important[3] and yielded the development by the International Accounting Standards Board (IASB) and Financial Accounting Standards Board (FASB) of the Staff Draft of Exposure Draft, IFRS X, financial statement presentation, which proposed far-reaching changes in the structure and informative content of financial statements (IFRS, 2010). The draft specifies the following components of the financial statements:

- Statement of financial position at the end of the period (balance sheet)
- Statement of profit or loss and other comprehensive income for the period
- Statement of cash flows for the period
- Statement of changes in equity for the period
- Notes, comprising a summary of significant accounting policies and other explanatory notes

In all components of the financial statements, except for explanatory notes, the following sections were distinguished:

a Business section containing (1) an operating category (with an operating finance subcategory) and (2) an investing category
b Financing section, containing a debt category, and an equity category
c Income tax section
d Discontinued operation section
e Multi-category transaction section

Other restructuring activities in the financial reporting area involved:

- Introducing a new concept (comprehensive income) of presenting an income statement
- Developing a proposal for changes in the scope of disclosure

- Work on changing the information structure of financial statements; that is, developing its business formula (Staff Draft of Exposure Draft)
- Introducing new information content of the management commentary
- Work on integrated reporting

Moreover, in connection with the need to disclose non-financial information, the conviction of the need to integrate financial and management accounting is growing, and the recognition of the mutual interpenetration of financial and managerial information in the financial statement yields an increase in the scope of financial statements (Sobańska, 2003, p. 248).

The growing significance of non-financial reporting stems from enterprises' pursuit of social responsibility. Stakeholders require information on an organization's ecological, social responsibility, and ethical performance (Ernst and Young, 2011), which is not fully provided by financial statements. Hence, there is a need to include non-financial information in the content of the report or supplement existing financial statements with new, separate reports to ensure all stakeholders are satisfied. Further, according to the literature, voluntary non-financial disclosures reduce information asymmetry between organizations and investors (Albers and Günther, 2010).

The disclosure of non-financial information together with financial statements helps stakeholders understand the organization's business model and the ability to create value and enable rational investment decisions.

Considering these facts, reporting should be based on two main types of reporting: financial and non-financial. Disclosing non-financial information with financial statements can help stakeholders understand the general condition of the organization and enable more rational business decisions. Therefore, non-financial information should supplement financial information beyond traditional financial indicators.

Based on a review of the literature, the development of company reporting makes it possible to distinguish the stages in the development of reporting (Table 1.1): financial reporting, sustainability reporting, and integrated reporting (Bobitan and Petru, 2017). According to Marcinkowska (2004), "the changes observed in reporting can be divided into four aspects: financial information is supplemented by non-financial data, quantitative information is supported by descriptions, disclosure of information is not only mandatory but also voluntary, and information is both retrospective and with some prospective view."

Despite significant changes in recent years, the current reporting model still requires improvement. The improvement of financial statements and the increase in information scope remain ongoing because in a dynamically changing environment, there is a growing demand for transparent and reliable financial and non-financial information. Thus, to obtain a credible picture of the organization and demonstrate its sustainability and attractiveness to investors, companies must meet the needs of stakeholders by disclosing financial and non-financial information, which would show a sustainable development

Table 1.1 Evolution of organizational non-financial reporting

Stages in the development of non-financial reporting	*New regulations, practices, and literature*
The beginnings of non-financial reporting	White (1999) – first mention of integrated reporting in the literature
	2000 – Global Reporting Initiative (GRI), Sustainability reporting guidelines
	2000 – UN Global Compact Leaders' Summit – call for adopting sustainable and socially responsible policies, and to report on their implementation
	2002 – Sarbanes-Oxley ACT (rising questions about the transparency of corporate environmental disclosure)
The CSR and sustainability reporting	White (2005) – Fade, Integrate or Transform? The Future of CSR
	2005 – KPMG International Survey of Corporate Responsibility Reporting, Amsterdam, KPMG
	March 2006 – European Alliance for Corporate Social Responsibility launched by the European Commission
	2008 – KPMG International Survey of Corporate Responsibility Reporting, Amsterdam, KPMG
	2008–2009 – firsts responsibility reports issued
The integrated reporting	Eccles and Krzus (2010b) – Integrated Reporting for a Sustainable Strategy
	2011 – IIRC Discussion Paper Towards Integrated Reporting – Communicating Value in the 21st Century
	Adams and Simnett (2011) – integrated reporting for Australia's not-for-profit sector
	Eccles and Saltzman (2011) – survey on determinants of integrated reporting
	Maroun and Solomon (2012) – integrated reporting in South Africa
	2012 – Raddley Yelda, socially responsible investors and analysts
	2013 – IIRC, The International <IR> Framework
	2014 – The EU Non-Financial Reporting Directive (which requires large companies in the EU to disclose social, environmental, and diversity information)
	2021 – IIRC, The International <IR> Framework, amended

Source: Own elaboration, based on Dragu and Tudor-Tiron (2013).

strategy in various types of reports. However, there are questions regarding how stakeholders understand the information disclosed. Can stakeholders understand the links between financial and non-financial information?

The process of improving the quality of the reporting model is accompanied by changes to increase information on non-financial companies' activities and social responsibility. Therefore, following a firm's reporting changes, the five basic stages of its development include the following (Walińska, 2015):

1 Financial statement covering only financial data
2 Financial statement extended by non-financial information contained in the explanatory notes

3 Annual report covering financial statements (financial data and explanatory notes) and other non-financial information
4 Management commentary next to the annual report
5 Multiple reports: beyond the annual report and the management commentary, other reports have been created, such as corporate social responsibility (CSR) reports, environmental reports, sustainability reports, and reports on corporate governance (Walińska, 2015, p. 154)

Currently, the next stage in the development of the organization's reporting can be distinguished: the modern concept of integrated reporting, combining the features of many different reports in the form of a comprehensive document.

The key stages in the development of organizational reporting involve (Bobitan and Petru, 2017, p. 95):

1 Financial statement
2 Financial report – financial statement supplemented by additional information and reports: management decisions, governance and remuneration, and environment reporting
3 Business report – financial statement extended with additional reports, focused on a business model:
    - Report on CSR
    - Report on intellectual capital
    - Other reports
4 Integrated report – statement providing financial and non-financial information to create and sustain value over time

Non-financial information should complement mandatory financial reporting to go beyond traditional financial ratios. Undoubtedly, non-financial reporting is currently the most important trend in the development of corporate reporting to improve the information in annual reports, given the growing needs of stakeholders. In a highly competitive economy driven by globalization, one of the most important issues critical to business development is the information and communication process.

The path to better reporting continues with the new Directive (2014/95/EU) (Bobitan and Petru, 2017) on non-financial and diversity disclosures to ensure that large public-interest entities in Europe provide a comprehensive and substantive picture of their position and performance. Starting in 2017, this directive requires entities subject to regulations to reveal an annual non-financial report in the management commentary. The report should contain, at a minimum, information on environmental, social, and governance (ESG) issues that should enable stakeholders to understand the organization's performance, including

- A short description of the organization's business model
- Information on the policies applied in the noted areas, including all implemented due diligence processes

- Result and effects of the policies
- The main risks associated with the organization's activities, business relationships, products, and services, which may adversely affect the noted areas and how the organization manages these risks
- Presentation of the most important key indicators of non-financial performance

Entities that will apply this new directive must provide non-financial reports containing information on social, employee, and anti-corruption issues; ecological issues; and respect for human rights. The European Union (EU) Commission has published non-binding guidelines to help companies disclose relevant non-financial information more consistently and comparably, including key indicators of non-financial, general, and sectoral performance.

Summing up the development of non-financial information is already a reality; however, there remain problems and dilemmas related to its disclosure. Currently, integrated reporting is the latest trend in reporting models.

Integrated reporting, as a new global trend of corporate reporting, presents a business model of the organization and the process of creating value. The types and effectiveness of resources used in the organization's activity enable stakeholders to assess the ability of the organization to create value in the short, medium, and long term and help users assess the long-term profitability of enterprises. Thus, they can more effectively allocate limited resources.

1.2 Disclosure of non-financial information in organization's reporting – Research review

The issue of disclosing non-financial information is a subject of interest to various authors. Most studies are primarily concerned with reporting CSR activities (CSR reports) and integrated reporting. The following issues were raised in this area of research:

- Scope and quality of the information presented
- Standards and guidelines for reporting non-financial information
- Relationship between non-financial disclosures, mainly in the CSR field, and financial results
- Usefulness of non-financial information

Studies on integrated reporting concerns

- Factors affecting the development of integrated reporting
- The relationship between integrated reporting, sustainability reports, and CSR reports
- The problem of verification of non-financial information included in the integrated report
- Costs and benefits of implementing integrated reporting
- Information base for integrated reporting

- Use of performance measurement systems (PMSs) in the process of preparing an integrated report
- The quality of disclosures in integrated reports (Bek-Gaik and Surowiec, 2019)

An important part of this research concerns the practice of integrated reporting and focuses on the following problems:

- The information content of integrated reports
- The compliance of published integrated reports with the integrated reporting framework
- Determining the benefits of implementing integrated reporting within the organization

The conducted research on non-financial disclosures in the organization's reporting involves

- An analysis of the content of non-financial disclosures (CSR reports, integrated reports, and management commentary)
- A relationship of non-financial disclosures with the financial performance of the organization
- The usefulness of non-financial information
- The quality of non-financial disclosures

Many CSR studies focus on CSR regarding the content[4] and impact of CSR disclosures on organizational performance (Table 1.2), especially its impact on financial performance (Bek-Gaik and Rymkiewicz, 2014; Li and Li, 2018; Chen et al., 2019). In general, the noted studies can be divided into those that show a positive relationship between CSR and financial performance indicators, a negative relationship, and no statistically significant relationship.

Vance (1975) and Cochran and Wood (1984) demonstrate the negative impact of CSR on financial performance. Vance (1975), in his research on a sample of socially responsible companies in "Survey of Businessmen" from 1972 and in "How Business School Students Rate Corporations" from 1972, showed that companies with higher social responsibility have a lower stock exchange value. In turn, the study by Cochran and Wood (1984) was conducted on a sample of 61 companies in two periods: 1970–1974 and 1975–1979. The results show a strong correlation between CSR and the age of assets.

The second group includes studies that show a positive relationship between CSR disclosure and financial performance indicators. Ngwakwe (2008) studies 60 production companies in Nigeria during the 1997–2006 period and shows a positive relationship between CSR (expressed by three indicators: health and safety of employees, waste management, and social development) and the return on total assets. In turn, Cheng et al. (2014b), based on a sample of 10,078 observations from 2002 to 2009, show a positive relationship

Table 1.2 Selected studies on CSR disclosures and their impact on financial performance measures

Authors	*Research description*	*Outcomes*
Bowman and Haire (1975)	Research on the interaction between corporate social responsibility (CSR) and profit performance; the study analyzed 82 companies in the food-processing industry during 1973	Companies presenting data on CSR obtain a higher return on equity (ROE)
Vance (1975)	Survey of the relationship between social responsibility and a change in stock prices in 1972 (90 companies)	There is a negative relationship between the results of a survey conducted among businessmen and students and a change in stock prices
Waddock and Graves (1997)	Examination of the relationship between corporate social performance (CSP) and financial performance among 469 companies (1989–1990)	CSP is positively associated with prior financial performance. CSP is also positively associated with future financial performance
Orlitzky et al. (2003)	Quantitative study on the relationship between CSP and financial performance; the study conducted a meta-analysis of 52 studies, with a total sample of 33,878 observations	The meta-analytic findings suggest that CSR and, to a lesser extent, environmental responsibility are likely to pay off, although there is no strong positive association between CSP and corporate financial performance (CFP)
Fiori et al. (2007)	The research on the impact of voluntary CSR disclosures on the price of shares in the 2004–2006 period on the example of 25 companies	There is a lack of correlation between CSR and the price of shares, a statistically insignificant correlation
Mittal et al. (2008)	Examination of relationships between economic value added (EVA) and CSR, 50 companies from the S&P CNX index in the 2001–2005 period	There is little evidence that companies with a code of ethics would generate significantly more EVA and market value added than those without codes
Ngwakwe (2008)	Research on the relationship between sustainable business practice and firm performance; the study employed a field survey to study 60 manufacturing companies in Nigeria in the 1997–2006 period	The sustainable practices of the "responsible" firms are significantly related to firm performance, and sustainable practices are inversely related to fines and penalties
Godfrey et al. (2009)	Research on the relationship between CSR and shareholder value among 160 companies, with 180 observations on events affecting the price of shares in the 1993–2003 period	Participation in institutional CSR activities (aimed at a firm's secondary stakeholders or society at large) provides an "insurance-like" benefit, while participation in technical CSRs (activities targeting a firm's trading partners) yields no such benefits

(*Continued*)

Table 1.2 (Continued)

Authors	*Research description*	*Outcomes*
Cellier and Chollet (2010)	Research on market response to publishing CSR ratings among 739 companies, with 1,838 events in the 2004–2009 period	Publishing information on CSR has a positive effect on the stock market
di Donato and Izzo (2012)	Research on the impact of CSP on stock prices of Italian listed companies among 32 firms listed at the Milan Stock Exchange in the 2004–2008 period	A good social performance negatively influences stock prices in the Italian Stock Exchange Market
Pawłowski and Wąsowska (2012)	The study compared the letters of management boards to shareholders of socially responsible companies (i.e., those in the Respect index of the Warsaw Stock Exchange) and companies that are not socially responsible. It determined whether the vocabulary regarding CSR is used to a greater extent in socially responsible companies	A comparative study using Wilcoxon Matched-Pairs Signed-Ranks Test confirmed the examined relationship
Tang et al. (2012)	Research on the CSR and CFP relationship; longitudinal data collected from 130 firms from 1995 to 2007–2007	Firms benefit more when they adopt a CSR engagement strategy that is consistent, involves related dimensions of CSR, and involves aspects of CSR that are more internal to the firm. However, the pace of the CSR engagement strategy does not moderate the relationship between CSR and CFP. This study shows that, regardless of contextual factors, a firm can choose the proper strategy to enhance the financial benefits of CSR engagement
Dobrescu (2013)	Research on the correlation between CSR actions and companies' value on the sample of 101 important companies in Romania (2011–2012)	CSR activity is partially influenced by financial strength, market position, and value for a company, not the other way around; second, CSR activity is facilitated by companies having a larger number of employees

(*Continued*)

Table 1.2 (Continued)

Authors	*Research description*	*Outcomes*
Bek-Gaik and Rymkiewicz (2014)	Research on the relationship between CSR and financial performance measures on the sample of companies included in the WIG30 index; the study employed a dichotomic variable indicating whether a given company revealed information on CSR in annual, social, or environmental reports to describe the social responsibility of business. The following measures of financial performance were used: accounting variables (ROE, return on assets [ROA], net profitability, operational profitability) and market variables (market price to profit [p/e], market price to book value [P/bv], market price to cash flow [p/cf], and dividend rate)	The correlation analysis showed a poor correlation between the variable describing CSR and other variables; the strongest relationship occurred between CSR and P/BV. Linear regression analysis showed that social reporting negatively (positively) impacts the p/bv (operational profitability ratio)
Cheng et al. (2014b)	Research on whether superior performance on CSR strategies induces better access to finance on the sample of 10,078 observations in the 2002–2009 period	Firms with better CSR performance face significantly lower capital constraints, and better stakeholder engagement and transparency around CSR performance are important in reducing capital constraints
Gregory et al. (2014)	Research on the effect of CSR on firm value seeks to identify the source of that value, with 13,089 firm-year observations over the 1992–2009 period	The valuation effects are principally driven by CSR performance associated with better long-run growth prospects
Bek-Gaik and Rymkiewicz (2015a)	Research on the relations between CSR and the CFP on the sample of companies included in the WIG30 Index and mWIG40 Index (financial institutions were excluded from the study, i.e., banks and insurance companies)	Companies reporting CSR issues gain higher revenues and profits and have a greater asset value
Otola and Tylec (2016)	Research on the relation between expenditure on CSR and the profitability of the company (ROA, ROE, and the gross margin to sales ratio) on the sample of selected companies listed on the Warsaw Stock Exchange (including NewConnect)	It cannot be concluded that CSR expenditure increases with the increase in the profitability of assets

(*Continued*)

Table 1.2 (Continued)

Authors	*Research description*	*Outcomes*
Sobczyk (2016)	Research to determine the impact of CSP on CFP in the example of companies included in the RESPECT Index portfolio of the Warsaw Stock Exchange. Thus, the study employed a literature review and statistical analysis (descriptive statistics) for the 2008–2014 period	The social responsibility of companies included in the RESPECT Index, as reflected in financial performance, cannot be expected
Wang et al. (2016)	The study empirically tests the curvilinear relationship between CSP and CFP, using a data set of 30 international construction companies and 210 firm-year observations over the sample period from 2007 to 2013	The curvilinear relationship of CSP on return on assets and earnings per share as specific CFP measures is strongly supported

Source: Own elaboration.

between better CSR performance expressed in the Composite CSR Index (based on ESG indicators developed by Thomson Reuters ASSET4, 2013)[5] and significantly lower capital constraints. Tang et al. (2012), based on a research sample covering 130 companies from the MSCI ESG database from 1998 to 2007, show that the company's financial performance decreases if the disclosures regarding CSR performance are inconsistent (i.e., sporadic or occasional) (Tang et al., 2012).

Studies that did not show a statistically significant relationship between financial and CSR performance include Mittal et al. (2008) and Brine et al. (2006). Notably, Orlitzky et al. (2003) study the relationship between the social and environmental performance of an enterprise and its financial performance. They show a positive correlation between corporate social performance and corporate financial performance (CFP).

The relevant literature also includes studies conducted to assess the impact of CSR on share prices, including Donato and Izzo (2012), who show a negative impact of CSR practices on share prices, based on a sample of 32 Italian companies listed on the Milan Stock Exchange that published social reports from 2004 to 2008. Cellier and Chollet (2010) show a positive relationship between Vigeo[6] rating announcements (2004–2009) and short-term European stock returns. The literature also shows a lack of significant impact on the share price of companies, demonstrated, inter alia, by Fiori et al. (2007).

These diverse research results confirm the challenges in determining the impact of disclosing CSR activities on an organization's financial performance. It has not been unequivocally proven that non-financial disclosures on CSR positively impact financial performance measures. Table 1.2 presents the list of related studies.

Another group of studies concerns the usefulness of non-financial information. However, their conclusions are ambiguous. For example, Coram et al. (2011) state that financial analysts pay attention to non-financial information, especially in companies where financial information shows a positive trend. Cohen et al. (2011) indicated that socially responsible investors use non-financial information when making decisions. However, they confirmed that financial analysts use non-financial information when valuing shares.

Research by Chojnacka and Jadanowska (2020) in Poland showed that respondents, in most cases, do not use non-financial information to evaluate companies. Szadziewska et al. (2018) assessed the quality of disclosed non-financial information and concluded that it was diverse. This finding accords with the results of other studies. A quality analysis of non-financial disclosure was conducted by Mazzotta et al. (2020). The authors examined whether the introduction of requirements to disclose non-financial information affects their credibility. From the material legitimacy theory perspective, the non-financial disclosures of 31 Italian Financial Times Stock Exchange (FTSE) MIB-listed companies for the 2017 fiscal year were examined. The credibility index was constructed based on content analysis using an operational framework based on Habermas idealism. The authors understood credibility as a multidimensional construct comprising three sub-dimensions: truth, sincerity, appropriateness, and understandability. The research results show that the obligatory disclosure of Italian FTSE MIB companies is credible. Tables 1.3 and 1.4 present studies on the usefulness and quality of non-financial information.

Another area of research on non-financial disclosures is integrated reporting, which contains the largest number of non-financial disclosures. These studies remain in dynamic development. Research results in this area are ambiguous. Some authors demonstrate the usefulness of this form of reporting in various stakeholder groups. Researchers also highlight the increasing complexity of such reports. Some identify a general tendency of not disclosing information that seems to be crucial to the IIRC's assumptions – information about the organization's value-creation process and insufficient disclosures on organizational performance – the lack of some indicators that would allow a full analysis of the organization's activities, and the lack of forward-looking disclosures. Other studies confirm these tendencies (Eccles et al., 2015).

Perego et al. (2016) conducted research on the perception of integrated reporting by management. In their interviews, key experts influencing global integrated reporting practices noted that, in most organizations, there is currently a poor understanding of the "value" of integrated reporting. They also indicate that the adoption of integrated reporting can stimulate internal organizational change and related benefits. Other studies on integrated reporting indicated an imbalance between the scope of information companies want to reveal and the scope of information required by users. Most studies also noticed that integrated reports are becoming increasingly extensive

Table 1.3 Research on the usefulness of non-financial information

Authors	*Research description*
Belkaoui (1976)	Research on the impact of disclosing information on expenditure on pollution control on company share prices using a sample of 100 companies. The disclosure of information on pollution control expenditure had a positive but temporary impact on the rate of return
Anderson and Frankle (1980)	Research on the impact of disclosures regarding social responsibility on the capital market using companies of the Fortune 500 list in the 1972–1973 period. The findings indicate that social disclosure has information content, and the market values this disclosure positively
Belkaoui and Karpik (1989)	An attempt to verify seven hypotheses on the relationship between deciding to disclose social information and social performance, political visibility, financial variables, and economic performance. The decision to disclose social information is mainly affected by social performance and political visibility
Luo and Bhattacharya (2006)	Examination of relationships between corporate social responsibility (CSR), customer satisfaction, firm market value, and corporate abilities (innovativeness capability and product quality) using a sample of 113 companies in the 2001–2004 period. CSR has a positive significant impact on customer satisfaction
Bescos et al. (2007)	Analysis of non-financial and financial information disclosed by 250 of the largest French-listed companies in their financial reporting. The study examined the usefulness, credibility, and comparability of this information, using a sample of the largest French companies listed on the Paris Stock Exchange. Generally – the quality of disclosed information is not bad, but it can be significantly improved
Coram et al. (2011)	Research on the usefulness of non-financial information when performing stock-price valuations. The study examined whether a wider disclosure of non-financial performance indicators affects the decision-making processes of financial analysts when valuing shares. The behavior related to information processing and types of information used by analysts in the valuation process was analyzed. Financial analysts focus on non-financial information, especially in enterprises where financial information shows a positive trend. Financial information received greater attention when the trend was negative
Krasodomska (2014)	The study identifies non-financial information and determines its significance in the reporting of public companies and develops a new disclosure model in business reports. The author formulated the hypothesis, according to which the evolution of enterprises' reporting aimed to expand non-financial information
Dyduch (2015)	The subject of the study is the consolidated annual reports for 2013 of six capital groups, whose parent units are listed at the Warsaw Stock Exchange (WSE). The scope of disclosed environmental financial information in supplementary information and management commentary is small and concerns mainly the rights to emit greenhouse gases, environmental protection reserves, and subsidies for pro-ecological investments. The diverse forms of revealing this information in the surveyed reports make it difficult to compare even within the same industry

(*Continued*)

Table 1.3 (Continued)

Authors	*Research description*
Dziawgo (2016)	The study presents the results of a survey conducted on a sample of over 400 Polish individual investors. This survey was conducted by the Association of Individual Investors. It employed the following research methods: descriptive method, comparative method, analysis of the literature on the subject, and survey method. Integrated reporting is positively evaluated by institutional investors and individual investors. Therefore, it is the expected direction of changes in the financial market. However, the question remains open on how to achieve this change at the lowest expenditure
Dyduch and Krasodomska (2017)	The study examined 60 non-financial listed companies included in the WIG30 and WIG40 indexes of the WSE. The analysis concerned CSR disclosures presented by firms in annual reports (management commentary) (56 cases) and integrated reports (four cases) published for 2014. The results indicate positive relationships between disclosure of CSR and the profitability of the organization, measured by company turnover and belonging to the environment-sensitive industry. However, no relationship was found between CSR disclosure and profitability, financial leverage, the board size, or the number of women on the board. The results of the research confirmed the relationship between the reputation of the organization and the quality of CSR disclosure in the case of two of the four considered variables: the duration of the stock exchange listing and inclusion in the Respect Index of WSE
Matuszak and Różańska (2017)	Research on 150 listed companies based in Poland. The analysis included CSR information published in management reports in separate CSR reports prepared at the end of 2015, presented on websites in July 2017. The results show that companies present the voluntary disclosure of CSR in annual reports. In most cases, the CSR disclosure did not comply with the new requirements. Companies put little emphasis on human rights-related and anti-corruption issues. It suggests that new reporting requirements should increase the scope and quality of non-financial disclosures of Polish-listed companies
Melloni et al. (2017)	Research on the quality of non-financial disclosure that determines the usability of this information. The study analyzed information presented in reports, focusing on conciseness, completeness, and objectivity of information. It employed a sample of early integrated reports, showing that companies with poor financial results prepare integrated reports that are usually much longer, less readable (less concise), and more optimistic (less complete). Moreover, companies with worse social performance prepare reports that are less illegible and contain less information on sustainability performance (less complete). The initially published integrated reports use thematic and verbal manipulation to make a positive impression. Such a strategy depends on the level of the company's performance between financial and non-financial companies. Generally, there is no confirmation of high-quality non-financial information, which reduces their usability

(*Continued*)

Table 1.3 (Continued)

Authors	*Research description*
Peršić and Halmi (2017)	Research on the scope and quality of non-financial information disclosed by Croatian hospitality companies in non-financial (sustainability) reports after the Directive 2014/95/EU and Croatian Accounting Act. The study employed the case study method to explore the specifics of non-financial reporting in the hospitality industry. Environmental issues, work practice, and social aspects (overall result is 7.67 out of 30) had the highest quality score on timeliness. Reliability and comparability of information and issues of products and human rights had the lowest quality score. The results indicate the need to determine the framework for the disclosure of non-financial information to make it useful for internal and external users
Walińska and Gad (2017)	The study, based on literature studies, analyzed the relations between the financial statement, the management report, the integrated report, and the reporting practice of public companies related to disclosing financial and non-financial data. It examined reports prepared for 2015 by companies listed at the WSE included in the WIG 30 index. Reports prepared by the Orlen Group in 2015 provided an in-depth analysis of the subject
Czaja-Cieszyńska (2018)	Research on the level of reporting non-financial information in non-governmental organizations in Poland. The study conducted a quantitative and qualitative analysis of non-financial reports of Polish NGOs published in the international register of Global Reporting Initiative and the Polish register of CSRinfo. The qualitative analysis showed that all analyzed reports mainly present information of a social nature, which is related to the specific nature of the non-governmental organizations. In other aspects (i.e., economic and environmental), most entities disclose little to no information
Dissanayake and Ekanayake (2018)	Research on the user preferences on environmental reporting of the companies listed in the Colombo Stock Exchange in Sri Lanka. The study investigated whether the environmental disclosures fulfill the information needs of the users, considering two fundamental (i.e., relevance and faithful representation) and four enhancing (i.e., comparability, verifiability, understandability, and timeliness) qualitative characteristics. The users of environmental reports do not read reports perceived to be irrelevant or faithfully represented; instead, the users need such reports to be shown in a balanced manner (containing positive and negative information) and be provided with future-oriented information, demonstrating top management's commitment to those issues
Szadziewska et al. (2018)	Research on 53 companies, revealing that the form of disclosures is diverse. Most often, non-financial information was presented in management reports. The scope of the information presented was also varied. Companies from the chemical and energy industry presented the most non-financial data. The following factors influenced the publishing of this type of information: the company's size, its market value, and the industry to which it belongs

(*Continued*)

Table 1.3 (Continued)

Authors	*Research description*
Walińska et al. (2018)	The main aim of the article was the attempt to classify the integrated report as a financial or non-financial report by analyzing its information content. The article also determines how the form of the integrated report was changing and what relations existed between this type of report, the financial statement, and the management report. The analysis comprised integrated reports published by companies listed on the WSE in the 2013–2016 period. There was no uniform structure and scope to this report, although the report contained mainly non-financial information. Financial information occurred occasionally or did not occur at all
Artene et al. (2020)	Research on the changes generated by the EU Directive 2014/95 regarding how oil entities listed at the Bucharest Stock Exchange and the Athens Stock Exchange between 2014 and 2018 reported environment-related information. The study examined whether polluting entities in industries were more sensitive to environmental factors and whether they tended to report more information relative to other business sectors. Entities operating in important polluting industries demonstrate transparency regarding the efforts and investments made to counteract the environmental impacts
Bilski and Zawadzki (2020)	Research on the evolution process of financial reports over the past five years on the example of selected companies listed on the WSE. Annual reports were analyzed. The results demonstrate the quantity, quality, and way of presenting the information to users
Chojnacka and Jadanowska (2020)	Research on 37 companies to ascertain two research hypotheses: (1) the disclosed non-financial information is useful for the enterprise in decision-making processes; (2) despite the existence of the benefits of disclosing non-financial information, enterprises publish it mainly for legal requirements. In most cases, respondents do not use non-financial information to evaluate other entities. Moreover, they do not include them in the strategic, decision-making process and operational management

Source: Own elaboration.

and contain much unrelated data, which makes them more challenging to understand and less substantive, creating informational chaos (Bek-Gaik and Surowiec, 2019). According to one study, organizations do not prepare and implement integrated reports because investors lack interest in such reports (Cheng et al., 2014a) (Table 1.5).

In summary, research on the disclosure of non-financial information shows that information on the organization's social responsibility and sustainability has been widely accepted as information of fundamental significance and a strategic element of external reporting. Studies also show that organizations that present such information gain market benefits, and some have proven the positive impact of non-financial disclosures on the performance and value of the organization. Other empirical research (Adams and Simnett, 2011, pp. 1–41; Cohen et al., 2012, pp. 65–90) indicates that stakeholder

Table 1.4 Research on the quality of non-financial disclosures

Authors	*Research description*
Gad (2015)	The study showed that the structure of the management report in practice is characterized by high flexibility regarding the detail and order of disclosed information
Bek-Gaik and Surowiec (2019)	Research on the quality of disclosure in the practice of integrated reports published by Polish companies in the 2013–2017 period. It employs content analysis (weighted disclosure index) to assess the quality of integrated reports developed by 20 capital groups during the considered period. Research results indicate gradual positive changes regarding the number of published reports and the quality of some areas of disclosure in published reports. Improvements are required in reporting elements such as the business model, outlook, value-creation process, and the presentation of the resources per the International Integrated Reporting Council (IIRC) guidelines
Agustia et al. (2020)	The study examined 63 entities in 2016 and 2017 and employed content analysis for the quality assessment of 126 integrated reports. European entities on average published integrated reports of a moderate quality level. There was also a partial improvement in the quality of integrated reporting in the 2016–2017 period, especially regarding readability, document transparency, and the area of content elements
Bek-Gaik and Surowiec (2020a)	Quantitative and qualitative analysis of forward-looking disclosures in integrated reports published by Polish companies. The analysis covered 33 integrated reports prepared by 20 capital groups in 2016 and 2017. The level of forward-looking disclosures is diverse. Moreover, most prospective disclosures are narratives regarding strategy, information on development opportunities, industry or market risk, and environmental risk; less attention was devoted to investment projects, products, development plans, and financial risk
Bek-Gaik and Surowiec (2020c)	Quality assessment of disclosure about the business model based on the case study of selected integrated reports of Polish companies. Companies mostly introduce their solutions while presenting information on their business models in integrated reports; only some examined companies revealed the business model per the <IR> Framework proposed by IIRC. However, the quality of disclosures in the integrated reports is not satisfactory
Mazzotta et al. (2020)	Quality analysis of non-financial disclosure. The study examined whether the introduction of requirements to disclose non-financial information affects their credibility, using non-financial disclosures of 31 Italian Financial Times Stock Exchange (FTSE) MIB-listed companies for 2017. The study constructed a credibility index using an operational framework based on Habermas idealism. The obligatory disclosure of Italian FTSE MIB companies tends to be credible in terms of three dimensions: truth, sincerity and appropriateness, and understandability

Source: Own elaboration.

Table 1.5 Research on non-financial disclosures in integrated reports

Authors	*Research description*	*Outcomes*
Adams and Simnett (2011)	Research on the application of the principles of integrated reporting and the possibilities of its implementation in the Not-for-Profit sector in Australia	It is possible to use the concept of integrated reporting in the Not-for-Profit sector
Jensen and Berg (2012)	Research on the factors that influence the decision to prepare integrated reports. The authors explained the decision to adopt integrated reports regarding institutional factors	Important factors influencing the implementation of integrated reporting into practice include the level of investor protection and the status of economic development
Krasodomska (2012)	Analysis of the assumptions of integrated reporting – theoretical considerations. The study presents the reasons for modifying the current reporting solutions and the basic assumptions of integrated reporting	It presents the reasons for modifying the current reporting solutions and the basic assumptions of integrated reporting
Dragu and Tudor-Tiron (2013)	Analysis of the impact of political, economic, and cultural factors on integrated reporting practices	There are positive and negative correlations between integrated reporting and political, economic, and cultural conditions
Frias-Aceituno et al. (2013a)	Research on the role of the management board in the dissemination of integrated social corporate reporting	Growth opportunities, the size of a company and its management bodies, and gender diversity are the most important factors in the integrated dissemination of information
García-Sánchez et al. (2013)	Research on the impact of the Hofstede national cultural system, representative of the values of local stakeholders, on integrated reporting, relative to various unrelated documents on corporate performance. The study employed a sample of companies from 20 countries (2008–2010), with 3,042 observations from 1,590 companies	Companies in societies with stronger collectivist and feminist values are in the vanguard of information integration
Sierra-Garcia et al. (2013)	Research on why companies are producing integrated reporting, paying special attention to the links with the assurance of the corporate social responsibility (CSR) report. The analysis covered the 2009–2011 period, with 7,144 worldwide observations	The likelihood of disclosing an integrated report is positively associated with having the CSR report assured, year, size, and supplement industry

(*Continued*)

Table 1.5 (Continued)

Authors	*Research description*	*Outcomes*
Sobczyk (2013)	Analysis of the theoretical basis of the concept of integrated reporting	An attempt to present the theoretical basis of the concept of integrated reporting, using the analysis of the literature on the subject and the method of deduction
Churet and Eccles (2014)	Using the database of over 2,000 companies surveyed during its annual Corporate Sustainability Assessment, the study discussed the extent and recent growth of integrated reporting and its likely effects on important indicators of ESG quality of management and financial performance	The relationship between integrated reporting and financial performance is significant for two sectors: healthcare and information technologies
Eccles and Krzus (2014)	The study analyzed English-language integrated reports of 124 companies around the world for 2012 and assessed the quality of disclosure	The study provides insight into opportunities and challenges in integrated reporting
Eccles and Serafeim (2014)	The study discusses, through a series of case studies, what constitutes an effective integrated report (Coca-Cola Hellenic Bottling Company) and the role of regulation in integrated reporting (Anglo-American)	The study presented the two primary functions of corporate reporting (information and transformation) and why currently isolated financial and sustainability reporting are not likely to perform effectively those functions
Haller and van Staden (2014)	The study discussed the concept of integrated reporting and proposed a practical and useful instrument that could help to apply the integrated reporting concept in corporate practice, a structured presentation of the traditional measure of "value-added" in a so-called "value-added statement"	The study proposed the structure of value-added statements to meet the guiding principles and concepts developed in the integrated reporting framework and help report on the monetary effects of different types of capital included in integrated reporting
Stubbs and Higgins (2014)	The study verifies the internal mechanisms of implementation of integrated reporting in Australian companies and finds the answer to the question of whether integrated reporting stimulates innovative mechanisms of information disclosure. A study was conducted on a sample of 23 managers responsible for company sustainability, communication, and finances, representing 15 organizations	Organizations producing some form of an integrated report are changing their processes and structures; their adoption of integrated reporting has not necessarily stimulated new innovations in disclosure mechanisms or reporting processes beyond incremental changes to processes and structures that previously supported sustainability reporting

(*Continued*)

Table 1.5 (Continued)

Authors	*Research description*	*Outcomes*
van Bommel (2014)	This study examines the multiplicity of views on integrated reporting to consider the possibility of gaining legitimacy through a compromise. The authors applied Boltanski and Thévenot's sociology of worth framework to analyze integrated reporting in the Dutch reporting field	Integrated reporting requires a compromise of common interests, avoidance of clarification, and maintenance of ambiguity to become a legitimate practice
Bek-Gaik (2015)	The study aims to present the views and opinions on the business model disclosure in the organization's financial and non-financial reporting	The study indicated the potential benefits and problems regarding implementing integrated reporting. Key problems include the following: • Credibility of the presented data, mainly of a non-financial and forward-looking nature • No uniform structure of integrated reporting • Lack of an appropriate database for integrated reporting • Too much information • Lack of defined key performance indicators
Bek-Gaik and Rymkiewicz (2015a)	Research on integrated reports published by companies included in the WIG30 index of the Warsaw Stock Exchange for 2013	Key findings include the following: • Large volumes of integrated reports • Information presented is often reproduced from other published reports • Challenge in assessing the quality and credibility of the presented non-financial information • Lack of clear links between non-financial and financial data • Small number of performance indicators, which significantly reduces the credibility of published information • Information on the business model is dispersed in different parts of the report

(*Continued*)

Table 1.5 (Continued)

Authors	*Research description*	*Outcomes*
Chersan (2015)	The latest integrated reporting practices were presented by analyzing annual reports published on the IIRC website (all for 2014)	The content analysis allowed for describing and explaining the identified tendencies and extracted inferences. The results of the study were used to identify features of integrated reports and positive and negative tendencies regarding their content and shape
Eccles et al. (2015)	The study reviewed the integrated reports of 25 multinational companies that participated in the IIRC's Pilot Programme Business Network. It provides a summary of the best reporting practices, assuming three main distinguishing features of a truly integrated report: an explanation of a company's value-creation strategy and how it uses and affects the IIRC's concept of "six capitals," a clear and detailed explanation of the relationships between financial and non-financial performance, and the materiality of information	The study showed the compliance of the content of the analyzed reports with the integrated reporting framework, transparent presentation of the organization's business model, and presentation of social and environmental activities
Flower (2015)	Theoretical discussion	On its foundation, the IIRC's principal objective was the promotion of sustainability accounting. However, in the proposed <IR> Framework, the IIRC has abandoned sustainability accounting. Moreover, the IIRC's proposals have little impact on corporate reporting practices because of their lack of force
Garstecki (2015a)	Analysis of integrated reports of selected Polish companies	The study draws attention to the need for the unification of integrated reports, primarily the financial part. Although integrated reporting does not focus mainly on financial information, its appropriate selection and presentation may increase the usability of the integrated report
Garstecki (2015b)	Research on the financial data disclosure integrated reports of Polish companies. The study analyzed five integrated reports from 2013	The study indicates the lack of standardization of integrated reporting in the financial part and the area of other financial information

(*Continued*)

Table 1.5 (Continued)

Authors	*Research description*	*Outcomes*
Gregorczyk (2015)	The study presents the role of integrated reporting in creating shared value, which is implementing economic objectives while meeting social needs	The study describes the role of the state as a regulator to create shared value, particularly in the development of reporting requirements, and the role of integrated reporting as a crucial factor in creating shared value
Jinga and Dumitru (2015b)	This study furnishes insight into the reporting practices of an experienced preparer of integrated reports on the example of Takeda Pharmaceutical Company	The experience in the field of integrated reporting supported the company's assimilation of the integrated reporting framework guidelines for organizational legitimacy
Walińska (2015)	This study identifies the relationship between the integrated report and financial statements	The proper solution is the coexistence of both forms of company reporting, and their integration should not be understood as only a combination of financial and non-financial data in one report. The effect of integration should be a value report that should show linked information
Walińska et al. (2015)	Analysis of disclosure methods of non-financial information by selected public companies included in the WIG20 index of Warsaw Stock Exchange (WSE)	The publication of many different types of reports hinders the analysis of a firm's performance; information is repeated in different reports
Veltri and Silvestri (2015)	The research explored the integrated report of a South African public university by comparing it with the International Integrated Reporting Council (IIRC) <IR> Framework	The examined report does not follow the <IR> Framework: the data do not have an outlook orientation, the information is not interconnected, the stakeholder relationships are not highlighted, and the organizational ability to create value is not disclosed
Zyznarska-Dworczak (2015)	Analysis of the reliability of integrated reporting in the light of the strategic-information paradigm of accounting	The study suggested increasing the reliability of integrated reporting by including social responsibility management accounting in the implementation of a CSR policy, which promotes the transparent communication of information on the current and future economic, environmental, and social performance of the enterprise

(*Continued*)

Table 1.5 (Continued)

Authors	*Research description*	*Outcomes*
Bek-Gaik and Rymkiewicz (2016)	The study was conducted on the sample of 60 companies included in the WIG20 and mWIG40 of WSE indexes, analyzing 337 corporate reports for the 2013–2014 period	Integrated reports are mainly prepared by companies that are leaders in their industries, the structure of reports is very diverse, and the quality of disclosure varies
Lai et al. (2016)	The study seeks to ascertain whether the decision to adopt integrated reporting is an element of the legitimacy strategy to improve the negative image of the company regarding its sustainability. The study sample comprises enterprises that participate in the IIRC Pilot Program	Enterprise involvement in integrated reporting is not a matter of strategic legitimacy
Lueg et al. (2016)	The study shows how standards and guidelines for CSR can help a company in its integrated reporting. It probes the motivations of diverse stakeholders in fostering the adoption of CSR standards and guidelines after integrated reporting became mandatory in Denmark	Strategy, in which CSR is an essential value driver, fostered integrated reporting with guidelines and standards for CSR
Perego et al. (2016)	Research on the perception of integrated reporting by the management staff. Interviews were conducted with three key experts influencing integrated reporting practices at a global level	Experts perceive integrated reporting as fragmented and believe most companies currently have a weak understanding of the business value of integrated reporting
Remlein (2016)	Research on the costs and benefits of implementing and using integrated reporting	The study noted the following benefits: • Better satisfaction of the information needs of long-term investors • Showing links between factors inside and outside the entity and the impact of the entity on other members of the supply chain • Higher level of trust of key stakeholders • Better resource allocation decisions • Lower reputational risk • Easier access to capital

(*Continued*)

Table 1.5 (Continued)

Authors	*Research description*	*Outcomes*
Świderska and Bek-Gaik (2016)	Analysis of the pros and cons of integrated reporting. The study ascertains whether the current integrated can replace present reporting and improve its imperfections	Indicated problems: data reliability, lack of consistency and substantive links of presented data, impact of the involvement and cooperation of stakeholders on the scope of the report, and completeness of the issues covered in the report
Feng et al. (2017)	The study explores how integrated reporting stakeholders in Australia interpret integrated thinking, and how pilot organizations put integrated thinking into practice	The study suggests a lack of understanding of integrated thinking by practitioners and the need to accurately present the potential contribution of integrated reporting into organizational practice
Caraiani et al. (2018)	The study investigated the perspectives of integrated reporting as an emerging field in mainstream academic literature. The current state of research and its development were explored using the structured literature review method on publications indexed in Clarivate Analytics' Web of Science	The findings suggest an evolution of integrated reporting research from the phase of spreading awareness regarding the new reporting paradigm toward an impact analysis phase. The accounting and audit journals have greatly contributed to the shift in the integrated reporting literature toward studying integrated reporting as a reporting practice and the need to discuss possible links between integrated reporting, governance, and integrated thinking
Kiliç and Kuzey (2018)	The study examined the nature and scope of forward-looking disclosures in early examples of integrated reporting and investigated the determinants of those disclosures. The sample for research involved 55 non-financial companies whose reports are available in the integrated reporting examples database for 2014. The study employed content analysis to investigate the quantitative and qualitative forward-looking disclosures among early adopters of integrated reporting	Most of the entities tended to provide qualitative rather than quantitative forward-looking disclosures; gender diversity and firm size are positively related to forward-looking disclosures, whereas leverage is negatively related to forward-looking disclosures; there was no significant impact created by board size, board composition, profitability, or industry on forward-looking disclosures

(*Continued*)

Table 1.5 (Continued)

Authors	*Research description*	*Outcomes*
Lai et al. (2018)	The study analyzed how the preparers' mode of cognition influences the patterns of accountability associated with integrated reporting. It conducted in-depth interviews with the integrated reporting preparers of a global insurer that has used integrated reporting since 2013 were conducted	The preparers' narrative mode of cognition facilitates dialogue with users of integrated reports
Pistoni et al. (2018)	Research on the quality of integrated reports issued by firms, proposing a scoring model and an integrated reporting scoreboard, which were applied to analyze 116 integrated reports issued in 2013 and 2014	The quality of integrated reports is low
Higgins et al. (2019)	The study employs Morgan's analysis of the role of metaphors in understanding and managing organizations to assess in what respects organizations using integrated reporting are on a "journey" of organizational change. The study analyzed the integrated reporting practitioner literature and used in-depth interviews to assess the extent to which this metaphor captures how six early adopter organizations in Australia implement integrated reporting, and what changes resulted over four years	The journey metaphor implies substantive and holistic organizational change. By contrast, organizations use integrated reporting in contextual, instrumental, and piecemeal ways. The study proposed a "toolbox" metaphor to help present how organizations adapt their reporting to fit decisions already made and challenges presented through ordinary and ongoing strategic management
Guthrie et al. (2017)	Research on the links between integrated reporting and the internal processes of the organization, focusing on examining the internal mechanisms of change that can contribute to the implementation of integrated reporting; the study analyzed five Italian public sector organizations	The study highlights that the change processes in organizations implementing integrated reporting involve the adoption of an integrated mindset by these organizations given the internalization process

Source: Own elaboration.

engagement and participation are integral to day-to-day operations of organizations, and information on social issues and corporate governance has become an indicator of future cash inflows for investors.

The findings show several benefits of disclosing non-financial information. Non-financial disclosures improve communication with stakeholders, improve the image and reputation of the organization, improve the quality and reliability of information about the organization, increase the decision-making comfort of investors, provide a more accurate valuation, and lower the investment risk (Adamek et al., 2018). It accords with the statement of Lament (2017, pp. 68–69), which points to two main groups of reasons for non-financial reporting – marketing and image-related reasons – which are part of the company's information policy. Moreover, financial reasons regard the impact on the firm's financial performance. Further, the disclosure of non-financial information is part of the legitimization strategy to improve the negative image of the company in terms of sustainability.

The indicated benefits of disclosing non-financial information may also constitute a basic motivation for such reporting. The relevant literature (Remlein, 2016, pp. 51–59; Morros, 2016, pp. 336–356) emphasizes the multiple benefits of reporting non-financial information, increasing transparency, and building a competitive advantage. These benefits are mainly the result of disclosing prospective non-financial information, information about the value-creation process, information about all the capital the organization uses (business model), and comprehensive information about the organization's performance. Notably, non-financial information helps to understand the business logic of an organization, mainly its business model. The non-financial disclosure also presents the full range of factors that significantly affect an organization's ability to create long-term value and inform about all the organization's resources that enable value creation.

Based on the considerations, while investors' demand for non-financial information has increased over time, interpreting the impact of non-financial disclosures on an organization's financial performance is challenging. Another challenge is the lack of a uniform reporting format for non-financial disclosures (despite guidelines and standards), which induces differences in the presentation of information by various entities and increases the complexity of the analysis of non-financial information. Companies often adopt their solutions by presenting, for example, an integrated report. Investors' lack of knowledge about the impact of non-financial information on valuation increases the incentives for financial analysts to explain how that information affects an organization's performance and value.

The presented considerations raise the following question about the future of disclosing non-financial information: is an orthodox division into financial and non-financial information at all possible and justified? (Sobczyk, 2017, p. 396). Undoubtedly, arriving at an answer is challenging because non-financial information is often supplemented by financial data. Thus, this division is only conventional.

1.3 Non-financial reporting's voluntary and legal standards and requirements

In recent years, there has been intensive development in the reporting of financial and non-financial information. The development of the trend of non-financial information in organizational reporting and the huge increase in its importance are undoubtedly associated with the transition to a knowledge-based economy, globalization, increased competition, and the harsh criticism of the informational content of financial reports (Eccles et al., 2010). Moreover, non-financial reporting is a response to modern market conditions, which bring new challenges for organizations and make stakeholders expect more transparent reports. It is closely related to the evolution of the approach to an organization's value creation (White, 2005; Eccles et al., 2010).

New forms of corporate reporting, particularly colloquially defined non-financial reports, help organizations provide information on value creation and business models and help all stakeholders understand the overall condition of the organization, enabling them to make more informed and rational business decisions. Notably, non-financial information is becoming increasingly important given the transition to a knowledge-based economy, globalization, and increased competition. Certainly, non-financial information should complement mandatory financial reporting beyond traditional financial ratios and link them to non-financial achievements. Currently, the integrated report, which has proven to be controversial, is considered the perfect form of reporting non-financial information. According to Eccles and Krzus (2010b), organizations will see integrated reporting as an opportunity to communicate and implement a sustainable development strategy that creates value for shareholders in the long term while contributing to a sustainable society.

The literature on the subject also indicates that, given the weaknesses of traditional reporting and the increasing complexity of business activities, reporting should be based on two main types of reporting: financial and non-financial. Non-financial information should complement mandatory financial reporting beyond traditional financial ratios.

The journey to better business reporting continues, given a new Directive adopted by the European Parliament – Directive 2014/95/EU on the disclosure of non-financial and diverse information – to ensure that large public-interest entities in Europe provide a comprehensive and substantively meaningful picture of their positions and achievements. Moreover, non-financial reports are published in various forms, which is also problematic. Over the past 20 years, many proposals have been made to improve non-financial reporting, almost all of which focus on disclosing more non-financial information and improving its quality and comparability. Since 2008, many organizations have published frameworks and guidelines for reporting non-financial information (Eccles et al., 2011). Various bodies, such as the American Institute of Certified Public Accountants (AICPA), the FASB, and the Institute of Chartered Accountants in England and Wales (ICAEW), have developed reporting models that formulate recommendations for the presentation of non-financial indicators (Orens and Lybaert, 2013). Other recommendations for voluntary reporting of non-financial information have been developed by numerous international organizations, such as the Global Reporting Initiative (GRI),[7] United Nations Global Compact (UN GC),[8] UN Environment Programme,[9] International Petroleum Industry Environmental Conservation Association (IPIECA),[10] OECD (Guidelines for Multinational Enterprises), the International Organization for Standardization (ISO 26000 Guidelines),[11] and the International Integrated Reporting Council (IIRC). In 2013, the IIRC published the integrated reporting framework (revised in 2021), which provided guidelines for the preparation of integrated reports. Changes were made to Directive 2014/95/EU.

In global corporate reporting practice, many different regulations are related to non-financial issues, including CSR and sustainability. Some were developed for a specific industry, but their universality allows for their widespread use by various industries. All the developed standards accord with Directive 2014/95/EU. The following standards or guidelines can be distinguished:

1. GRI Standards
2. Communication on Progress (CoP)
3. International integrated reporting framework
4. Guidance on Corporation Responsibility Indicators in Annual Reports
5. Key performance indicators (KPIs) for ESG
6. Model Guidance on Reporting ESG Information to Investors
7. Carbon Disclosure Project (CDP)
8. Greenhouse Gas Protocol (GHG Protocol) Corporate Standard
9. Principles for Responsible Investment (PRI)
10. PN-EN ISO 26000: 2021-04 related to social responsibility
11. Standard of Non-Financial Information (SIN)

The GRI Standards are global standards for sustainability impacts, containing guidelines for reporting economic, environmental, and social performance used most widely in the preparation of non-financial reports. The GRI was founded in 1997 in the United States to create a general global framework to report the economic, social, and environmental aspects of the organization. The first version of the GRI-G1 standards was published in 2000. A subsequent version of the guidelines was the GRI-G4, published in 2013. It was replaced by the GRI Sustainable Development Reporting Standards (GRI Standards), published in 2016. The latest changes were introduced in 2021.

The GRI Standards guidelines are the most advanced standards for reporting non-financial issues, particularly regarding sustainable development and CSR. The GRI Standards are a modular system comprising three series of standards: the GRI Universal Standards, incorporating reporting on human rights and environmental due diligence; the GRI Sector Standards; and the GRI Topic Standards. The GRI Standards previously comprised two types of standards:

- Universal standards that apply to all reporting organizations (101, 102, and 103)
- Issue-specific standards that focus on specific topics of sustainable development, such as human rights, waste, and emissions (Series 200, 300, and 400)

The GRI reporting system has been updated with a revision of the universal standards. The GRI Universal Standards were renamed as follows:

- GRI 1: Foundation 2021
- GRI 2: General Disclosures 2021
- GRI 3: Material Topics 2021

One of the key concepts for reporting sustainable development is materiality, and reports must focus on issues relevant to the results of the reporting organization in the field of sustainable development. The definition of materiality in the 2016 version is based on two axes: the impact on stakeholders' decisions and the materiality of economic, environmental, and social impacts. Given the last change, the focus was completely shifted to the impact: reporting organizations must ensure they understand their real and potential economic, environmental, and social impacts. The goal is to understand the priorities of stakeholders and gather information and prospects for a better understanding of the impact of the organization.

Focusing on the impact means that reporting organizations must establish the process of identifying and managing their impacts with due diligence. The concept of due diligence was almost completely absent in the first version of the standards; it is now central. Due diligence is a process through which an organization identifies, prevents, mitigates, and accounts for how it addresses its actual and potential negative impacts on the economy, the environment, and people. One of the most important issues reporting companies must reveal in their approach to due diligence is their impact on human rights. Therefore, the GRI Standards update ensures better compliance with the UN GC Guidelines for Business and Human Rights and various national legislative initiatives.

The updated structure of Global Reporting Initiative (GRI) Standards comprises[12]:

- **The Universal Standards** – that apply to all organizations, incorporate reporting on human rights and environmental due diligence, in line with intergovernmental expectations, and include:
  - Requirements and principles for using the GRI Standards
  - Disclosures about the reporting organization
  - Disclosures and guidance about the organization's material topics
- **The Sector Standards** enable more consistent reporting on sector-specific impacts;
- **The Topic Standards** – adapted to be used with the revised Universal Standards – list disclosures relevant to a particular topic.

These documents show the rules regarding reporting per the GRI Standards. Reporting per the GRI Standards is voluntary and can be used to prepare any type of report covering the topics included in the standards. GRI 1: Foundation 2021 comprises the following.

- Purpose and system of GRI Standards
- Key concepts
- Reporting per the GRI Standards
- Reporting principles
- Additional recommendations for reporting

The key concepts explain those that lay the foundation for sustainability reporting. Those covered in this section are as follows:

- Impact refers to the effect an organization has or could have on the economy, environment, and people, including the effects on their human rights, because of the organization's activities or business relationships.
- Material topics: the organization prioritizes reporting on topics that represent the most significant impacts on the economy, environment, and people. Examples of material topics include anti-corruption, occupational health and safety, and water and effluents.
- Due diligence refers to the process through which an organization identifies, prevents, mitigates, and accounts for how it addresses its actual and potential negative impacts on the economy, the environment, and people.
- Stakeholders: individuals or groups with interests that are affected or could be affected by an organization's activities.

Reporting per GRI Standards means reports should comply with the reporting principles:

- Accuracy: the characteristics that determine accuracy vary per the nature of the information (qualitative or quantitative) and the intended use of the information
- Balance: the reporting organization shall report information in an unbiased way and provide a fair representation of the organization's negative and positive impacts
- Clarity: the reporting organization shall present information in a way that is accessible and understandable
- Comparability: the reporting organization shall select, compile, and report information consistently to enable an analysis of changes in the organization's impacts over time and an analysis of these impacts relative to those of other organizations. Information reported in a comparable way should enable the organization and other information users to assess the organization's current impacts against its past impacts and its goals and targets
- Completeness: the reporting organization shall provide sufficient information to enable an assessment of the organization's impact during the reporting period

- Sustainability context: the reporting organization shall report information about its impacts in the wider context of sustainable development. Sustainability reporting using GRI Standards aims to provide transparency on how an organization contributes or aims to contribute to sustainable development
- Timeliness: the reporting organization shall report information on a regular schedule and make it available in time for users to make decisions
- Verifiability: the organization should gather, record, compile, and analyze information such that the information can be examined to establish its quality

The organization must comply with nine requirements per the GRI Standards:

- Requirement 1: apply the reporting principles
- Requirement 2: report the disclosures in GRI 2; General Disclosures 2021
- Requirement 3: determine material topics
- Requirement 4: report the disclosures in GRI 3; Material Topics 2021
- Requirement 5: report disclosures from the GRI Topic Standards for each material topic
- Requirement 6: provide reasons for omitting disclosures and requirements the organization cannot comply with
- Requirement 7: publish a GRI content index
- Requirement 8: provide a statement of use
- Requirement 9: notify GRI

General Disclosures contain disclosures for organizations to provide information about their reporting practices, activities and workers, governance, strategy, policies, practices, and stakeholder engagement. This information provides insight into the profile and scale of organizations and provides a context for understanding their impacts. This Standard is structured as follows:

- Section 1 contains five disclosures that provide information about the organization, its sustainability reporting practices, and the entities included in its sustainability reporting.
- Section 2 contains three disclosures that provide information about the organization's activities, employees, and other workers.
- Section 3 contains 13 disclosures that provide information on the organization's governance structure, composition, roles, and remuneration.
- Section 4 contains seven disclosures that provide information about the organization's sustainable development strategy and its policies and practices for responsible business conduct.
- Section 5 contains two disclosures that provide information about the organization's stakeholder engagement practices and how it engages in collective bargaining with employees.
- The glossary contains terms with specific meanings when used in GRI Standards. The terms are underlined in the text of the GRI Standards and linked to the definitions.

- The bibliography lists authoritative intergovernmental instruments and additional references used in developing this standard and the resources that the organization can consult.

An important change introduced in 2021 removes the distinction between reporting, which applies only to core information, reporting, and comprehensive information. This change means that reporting organizations must present all disclosures for all topics considered important. The use of a new version of the GRI Universal Standards became mandatory on January 1, 2023. Table 1.6 lists the groups.

The Sector Standards provide information for organizations about their likely material topics. An organization uses the applicable Sector Standards

Table 1.6 Global reporting initiative standards general disclosures

The group of disclosures	*Description*
Organization and reporting practices	Organizational details Entities included in the organization's sustainability reporting Reporting period, frequency, and contact point Restatements of information External assurance
Activities and workers	Activities, value chain, and other business relationships Employees Workers who are not employees
Governance	Governance structure and composition Nomination and selection of the highest governance body Chair of the highest governance body Role of the highest governance body in overseeing the management of impacts Delegation of responsibility for managing impacts Role of the highest governance body in sustainability reporting Conflicts of interest Communication of critical concerns Collective knowledge of the highest governance body Evaluation of the performance of the highest governance body Remuneration policies Process to determine remuneration Annual total compensation ratio
Strategy, policies, and practices	Statement on sustainable development strategy Policy commitments Embedding policy commitments Processes to remediate negative impacts Mechanisms for seeking advice and raising concern Compliance with laws and regulations Membership associations
Stakeholder engagement	Approach to stakeholder engagement Collective bargaining agreements

Source: Own elaboration based on GRI 2: General Disclosures 2021, https://www.globalreporting.org/standards/

to its sector when determining its material topics and what to report for each. The New GRI Sector Standards have two-digit code numbers. Standards for individual sectors do not contain any new disclosures but help companies identify their important topics. They defined and described key economic, environmental, and social impacts in a given sector, creating a context for reporting. The first sectoral standards were published for the oil and gas industry (2021), coal sector (2022), and Agriculture Aquaculture and Fishing Sectors (2022).

GRI Topic Standards remain in force, and only three topic standards have been withdrawn and included in the revised GRI Universal Standards. After the revision, there are currently 31 topic standards with three-digit code numbers. The topic standards contain disclosures the organization uses to report information about its impacts on particular topics. The organization uses topic standards according to the list of material topics determined using GRI 3.

The **Communication on Progress (CoP)**[13] is a questionnaire through which a company informs stakeholders about the implementation of the Ten Principles of the UN Global Compact. The main objective of the CoP is to provide information on sustainability performance and foster transparency and accountability in corporate sustainability performance. The CoP can be an effective tool for stakeholder dialogue and sharing best and emerging practices. CoP is particularly useful for smaller organizations.

The International Integrated Reporting Framework introduced by the IIRC is dedicated to companies preparing integrated reports.

Guidance on Corporate Responsibility Indicators in Annual Reports[14] is a standard developed by the UN Conference on Trade and Development. It guides enterprises on annual sustainability reporting. Although the number of indicators is limited, they are described to help the organization select the content of the report. These indicators regard many important issues: trade and investment, employment creation and labor practices, technology and human resource development, health and safety, government and community contribution, and corruption. The guidelines concern social and employee issues and counteracting corruption. It aims to assist preparers of enterprise reporting in producing concise and comparable corporate responsibility indicators in annual financial reports.

Another standard was developed for all entities, with particular emphasis on companies listed on stock exchanges or issuing bonds. **KPIs for ESG**[15] present indicators in 114 subsectors, which enables the adjustment of the content to the specificity of the entity. Given the division of indicators into subsectors, each entity can find content most suited to its business. The issues addressed in this standard regard environmental, social, and labor aspects, human rights, and anti-corruption.

The UN Sustainable Stock Exchange Initiative created a voluntary tool for stock exchanges to guide issuers worldwide. However, the general recommendations of this tool may be useful for all reporting units. **Model Guidance on Reporting ESG Information to Investors**[16] helps exchanges promote sustainable business practices in their markets. It includes recommendations for companies in the field of non-financial reporting and for selecting appropriate publications and a set of indicators. It covers environmental, social, and employee issues; human rights; and counteracting corruption.

Carbon Disclosure Project (CDP),[17] a not-for-profit charity, provides a disclosure system for investors, companies, cities, states, and regions to manage their environmental impacts. The CDP standard of environmental reporting includes indicators related to climate, water, and forests and is dedicated to companies, supply chains, public authorities, cities, investors, private markets, governments, states, and regions.

The GHG Protocol Corporate Accounting and Reporting Standard (GHG Protocol Corporate Standard),[18] designed by the GHG Protocol Initiative, provides requirements and guidance for companies and other organizations preparing corporate-level GHG emissions inventories. The standard covers the accounting and reporting of greenhouse gases covered by the Kyoto Protocol, such as carbon dioxide (CO_2) or methane. The GHG Protocol Corporate Standard allows companies to measure and report emissions from purchased or acquired electricity, steam, heating, and cooling. The GHG information allows for tracking and comparing GHG emissions information over time to identify trends and assess the performance of the reporting company.

The Principles for Responsible Investment (PRI)[19] contains recommendations on the inclusion of social, environmental, and corporate governance issues in investment practices. Reporting guidelines refer to responsible investing; therefore, their recipients are enterprises that invest their funds. The PRI offers recommendations for possible actions to incorporate ESG issues into investment practice.

PN-EN ISO 26000:2021-04[20] is an international standard containing guidelines for all organization types, regardless of their size, location, concepts, terms, and definitions regarding the context, trends, characteristics, principles, practices, key areas, and issues regarding social responsibility. This standard was developed to help organizations take actions that contribute to sustainable development. The purpose of the standard is to promote a shared understanding of social responsibility and complement other social responsibility tools and initiatives, not replace them. When applying this standard, a firm should consider social, environmental, legal, cultural, political, organizational, and economic differences while maintaining consistency with international standards of conduct.

The Standard of Non-Financial Information (SIN), introduced in 2017 in Poland, is a national environmental regulation, the development of which was coordinated by the Reporting Standards Foundation and the Polish Association of Listed Companies (SEG), which has been approved and supported by several institutions and organizations. The SIN enables Polish companies to fulfill the obligations of reporting non-financial information set out in Directive 2014/95/EU, as implemented in Polish law by the Act of December 15, 2016, amending the Act of September 29, 1994, on accounting (Journal of Laws of 2017, item 61). SIN can be used by listed companies and other enterprises, institutions, and organizations. Its structure includes basic parts and annexes. The basic part is divided into non-financial reporting and its scope, national and industry specifications, significance of indicators and their selection from the point of view of capital markets, and scope of the standard and descriptions of individual reporting areas. The annexes contain additional descriptions of the areas subject to reporting, legal interpretations of the EU directive and the Accounting Act, and guidelines for determining the significance of indicators. The standard covers managerial, environmental, social, and labor issues.

Despite several regulations and guidelines, the disclosure of non-financial information remains disordered. Generally, we address the freedom to choose possible standards and regulations for reporting non-financial information, combined with the lack of an obligation to verify them externally. The situation in Poland regarding non-financial reporting is also unregulated. Before 2019, non-financial disclosures in Poland were voluntary. Several studies have investigated different aspects of corporate practice in this regard (Bek-Gaik and Rymkiewicz, 2016; Dyduch and Krasodomska, 2017; Bek-Gaik and Surowiec, 2019). Significant changes in Poland were made by introducing the SIN.

1.4 Management commentary, sustainability reports, and integrated reports

1.4.1 Management commentary

Management commentary is an important source of non-financial information as part of an organization's reporting.[21] Currently, it is considered a basic non-financial report accompanying the financial statements of selected entities and is the subject of regulations and guidelines in accounting.

The management commentary is a narrative report that provides an interpretative context, enabling a better understanding of the financial situation and the results of the activity and cash flows of the entity. The management commentary also allows for understanding the goals chosen by the management board and the strategies undertaken to achieve them (IASB, 2010).

The management commentary provides users with financial statements with integrated information for a full picture of the company. It should also present the basic trends and factors that may affect the future financial performance of the entity, its financial position, and development. Hence, the management commentary applies to the present, past, and future and should help users understand

- Risk exposure
- Implemented risk management strategies and their effectiveness
- The impact of intangible business resources on an entity's operations
- The impact of non-financial factors on the information presented in financial statements

Legal requirements regarding the content of management commentary are presented in the IFRS Practice Statement *Management Commentary*, published by the IASB in 2010 (IASB, 2010).[22] Important requirements in the management commentary content were introduced by Directive 2014/95/EU.

The management commentary is crucial to the modern reporting model. As a narrative report, the management commentary explains the situation of the company. It is an enterprise tool used to highlight its capital market history. This history concerns business, types of activity, strategies, goals, financial performance, financial position, cash flow, various types of risk, and possibilities and threats that may affect the future business activity of an enterprise (KPMG, 2011, p. 2). The management commentary is like a "lens" through which investors can see and understand the value-creating process of the enterprise and the results of activities (CFA Institute, 2007, p. 1). It also allows stakeholders to control managers. As Gad (2013) highlights, management commentary is particularly important from the perspective of the tasks facing the management board.

The IASB presented the scope of disclosures that should be included in management commentary. Basic elements of management commentary have been divided into five basic parts[23]:

- The nature of the business comprising the knowledge of the business in which an entity is engaged and the external environment in which it operates
- Management's objectives and its strategies for meeting those objectives in order to assess the strategies adopted by the entity and the likelihood that those strategies will be successful in meeting management's stated objectives
- The entity's most significant resources, risks, and relationships comprising a basis for determining the resources available to the entity and obligations to transfer resources to others; the ability of the entity to generate long-term, sustainable net inflows of resources; and the risks to which those resource-generating activities are exposed, both in the near and long term
- The results of operations and prospects including the ability to understand whether an entity has delivered results per expectations and, implicitly, how well management has understood the entity's market, executed its strategy, and managed the entity's resources, risks, and relationships
- The performance measures and indicators that management uses to evaluate the entity's performance against stated objectives comprising the ability to focus on the critical performance measures and indicators that management uses to assess and manage the entity's performance against stated objectives and strategies

According to the IASB concept, management commentary should include the following detailed items (IASB, 2010):

- Description of the nature of the entity's activity
- Disclosure regarding goals and strategies that allows us to understand the priorities of the management board
- A clear description of the most important resources of the entity, various types of risk, and relations in the management board's opinion may affect value creation in the long term
- Description of resources specific to an entity
- Disclosure of the main types of risk to which the unit is exposed, management plans, strategies regarding the mitigation of this risk, and the efficiency of risk management strategy
- Disclosure regarding the identification of significant unit-stakeholders relations
- A clear description of the financial and non-financial outcomes that can affect future results and the assessment of perspectives
- Explanations of the development potentials of the entity and its competitive position
- Analysis of the perspective of the entity, considering the goals regarding financial and non-financial resources
- Disclosure of measures and indicators of efficiency (financial and non-financial) used by managers to assess progress regarding established goals

In summary, the management report is a commentary on the company's financial situation and performance. An additional advantage is that it is created from two perspectives, both presenting the company's performance and future assumptions and forecasts. This information complements the financial statement and allows for a better understanding of the activities aimed at value creation for the enterprise.

1.4.2 Corporate social responsibility report

Reporting activities of social responsibility is considered good practice in enterprises (Śnieżek and Piłacik, 2016, p. 141) because of its many benefits, including communication on the process of implementing and monitoring social, economic, and environmental activities.

Notably, in the global relevant literature, many terms regarding the reporting of CSR and sustainable development results stem from the diversity of the synonyms used, such as sustainability, triple bottom line, corporate responsibility, ESG, and non-financial reporting (Urbaniec, 2015).

According to the relevant literature, the first disclosure of information on business responsibility activities appeared in the late 1950s and the early 1960s, and their dynamic development took place since the 1970s (Szadziewska, 2013, p. 262). At the end of the 1980s and early 1990s, companies in Anglo-Saxon countries began to publish separate reports on social and environmental issues. According to Roszkowska (2011, p. 77), CSR or sustainability reporting is a voluntary presentation of information on non-financial activities and economic, social, and environmental performance during the reporting period. That is, such a report, issued in print or published on the website, presents the company's strategy, social policy, and social responsibility performance regarding the key groups of stakeholders in a comprehensive manner. Śnieżek and Wiatr (2017, p. 119) emphasize that modern accounting has already begun to implement the assumption of presenting comprehensive financial and non-financial information, and an example of such practice is social accounting, considering many forms and tools of data collection and reporting beyond the framework of economic issues.

In summary, disclosing information on socially responsible activities is crucial, especially for building proper relationships with stakeholders. It provides a valuable source of information that enables the assessment of the level and effects of socially responsible activities and the level of implementation of the CSR concept by organizations. It occurs primarily in the practice of public companies, which are increasingly transparent in the field of disclosing information on the positive and negative social and environmental results of their activities.

A high level of advancement of the GRI Standard regarding the information content of the report and the presentation scheme allows for obtaining reliable and complete data on all areas of the company's activity (e.g., economic, social, and environmental), which precisely characterize the concept of CSR.

1.4.3 *Integrated report*

Integrated reporting, the latest approach to corporate reporting, is a hot topic. Recently, organizations and users of corporate reports realized that the previous profit-based reporting model must be revised and changed such that companies can report on broader goals beyond financial goals and, in particular, the organization's value.

Integrated reporting quickly gained importance and recognition since its guidelines were formulated in 2010 by the International Integrated Reporting Committee, renamed as the IIRC. Although the IIRC now leads in determining integrated reporting policy and practice, it is not the first to determine such guidelines. The pioneers include innovative organizations in South Africa, where applying integrated reporting was among the eligibility criteria for a company to be listed on the stock exchange.[24]

In 2010, the IIRC developed an Integrated Reporting framework. This framework facilitates the preparation of one integrated report; that is, one document in which the organization synthesizes all reporting aspects and indicators important for stakeholders: an integrated report. Eccles and Krzus (2010) defined integrated reports as a single report that combines financial and narrative information published in the entity's annual report with non-financial information (e.g., ESG issues) and narrative information found in CSR reports or corporate sustainability reports.

Notably, the literature on the subject draws attention to the fact that integrated reporting is a logical consequence of the development of two threads (trends) of corporate reporting developed in recent years: reporting of sustainable development and reporting CSR[25] (Walińska et al., 2016). Integrated reporting combines important financial and non-financial information reported in separate documents in a way that shows the interlinkage and explains how the organization's activities affect its ability to create and maintain values in the short, medium, and long term. Thus, it can be called a value report.

The integrated report[26] shows a holistic picture of the firm and its perspective and interrelations between financial and non-financial performance. Practitioners and proponents of integrated reporting claim that integrated reporting brings greater transparency regarding an organization's engagement in sustainable development by showing the links between financial and non-financial performance in one document (Eccles and Krzus, 2010). Further, it "brings governance, financial capital, intellectual capital, social capital, and environmental capital onto a common platform" (Morros, 2016, p. 338). Integrated reporting is an element of better business reporting with more benefits.

Integrated reporting should improve the quality of information available to stakeholders by combining various reporting areas (finance, management commentary, corporate governance, remuneration, and sustainable development) comprehensively, explaining the organization's ability to create and maintain value. Detailed information on the integrated report is presented in Chapter 2.

1.5 Problems and dilemmas in reporting non-financial information

The practice of non-financial reporting is diverse; some non-financial reports (in particular, integrated reporting) are at an early stage of development. Currently, organizations and stakeholders are observing the gradual acceptance of this reporting form. Studies on integrated reporting to identify its practice and the costs and benefits of its implementation are constantly increasing. The development of non-financial information is already a reality, but there remain problems and dilemmas associated with its disclosure. They relate, in particular, to the reliability of the presented data, mainly of a non-financial and prospective nature; lack of uniform structure of non-financial reporting; information overload and, thus, challenges with filtering information relevant for investors to make decisions; large freedom in "creating" non-financial information; the absence of a set of organization's performance indicators, preferred for disclosure in non-financial reporting; organizations' concerns about the possibility of losing competitive advantage (e.g., disclosure of business model); the possibility of bringing legal actions by investors who, using prospective data, have not achieved the expected rates of return; and financial market response to published non-financial data, creating an appropriate database for integrated reporting.

Emergent questions include the following:

- How will organizations, especially business organizations, handle risk in disclosing future information as required by integrated reporting?
- How do institutional and cultural factors in different countries affect non-financial reporting practices?
- Will non-financial reporting encourage auditors to seek innovative ways of expressing opinions on forward-looking information?

Although the non-financial information literature on business reporting is relatively new, theoretical and practical research on this issue is developing rapidly. However, it remains controversial and unresolved. There seems to be a poor understanding of the business value of non-financial reporting. In Poland and globally, there is a lack of research on the perception of non-financial reporting by management, and no consensus has been reached on the main objective and purpose of non-financial reporting. For example, Steyn (2014) conducted a survey to determine the opinions of representatives of management boards of listed companies regarding the expected benefits and challenges and the motives for developing integrated reporting and its role in providing information to stakeholders. In turn, Churet and Eccles (2014) analyzed the diversity of integrated reporting, examining the reports of many industries over two years, and observed a statistically significant relation between integrated reporting and quality of management in the long term. They discussed the information base issues for integrated reporting, its reliability, and the role of management accounting specialists in preparing integrated reports. The decision-making significance of non-financial statements is also a problem.

The problems clearly show that there are several unresolved issues regarding non-financial reporting and its future. The most common question is whether the decision to prepare a non-financial report is significant from a value-creation perspective. Do financial markets respond to the publication of non-financial reports? The quality of non-financial statement disclosures and elements of content raises great doubts. For example, what measures best adapt to market expectations or reflect the created value?

The development of non-financial reporting is a modern requirement, as stakeholder expectations have changed significantly. Modern reporting landscapes are diverse and constantly expanding. Despite critical opinions on non-financial disclosures, it is challenging to imagine a lack of reports on the non-financial activities of organizations. The legitimacy,[27] stakeholder, and institution theories forced the need to disclose non-financial information. The emergence of non-financial reporting can be interpreted as the next stage of corporate reporting development, which is the result of changes in the approach to organizational management and illustrates the ethical image of the organization and its corporate responsibility. Moreover, a firm can legitimize its activities via non-financial reports.

Strategic legitimacy stems from conflicting interests between the management board and stakeholders, and reporting in this context is an organizational mitigating factor. Therefore, legitimacy may be unique to a given organization and can be achieved through engagement in cooperation with external stakeholders to build or improve reputation. The management board consistently cooperates with stakeholders and selects various forms of non-financial reporting.

Non-financial reporting from an accountability perspective is the best way to inform key organization stakeholders about business. The management board must specify key stakeholders and the kind of reporting that should be implemented. Management must also quantify the cost-effectiveness of reporting, which reports will draw the attention of stakeholders, and what transparency level the organization can achieve by publishing mandatory and voluntary reports. However, these issues still raise many doubts. There are also problems and dilemmas regarding what information to reveal and to what extent.

Notes

1 The criticism of the information content of financial statements has been widely discussed in the relevant literature, including Hansen (2001), Teixeira (2004), ICAEW (2010), IASB (2011a), IASB (2011b), Parameter (2010), Kranacher (2011), Deloitte (2012), Pounder (2012), and Walińska et al. (2016).
2 IFRS (2010), Staff Draft of Exposure Draft, IFRS X, Financial Statement Presentation, developed by International Accounting Standards Board (IASB) and FASB.
3 As per Walińska (2012), many organizations are reconstructing the financial reporting model, including IASB, which published the document "Agenda Consultations 2011 – Request for Views" on July 26, 2011. It designated two strategic areas of action: the development of financial reporting and maintenance of applicable IFRS.
4 Such studies include Ciechan-Kujawa (2013), Dyduch and Krasodomska (2017), Hąbek and Wolniak (2015), Macuda et al. (2015), and Szadziewska et al. (2018).
5 See https://www.thomsonreuters.com/content/dam/openweb/documents/pdf/tr-com-financial/methodology/corporate-responsibility-ratings.pdf
6 The leader of extra-financial analysis, currently Vigeo Eiris (a global pioneer in ESG assessments, data, tools, and sustainable finance), affiliate of Moody's ESG Solutions Group
7 https://www.globalreporting.org/Pages/default.aspx
8 https://www.unglobalcompact.org
9 https://www.unep.org/
10 http://www.ipieca.org/about-us/
11 https://www.iso.org/iso-26000-social-responsibility.html
12 https://www.globalreporting.org/standards/
13 www.unglobalcompact.org
14 unctad.org
15 ec.europa.eu

16 sseinitiative.org
17 www.cdp.net
18 ghgprotocol.org
19 unpri.org
20 pkn.pl
21 Depending on the legal system, different terms may be used for the management commentary, such as "Management board report on the operations," "Report on the activities," or Director's report in Poland, Management report in Germany, Management's discussion and analysis (MD&A) in US, and Operating and financial review (OFR) in GB.
22 In Poland, guidelines regarding the preparation of the board's commentary were specified primarily in the following regulations:

   1 Accounting Act of September 29, 1994, consolidated text (Journal of Laws of 2021, item. 217, as amended)
   2 Regulation of the Minister of Finance of March 29, 2018, on current and periodic information provided by security issuers on conditions under which information required by the legislation of a non-Member State may be recognized as equivalent (Journal of Laws 2018, item 757)
   3 National Accounting Standard No. 9 "Director's Report" (Official Journal of the Minister of Development and Finance of 2018, item 4, as amended), applicable to management reports covering the financial year commenced in 2014.

23 https://www.ifrs.org/issued-standards/list-of-standards/management-commentary-practice-statement.html/content/dam/ifrs/publications/html-standards/english/2022/issued/ps1/
24 The first known company to produce an integrated report was the Danish industrial biotechnology company Novozymes, declared as "Integrated annual report, Environmental and Social Report." Further, firms listed on the Johannesburg Securities Exchange (JSE) were required to adopt Integrated Reporting from or after March 1, 2010. The driver for this initiative was the King Code of Governance Principles for South Africa 2009 (King III).
25 Sustainability and CSR reports and BSC Triple Bottom Line are considered the predecessors of integrated reports. According to this concept, the organization's activities and its performance are not only assessed through the prism of financial results but also through the impact that the organization exerts on the natural environment and on society (Fărcaş, 2015, pp. 106–113).
26 See IIRC (2011) and IIRC (2103d) regarding integrated reporting guidelines and framework.
27 Suchman (1995, str. 574) proposes a complex and broad-based definition of legitimacy as "a generalised perception or assumption that the actions of an entity are desirable, proper, or appropriate within some socially constructed system of norms, values, beliefs, and definitions."

2 Integrated report as a key non-financial statement

2.1 Essence of integrated reporting

The concept of integrated report (IR) has appeared in recent years to improve the usefulness and efficiency of business reporting. The new form of reporting entailed wide discussion in the scientific community and among practitioners.[1] The International Integrated Reporting Council (IIRC),[2] which developed the International <IR> Framework in 2013, had the greatest impact on the concept and integrated reporting system.

The idea of integrated reporting as the latest reporting practice was to replace the currently used reporting system by integrating financial and non-financial information in one document: an integrated report. Integrated reporting is considered to be a response to the limitations of traditional financial reporting, which is criticized primarily for focusing on the past, not considering intangible resources, lacking information about the value-creation process and all sources of value creation, having too much information, lacking a description of interrelations between sustainable development and financial performance, lacking information about the business model of an organization, and inconsistently presenting information (Eccles and Krzus, 2010b; Black Sun, 2012).

Undoubtedly, in recent years, the complexity of the business world has induced a growing demand for information on organizations' financial results, corporate governance, and their contribution to sustainable development (Frias-Aceituno et al., 2014; Lassini et al., 2016; Pistoni et al., 2016). Further, investors need an increasing amount of information on the process of creating value because financial reporting systems do not include all intangible assets produced or controlled by companies (Wyatt, 2008; Cohen et al., 2012; IIRC, 2017a). Moreover, companies' business models are increasingly based on transforming various forms of capital that together create value (Coulson et al., 2015).

In this context, integrated reporting may be a powerful means of fulfilling the growing demand for information about the process of creating value from the perspective of much capital to reduce information asymmetry (Adams, 2015; IIRC, 2017a,b). Walińska et al. (2016) also emphasized that the purely financial dimension of corporate value became too narrow, and the need appeared for

DOI: 10.4324/9781003336068-3

a more holistic view of the organization's activities and developing a report on the process of creating value.

To enable effective reporting practice, Eccles and Krzus (2010b) proposed the first version of integrated reporting by introducing a new concept: a single report. This concept aimed to present financial and non-financial information to show mutual relationships (Eccles and Krzus, 2010b, p. 10). This publication is in favor of integrated reporting practice, promoting two main reasons organizations should accept a single report as an external reporting procedure. The first motivation states that this innovative concept is a key element of true sustainability reporting because it allows for better risk management and creates the possibility of sustainable development. The second motivation is to improve corporate communication and transparency because a single report is concise and can communicate one message to all stakeholders (Eccles and Krzus, 2010b). The company's holistic perspective was later formulated in the advanced proposal of Eccles et al. (2014b) regarding a new concept of an annual board of directors' "Statement of Significant Audiences and Materiality" and a "Sustainable Value Matrix" tool that translates the statement into management decisions. A company's performance is perceived in the context of the value created for stakeholders.

As noted, integrated reporting is comprehensive and combines sustainable development and social responsibility reporting. Integrated reporting based on the <IR> framework was intended to provide a clear, concise, and comparable presentation of the organization's performance. Preparing an integrated report involves developing a single document that identifies the holistic story of the organization's activities by combining and confirming the organization's narrative with financial and non-financial data. Moreover, integrated reporting is a rational result of the debate and the gradual expansion of the guidelines for non-financial reporting, which in recent years have increasingly developed an equal footing with commonly accepted financial reporting standards (Figure 2.1).

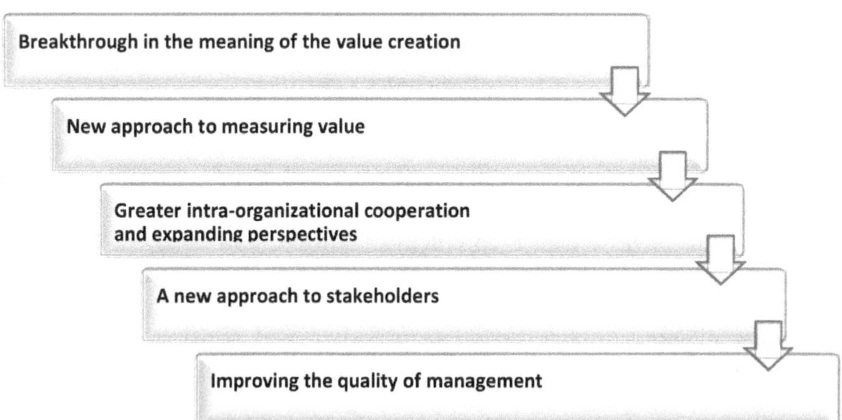

Figure 2.1 Integrated reporting development

Source: Own elaboration.

The IIRC has the greatest impact on integrated reporting development. The establishment of the IIRC and the development of the integrated framework are key turning points in the evolution of reporting and integrating financial and non-financial information. In 2013, the IIRC published the International <IR> Framework (IIRC, 2013d), the frame structure of integrated reporting, to organize the content of the report. The original version of the <IR> framework was replaced with a modified version of the same name in 2021 (IIRC, 2021). The IIRC proposed preparing a separate report containing financial and non-financial information (Cheng et al., 2014a). Thus, integrated reporting become a new reporting paradigm, providing a better picture of an entity, unlike the traditional financial statement, by combining financial and non-financial indicators of company performance (Brown and Dillard, 2014).

The key dates related to the integrated reporting development are as follows:

September 12, 2011
Discussion Paper Towards Integrated Reporting – Communicating Value in the 21st Century published
October 2011
Initial organisations participating in the IIRC Pilot Programme
July 2012
Draft Outline of the Integrated Reporting Framework
November 2012
Prototype of the International Integrated Reporting (<IR>) Framework
April 16, 2013
Consultation Draft of the International (IR) Framework
December 9, 2013
The International <IR> Framework
October 22, 2014
Directive of the European Parliament and of the Council
January 2021
The International <IR> Framework (2021) supersedes the International <IR> Framework (2013)

Per the fundamental concepts developed by the IIRC, integrated reports should contain information on financial results, the organization's strategy, corporate governance, social and ecological context, and companies' long-term forecasts, presented in a complex, organized, and coherent form. Although the main users of integrated reports are providers of financial capital or investors, the integrated report should benefit all stakeholders, including employees, clients, suppliers, regulatory bodies, and decision-makers interested in the ability of an organization to create value from short-, medium-, and long-term perspectives.

The guiding principles for integrated reporting emphasize the importance of coherent and multidimensional reporting, which communicates factors affecting the value of an organization in time (Maroun and Atkins, 2015). Strategic focus and future orientation are key principles of the integrated report developed by the IIRC. Future orientation relates to eight elements of the content described in the framework (IIRC, 2021). Thus, integrated reports enhance an organization's accountability toward stakeholders regarding future financial and non-financial performance.

Integrated reporting is primarily dedicated to creating value in the organization. To date, there remains a lack of compulsory reporting in this respect, which has enabled organizations to disclose their value-creating process or the impact of their activities on various capitals, either in the integrated report or in a separate report (Flower, 2015). Indeed, the approach proposed by the IIRC regarding the disclosure of the value-creation process considers the large diversity of situations in various organizations while ensuring an adequate degree of interorganizational comparison to meet the relevant information demand (IIRC, 2021). However, numerous requirements regard the scope of the report, and regarding information non-disclosure, companies must explain why the information was omitted (Flower, 2015).

Traditional reports do not disclose key performance indicators (KPIs). The lack of compulsory KPIs allows companies to decide what kind of information the process of value creation reveals and how (Coulson et al., 2015; Melloni et al., 2016). Indeed, the framework confirms that "quantitative indicators, including KPIs and monetized metrics and the context in which they are provided, can be very helpful in explaining how an organization creates, preserves, or erodes value and how it uses and affects various capitals"; however, the framework contains a clear statement that the purpose of integrated reporting is "not to quantify or monetize the value of the organization at a point in time, the value it creates, preserves, or erodes over a period, or its uses of or effects on all the capitals" (IIRC, 2021, p. 12).

Moreover, the framework recognizes that it is appropriate to make trade-offs between various forms of capital (IIRC, 2021, p. 27), and this assumption regards sustainability. A small range of guidelines offered by the IIRC regarding the method of measuring the use of various capitals can significantly increase the complexity of IR for those preparing this report. Indeed, the lack of performance indicators may increase the complexity of measuring capital and influence the decision to implement integrated reporting practices (Robertson and Samy, 2015). In this context, the question arises as to whether more companies, some for the first time, will consider and recognize in the report the direct and indirect negative effects their activities cause on human, social, and ecological capital, thus reducing information asymmetry (de Villiers et al., 2014).

Comprehensive capital reporting may reduce the comparison of information revealed over time and among companies. Therefore, it can be challenging to present the use of this capital coherently for comparison in the report (Thomson, 2015; Melloni et al., 2016). However, the "apply or explain" approach, according to which organizations should reveal the reason they consider any capital to be irrelevant and, thus, do not include it in the integrated report, may increase the interorganizational comparison of information (Flower, 2015). Hence, as part of signaling theory and based on current debates, the question emerges as to whether integrated reporting can reduce information asymmetry in reports effectively regarding multiple capitals.

Although integrated reporting is a relatively new area of theory and practice, it has attracted significant interest from scientists, with many studies on it. As it is a rapidly developing area of corporate reporting regulation, integrated reporting ensures the possibility of studying many aspects of regulation development in the field of accounting in a much shorter period than it usually happens in the case of financial reporting standards.

2.2 Information and transformational function of integrated reporting

Integrated reporting can be a powerful means of satisfying the growing demand for information on the process of value creation from the perspective of capital to reduce information asymmetry (Adams, 2015; IIRC, 2017a). The IIRC defines integrated reporting as "concise communication about how an organization's strategy, governance, performance and prospects, in the context of its external environment, lead to the creation, preservation or erosion of value in the short, medium, and long term" (IIRC, 2021, p. 53). The definition indicates its multidimensional character and emphasizes the transition from the concept of shareholder value to consistency and interrelations between the company's strategy, corporate governance, results of activity, and forecasts for the future. Moreover, the definition emphasizes the role of the external environment (e.g., globalization, demographic changes, resource deficiency, urbanization, and challenges related to the natural environment and technological conditions) as an important factor that exerts a long-term influence on the operational context of a given organization (Berndt et al., 2014, p. 196).

The framework emphasizes that an "integrated report should provide insight into the organization's strategy and how that relates to its ability to create value" (IIRC, 2021). Integrated reporting requires disclosure of the company's strategy and business model (De Villiers et al., 2014). Therefore, its implementation may aim to improve disclosures regarding the strategy and business model (Łęgowik-Świącik, 2018, p. 93) and improve the information quality for the benefit of investors.

The <IR> framework indicates two integrated reporting functions: information and transformation functions (Eccles and Serafeim, 2014). The executive summary of the <IR> framework notes that "integrated reporting promotes a more cohesive and efficient approach to corporate reporting and aims to improve the quality of information available to providers of financial capital to enable a more efficient and productive allocation of capital" (IIRC, 2021, p. 5). However, the IIRC also notes that the integrated report may also be interesting for other stakeholders: "An integrated report benefits all stakeholders interested in an organization's ability to create value over time" (IIRC, 2021, p. 5).

From the company perspective, the transformation function is achieved through "integrated thinking," which is "the active consideration by an organization of the relationships between its various operating and functional units and the capitals that the organization uses or affects" (IIRC, 2021, p. 3). Integrated reporting and integrated thinking are mutually strengthening, which yields an effective and productive allocation of capital and acts "as a force for financial stability and sustainable development" (IIRC, 2021, p. 5). The key to achieving this is measurement and reporting on all capital that the organization uses to create value (financial, manufactured, natural, intellectual, human, and relational capital) and information on the impact of one type of capital on the remaining capital.

The <IR> framework also provides insight into an external transformation by showing "how the organization interacts with the external environment" (IIRC, 2021, p. 15) and "by disclosing how key stakeholders' legitimate needs and interests are understood, taken into account, and responded to through decisions, actions, and performance, as well as ongoing communication" (IIRC, 2021, p. 29).

Providing this information to stakeholders enhances the transformation function. Stakeholders can "provide useful insights about matters that are important to them, including economic, environmental, and social issues that also affect the ability of the organization to create value" (IIRC, 2021, p. 28). It is possible by enabling the company to better understand how stakeholders perceive value, identify trends the company may not be aware of and trends that are gaining significance, identify the risks and possibilities, and contribute to the development and implementation of the company's strategy (IIRC, 2021).

Generally, the transformation function of integrated reporting stems from the company's engagement in stakeholder relations to obtain their feedback and contribution to the process of decision-making regarding the allocation of the company's resources. Separate financial statements and sustainability reports do not fulfill any of these functions. Investors need a better understanding of how companies' activities translate into financial and non-financial results. Integrated reporting also forces companies to interact with stakeholders in the preparation of the report and brings benefits in the form of feedback, completing the transformation function with the maximum possible efficiency.

Since the adoption of integrated reporting, there has been a significant increase in the scope and quality of non-financial disclosures, and companies have reported more non-financial information. Despite the increase in the volume of disclosed information, the key aspects of the disclosure are not presented comprehensively, financial and non-financial information is discussed in the management commentary, and the disclosures are general and not specific to the company (Robertson and Samy, 2015; Haji and Anifowose, 2016). However, in recent years, companies have increasingly adapted to the reporting requirements introduced in the <IR> framework.

According to Eccles and Krzus (2010b), enterprises will perceive integrated reporting to provide more detailed information about a company's sustainability strategy and how it contributes to stakeholders and a sustainable society. However, integrated reporting is much more than just a simple merger of financial statements and sustainability reports in one document. It also improves the level of dialogue and engagement with stakeholders.

Notably, integrated reporting induces a significant change in corporate behavior (Higgins et al., 2019) because it calls for a more holistic view of financial, natural, and human resource allocation and their interrelationships (Eccles and Krzus, 2010a). The International <IR> Framework notes the purpose of integrated reporting as a more consistent and effective approach to corporate reporting, which can improve the quality of information available to financial capital providers for a more effective allocation of capital.

The <IR> framework has also generated some controversy. Flower (2015) claims that the IIRC did not effectively resolve the issue of sustainable development reporting because the concept of value is value for investors, not society, and the IIRC does not impose the obligation to report damage caused to the environment. Although issues of sustainable development and ecology are pivotal, the <IR> framework published in 2013 emphasized the creation of long-term value for financial stakeholders (De Villiers et al., 2017). Thomson (2015) claims that "Integrated Reporting reduces sustainability into five sources of corporate value, but sources of value that need to be better managed in order to increase the wealth of individual investors not society's prosperity" (p. 19). Furthermore, Melloni et al. (2016) claim that companies adopt impression management strategies by manipulating the tone of business model disclosures provided in their integrated reports. Moreover, whether integrated reporting reduces information asymmetry is controversial.

Another issue that raises doubts is forward-looking disclosures. Academic researchers argue about its benefits (Bek-Gaik and Surowiec, 2020a). First, forward-looking disclosures reduce the information asymmetry that arises when some entities have private information on a company that is unavailable to investors and other stakeholders (Uyar and Kilic, 2012). Moreover, forward-looking disclosures on future operations, activities, plans, strategies, and financial objectives are useful for estimating the expected cash flows and future value of companies (Celik et al., 2006). Given that information about the past is insufficient for investors to anticipate possible opportunities and threats, forward-looking information plays a key role in their investment decisions (Menicucci, 2013; Bravo, 2016).

However, companies may be hesitant to disclose company-specific risks and prospects for several reasons. For example, sharing forward-looking information may indirectly increase the cost of sharing proprietary information that can be exploited by competitors (Kent and Ungs, 2003). Therefore, companies may avoid disclosing forward-looking information for fear of the possible negative impact of such disclosures on their competitive positions (Uyar and Kilic, 2012). Moreover, it may be difficult to predict a company's future performance with a certain accuracy owing to uncertainties related to the future (Aljifri and Hussainey, 2007). The potential inaccuracy of future forecasts reduces incentives for managers to disclose quantitative and forward-looking information because of potential litigation costs (Healy and Palepu, 2001; Oliveira et al., 2011).

2.3 Fundamental concepts and key content elements of an integrated report

The IIRC International <IR> Framework presents the fundamental concepts, guiding principles, and content elements of an integrated report and the rules for its preparation and presentation (IIRC, 2021).

At the foundation of the fundamental concepts of the <IR> framework is a belief that companies should expand their reporting to include all resources that contribute to their business. The IIRC uses the term "capita" to describe these diverse resources, identifying six types of capital: financial, manufactured, intellectual, human, social and relationship, and natural (IIRC, 2021), which accords with the view that the structure of resources determines the value of the company (Skowron-Grabowska, 2021). Moreover, high-quality information on environmental, social, and governance (ESG) issues disclosed in integrated reports signals that potentially important business risks are effectively managed, reducing information asymmetry and minimizing the cost of equity from the perspective of shareholders (De Villiers and Van Staden, 2011).

As per the IIRC framework, integration aims to ensure clear and complete disclosure, with a strategic perspective and special attention paid to communication with external stakeholders (Eccles and Krzus, 2010b; Cheng et al., 2014; De Villiers et al., 2014; Melloni et al., 2016). The essential goal of IR is to explain how organizations create value in time for financial capital providers (IIRC 2021). Therefore, the focus on creating value and a clear definition of the main stakeholders (providers of financial capital) are the characteristic features of the conceptual design of the <IR> framework (Milne and Gray, 2013; Flower, 2015). According to the IIRC framework, the main aspects of an integrated report are conciseness, interrelated information, and integrated thinking (IIRC, 2021). Information interrelations express the essence of integrated reporting, promoting the awareness of the organization regarding mutual relations between important factors of value-creation processes.

Reporting based on the <IR> framework should provide a clearer, more concise, and comparable representation of an organization's performance. Integrated report preparation involves developing a single document that reveals the holistic story of the company's activities by combining the non-financial narrative with financial data. However, though the IIRC determines significant developmental progress, it is also a measurable result of the debate and gradual expansion of the guidelines and frameworks of non-financial reporting, which in recent years have been increasingly sought as per highly regulated and widely accepted financial reporting standards.

Various resources (e.g., capital) have been noted as fundamental integrated reporting concepts. As part of IIRC, capitals are defined as "stocks of value that are increased, decreased or transformed through the activities and outputs of the organization" (IIRC, 2021, p. 6) to create value over time, which determines the business model of an organization (IIRC, 2013b, p. 10). Notably, the six capitals concept is one of the model assumptions suggested by the <IR> framework and is among the most distinguished integrated reporting features. Capital can be financial, manufactured, intellectual, human, social, relationship, and natural. The integrated report should explain how the organization cooperates with the external environment and how it uses and impacts various types of capital to create value for internal and external stakeholders (Eccles et al., 2014).

Financial capital refers to the pool of funds available to an organization for use in the production of goods or the provision of services obtained through financing, such as equity or grants, debt, or profit generated through operations or investments (IIRC, 2021, p. 19). Manufactured capital refers to manufactured physical objects (as opposed to natural physical objects) available to an organization for use in the production of goods or provision of services (IIRC, 2021, p. 19). It can be internal to the company, such as buildings and equipment, or external and renewable, such as infrastructure, roads, ports, waste, or water treatment plants. Intellectual capital regards knowledge-based intangible assets, including intellectual property and organizational capital (IIRC, 2021, p. 19). It is owned by the company (intellectual property) (e.g., patents, copyrights, software, rights, and licenses) or not (organizational capital) (e.g., tacit knowledge, systems, procedures, and protocols). Human capital includes people's competencies, abilities, experiences, and motivations for innovation. It includes their alignment with and support for an organization's governance framework; approach to risk management; ethical values; ability to understand, develop, and implement the organization's strategy, loyalty, and motivation to improve processes, goods, and services; and their ability to lead, manage, and collaborate (IIRC, 2021, p. 19).

The <IR> framework indicates that companies should extend their reporting to include all the resources they use as inputs to their business activities. The current IIRC framework aims to improve the quality of information available to providers of financial capital for a more efficient and productive allocation of capital (Dumay et al., 2016). The <IR> framework states that the primary purpose of integrated reporting is to explain how financial capital providers create value over time (IIRC, 2021). Further, IR benefits all stakeholders interested in an organization's ability to create value over time. Integrated reporting practitioners are now trying to gather information about strategies, corporate governance, performance, and social and environmental impacts, presented in the narrative part of financial statements (Melloni et al., 2016).

The concept of "capitals" according to IIRC includes the company's capital in a conventional sense and the capital of society, such as the natural environment. According to Flower (2015), this capital can be internal or external to the firm. The capital internal to the firm can either be owned or not by the legal entity, and if external, it is either renewable or not renewable.

Another fundamental concept on which the integrated report is based is value creation. The <IR> framework makes it clear that the primary function of integrated reporting is to communicate "value creation" and explain to providers of financial capital how an organization creates value over time. Such value manifests in the increases, decreases, or transformations of capital caused by the organization's business activities and their results. The value created has two main aspects: the value created for the organization, which enables the achievement of a financial surplus for financial capital providers (investors), and the value created for other stakeholders.

An important content element of integrated reporting is its business model. The <IR> framework requires that the description of the company's business model be included in the integrated report, with particular emphasis on how the business model and underlying strategies integrate the six capitals. According to the <IR> framework, capital preserves values (relationships), which are input elements to the business model.

A business model is a significant tool for capturing, visualizing, understanding, and communicating a company's business logic (Osterwalder 2004). It provides a platform to measure, track, and compare company performance and improve business management by improving the design, planning, change, and implementation of a company strategy. Disclosures about the business model in the integrated report allow for reacting to business environment changes; improving strategy, business organization, and technology alignment; and supporting innovations. Investors must understand the connection between a firm's business model and its strategy, corporate governance, performance, and prospects, which an integrated report provides. Further, integrated reporting overcomes the limitations of current reporting practices and the lack of a clear link between financial and non-financial information.

Integrated reporting also promotes integrated thinking. The IIRC framework (2021, p. 3) defines integrated thinking as "the active consideration by an organization of the relationships between its various operating and functional units and the capitals that the organization uses or affects. Integrated thinking induces integrated decision-making and actions that consider the creation, preservation, or erosion of value over the short, medium, and long term." It promotes a more holistic approach to building better companies and societies (Druckman, 2014).

The <IR> framework clearly states that integrated thinking considers the interrelations and interdependencies of a range of factors that affect an organization's ability to create value. These factors or capitals include all resources and relationships that form part of the organization's business model: financial, manufactured, intellectual, human, social, relational, and natural capital (IIRC, 2021). Such capitals are supposed to encourage companies to think from a broader perspective and consider all potential sources of value creation and then describe them in the report, providing investors with valuable data in a broader context (Druckman, 2014). Moreover, the <IR> framework states that the more integrated thinking is embedded into an organization's operations, the more naturally the connectivity of information flows into management reporting, analysis, and decision-making. It also induces a better integration of information systems that support internal and external reporting and communication, including the preparation of an integrated report.

The <IR> framework also lists the guiding principles of integrated reporting, which constitute the basis for developing an integrated report:

1 Strategic focus and future orientation – an integrated report should provide insight into the organization's strategy; how it relates to the organization's ability to create value in the short, medium, and long term; and its use of and effects on capital.
2 Connectivity of information – an integrated report should show a holistic picture of the combination, interrelatedness, and dependencies between the factors that affect the organization's ability to create value over time.
3 Stakeholder relationships – an integrated report should provide insight into the nature and quality of the organization's relationships with its key stakeholders, including how and to what extent the organization understands, considers, and responds to their legitimate needs and interests.
4 Materiality – an integrated report should disclose information on matters that substantively affect the organization's ability to create value over the short, medium, and long term.
5 Conciseness – an integrated report should be concise.
6 Reliability and completeness – an integrated report should include all material matters, positive and negative, in a balanced way and without material error.
7 Consistency and comparability – the information in an integrated report should be presented on a basis that is consistent over time to enable comparison with other organizations such that it is material to the organization's ability to create value over time (IIRC, 2021, pp. 25–36).

2.3.1 *Key content elements of the integrated report*

The IIRC's integrated report framework contains seven content elements, presented in the form of the following questions an integrated report should answer (Bek-Gaik and Surowiec, 2020b):

- Organizational overview and external environment: "What does the organization do and what are the circumstances under which it operates?"
- Governance: "How does the organization's governance structure support its ability to create value in the short, medium, and long term?"
- Risks and opportunities: "What are the specific risks and opportunities that affect the organization's ability to create value over the short, medium, and long term, and how does the organization deal with them?"

- Strategy and resource allocation: "Where does the organization want to go and how does it intend to get there?"
- Business model: "What is the organization's business model?"
- Performance: "To what extent has the organization achieved its strategic objectives for the period and what are its outcomes in terms of effects on the capitals?"
- Outlook: "What challenges and uncertainties are organizations likely to encounter in pursuing their strategy, and what are the potential implications for its business model and future performance?"
- Basis of preparation and presentation: How does the organization determine what matters to include in the integrated report and how are such matters quantified or evaluated?" (IIRC, 2021, pp. 38–48).

The "organizational overview and external environment" content element should include information on the company's purpose, mission, and vision, and basic messages, such as the ownership and organization structure, the number of employees, competition, and the markets in which the organization operates. Additional issues should also be considered, directly or indirectly affecting the activities of the organization regarding the external environment in which the company operates (i.e., legal, commercial, environmental, political, and social aspects). Detailed information in this area concerns the following issues (IIRC 2021, pp. 39–40):

- The organization's specific features:
    - Culture, ethics, and values
    - Ownership and operating structure
    - Principal activities and markets
    - Competitive landscape and market positioning
    - Position within the value chain
- Key quantitative information highlighting significant changes from prior periods
- Significant factors affecting the external environment and the organization's response (including legal, commercial, social, environmental, and political aspects)

The corporate governance content element requires an integrated report on the organizational structure and management skills impact on the management process, the nature of the processes used in decision-making, the influence of culture and ethics on the use of capital, and building relationships with key stakeholders. Detailed disclosures in this area should include the following (IIRC, 2021, p. 40):

- The organization's leadership structure, including the skills and diversity (e.g., range of backgrounds, gender, competence, and experience) of those charged with governance

- Specific processes used to make strategic decisions and to establish and monitor the culture of the organization, including its attitude to risk and mechanisms for addressing integrity and ethical issues
- Particular actions to monitor the organization's approach to risk management
- Information on how the organization's culture, ethics, and values are reflected in its use of and effects on capital, including its relationships with key stakeholders
- Information on whether the organization is implementing governance practices that exceed legal requirements
- Information on the responsibility those charged with governance assume to promote and enable innovation
- Information on how remuneration and incentives are linked to value creation in the short, medium, and long terms, including how they are linked to the organization's use of and effects on capital

The business model[3] content element should show the key features of the organization's activity, providing information to assess whether the organization can create value and achieve the assumed financial and non-financial goals. It should answer several questions of fundamental organizational importance: who are the unit's clients? What is the value proposition? How can this value be delivered to customers? At what cost and how does the company use its assets in business activities? The business model in the <IR> framework should include the following (IIRC, 2021, pp. 41–43):

- Presentation of the organization: what is the organization's profile, the organizational structure, or in what areas it is operating?
- Business strategy: key aspects of the company's strategy
- Positioning of the organization within the entire value chain and dependence on key inputs
- Financial results: how the business model controls the profitability or generation of revenues
- Creating value: how the inputs, outputs, activities, and interrelations lead to value creation and desired outcomes (IIRC, 2013b, p. 13)

The content element of risk and opportunities (IIRC, 2021, p. 44) requires an integrated report to answer the following questions: what are the specific risks and opportunities that affect a firm's ability to create values in the short, medium, and long term, and how do firms cope with them? In particular, integrated should present the following:

- Key risks and opportunities
- Sources of threats, risks, and opportunities, both internal and external

- Organization's judgment regarding the probability that a given risk will occur and determine the opportunities and threats related to it
- Organization activities in the field of risk management

The presentation of the content element of strategy and resource allocation (IIRC, 2021, pp. 44–45) is associated with answering the question: where is the organization going and what is it going to achieve? As the fundamental concepts of IIRC emphasize, the description of the connections between the organization's strategy and resource allocation and the information presented in other content elements is especially important. In particular, according to the IIRC guidelines, organizations should reveal:

- Strategic goals in a short, medium, and long term
- Strategies that the organization has developed or intends to implement to achieve these goals
- Resource allocation plans enabling the implementation of the adopted strategy
- Method of performance measuring and target effects for the short, medium, and long term

It is also vital to disclose the organization's activities aimed at adapting to changes, indicating factors that give organizations a competitive advantage and enable them to create value, including innovations, intellectual capital, and corporate social responsibility (CSR). Presenting performance in integrated reports (IIRC, 2021, pp. 45–46), the firm must reveal financial, non-financial, qualitative, and quantitative results and their impact on the company's resources. This section also discusses the linkages between past and current performance. An integrated report must contain qualitative and quantitative information regarding performance, in particular

- Quantitative indicators of targets, risks, and opportunities, explaining their significance, implications, and methods and assumptions used in compiling them
- The organization's effects (positive and negative) on capital, including material effects on capital up and down the value chain
- State of key stakeholder relationships and how the organization responded to key stakeholders' legitimate needs and interests
- The linkages between past and current performance and between current performance and the organization's outlook

As a content element, information on the future of the organization should appear in the integrated report (IIRC, 2021, pp. 46–47). The integrated report should answer the following questions: what challenges and uncertainties are organizations likely to encounter in pursuing their strategies? What are the potential implications for its business model and future performance?

The company should describe the issues in detail in the integrated report, including

- The organization's expectations about the external environment the organization is likely to face in the short, medium, and long terms
- How changes in the external environment affect the organization
- How organizations respond to critical challenges and uncertainties that are likely to arise

The integrated report should also include information based on its preparation and presentation (IIRC, 2021, p. 47).

The business model is perceived as among the most important elements of an integrated report. The International <IR> Framework (IIRC, 2021) emphasizes that integrated reporting should focus on the business model of a given organization and its resources and relations (e.g., capital). A firm's business model is among the key disclosures in integrated reporting. The business model is a fundamental concept for understanding how organizations operate and create value.[4]

The IIRC emphasizes that the integrated reporting should include complete disclosures about the business model regarding input elements, business activities, output elements, and outcomes to create value over the short, medium, and long term (IIRC, 2013b, p. 6). Table 2.1 presents the characteristics of the business model elements in the integrated report.

Business model reporting should also follow rules that can enhance the effectiveness and readability of the description, such as

- Identification of the key elements of the business model and their presentation in the form of a simple diagram, supported by an explanation of the relevance of business model elements to the organization
- A narrative that addresses all material matters for the organization
- Identification of critical stakeholders and other dependencies, key value drivers, and important external factors
- Positioning of the organization within the value chain and linkages to other aspects of reporting, including strategy, opportunities, and risks
- KPIs and financial considerations, such as cost containment and revenue (IIRC, 2013b, p. 13)

The IIRC suggests that considering the listed elements of the business model will bring specific benefits to the organization. First, the organization will develop a more consistent and effective approach to corporate reporting, thereby ensuring that all factors that significantly impact the organization's ability to create value over time are considered. Second, the implementation of this process will support integrated thinking and decision-making, and companies will focus on creating value via relationships with others. Society

Table 2.1 Elements of the business model in integrated reporting

Element	*Characteristic*
Inputs The capitals were divided into individual categories and described in the <IR> framework to prepare an integrated report (IIRC 2021, pp. 18–20)	Financial capital – funds available to the organization for use in the production of goods or provision of services or obtained by financing, such as equity or grants, debt, or profit generated through operations or investments Manufactured capital – manufactured (distinct from natural) physical objects that are available to an organization for use in the production of goods or the provision of services; in particular, buildings, equipment, infrastructure Manufactured capital is often created by other organizations, but includes assets manufactured by the reporting organization for sale or when retained for its use. Intellectual capital – organizational, knowledge-based intangibles, including • Intellectual property (e.g., patents, copyrights, software, rights, and licenses) • "Organizational capital," such as tacit knowledge, systems, procedures, and protocols Human capital – people's competencies, capabilities, and experience and their motivations to innovate, including their • Alignment with and support for an organization's governance framework, risk management approach, and ethical values • Ability to understand, develop, and implement an organization's strategy • Loyalties and motivations for improving processes, goods, and services, including their ability to lead, manage and collaborate Social and relationship capital – the institutions and relationships within and between communities, groups of stakeholders, and other networks, and the ability to share information to enhance individual and collective well-being Social and relationship capital includes • Shared norms and common values and behaviors • Key stakeholder relationships and the trust and willingness to engage that an organization has developed and strives to build and protect with external stakeholders • Intangibles associated with the brand and reputation an organization has developed • An organization's social license to operate Natural capital – all renewable and non-renewable environmental resources and processes that provide goods or services that support the past, current, or future prosperity of an organization. It includes: • Air, water, land, minerals, and forests • Biodiversity and ecosystem health

(*Continued*)

Table 2.1 (Continued)

Element	*Characteristic*
Business activities	Business activities include basic activities, that is, research and development, planning, design, production/conversion, product differentiation, market segmentation, distribution, service provision, quality control, operational improvement, relationship management, and after-sales service. The fundamental concepts of integrated reporting indicate that "at the core of the business model are activities that, through the consumption [or] transformation of inputs into outputs, aim to generate valuable outcomes" (IIRC, 2013b, p. 8). The description of key business activities can include • How the organization differentiates itself in the marketplace (e.g., through product differentiation, market segmentation, delivery channels, and marketing) • The extent to which the business model relies on revenue generation after the initial point of sale (e.g., extended warranty arrangements or network usage charges) • How the organization approaches the need to innovate • How the business model has been designed to adapt to change IIRC also pays attention to the description of the contribution to the organization's long-term success through initiatives such as process improvement, employee training, and relationship management
Outputs	Outputs include an organization's key products and services and other outputs, such as by-products and waste (including emissions), depending on their materiality for the organization
Outcomes	Outcomes are the internal and external consequences of capital given an organization's business activities and outputs. The description of outcomes includes internal (e.g., employee morale, organizational reputation, revenue, and cash flows) and external (e.g., customer satisfaction, tax payments, brand loyalty, and social and environmental effects) outcomes. The <IR> framework indicates positive (i.e., those that result in a net increase in the capitals and thereby create value) and negative (i.e., those that result in a net decrease in the capitals and thereby erode value) outcomes

Source: Author's elaboration based on IIRC (2013b) and IIRC (2021).

will also benefit from the proper, information-based allocation of capital, increased accountability, and improved quality of management of the six types of capital (IIRC, 2021, p. 29). Moreover, there is evidence that organizations publishing sustainability or CSR reports can benefit from the reduction of equity capital, as noted by Dhaliwal et al. (2011).

The proposed <IR> framework will certainly facilitate the process of preparing an integrated report and will logically organize the information presented by organizations. It is also an important factor that enhances the coherence and connectivity of information. The following information requires linkages with other aspects:

- Various sections/chapters of the integrated report
- Past performance and a strategy for the future
- Six capitals
- Integrated report and other corporate reports

The <IR> framework also indicates the guiding principles that should be followed when preparing the integrated report:

- Strategic focus and orientation for the future
- Connectivity of information
- Stakeholder relationships
- Materiality
- Conciseness
- Reliability and completeness
- Consistency and comparability[5] (IIRC 2021, pp. 25–36)

The guidelines for integrated reporting emphasize the importance of coherent and multidimensional reporting that communicates factors affecting the value of the organization over time. Future orientation is among the key principles of the integrated report framework developed by the IIRC. Moreover, forward-looking information is contained in eight content elements of the report, described in the <IR> framework (IIRC, 2021, p. 8). Thus, integrated reports enhance the accountability of organizations from past and future financial and non-financial perspectives toward all stakeholders.

2.4 Integrated reporting and processes of organizational change

The adoption of integrated reporting, as research on the subject highlight, entails many organizational changes and facilitates the process of integrated thinking of managers. According to the <IR> framework, integrated thinking facilitates the continuous improvement of reporting and implements a more holistic corporate strategy. The IIRC expects that organizations implementing integrated reporting will introduce changes in their internal processes and practices.

Studies of entities that are early adopters of integrated reporting reveal a change in their reporting practice, though limited and in individual cases (Busco et al., 2013; Perego et al., 2016; Beck et al., 2017; Zhou et al., 2017; Zhou et al., 2019). In other cases, the change did not materialize (Higgins et al., 2014; McNally and Maroon, 2018), and integrated thinking can be a preliminary condition (not the result) of integrated reporting (Al-Htaybat and von Alberti-Altaybat, 2018). According to Dumay and Dai (2017), some aspects of integrated thinking may be undesirable, and a case study conducted by the authors showed that integrated thinking clashes with the existing organizational culture rather than driving a new organizational culture. Therefore, it is doubtful as to what the journey to change is associated with and how companies approach the idea of "integrated thinking." However, the literature identifies several benefits from the implementation of integrated reporting to the organization's reporting practice.

Higgins et al. (2019) divided the benefits of implementing integrated reporting into three basic groups: structural, cultural, and reporting practices. As part of the first group, the authors indicated:

- Better internal collaboration across organization (break down silos) ("Better internal collaboration between different teams, moving away from operating in silos, to more productive environments and increased efficiency," IIRC and Black Sun, 2015; IIRC, 2017a, p. 8).
- Ongoing changes to management information and systems ("[...] ongoing changes are made in management information and systems even in organisations with a number of years of IR experience," IIRC and Black Sun, 2014; IIRC, 2017a, p. 16).
- Use of capital, creation of value, and business model improvement occur concurrently as a holistic exercise ("[...] tackling key interconnected areas of Integrated Reporting: the use of capitals, the creation of value, and the definition of the organisation's business model," IIRC, 2013c, p. 4, 2016).

The authors described subsequent benefits of implementing integrated reporting as cultural elements, distinguishing:

- Change in a firm's mindset and approach to value creation ("The research also reinforces the point that IR in most cases is an outcome of changes in an organisation's approach to value creation and management" (IIRC and Black Sun, 2012, p. 1); "[...] to understand the interconnections between the full range of functions, operations, resources, and relationships, which have a material effect on the organisation's ability to create value over time. The journey towards integrated reporting, therefore, also entails a mindset change about how the company makes its money" (IIRC and Black Sun, 2012, p. 1))
- Improved self-insight into business activity ("As reporters become more in tune with integrated thinking and reporting, companies are beginning to experience improved insights into its business," IIRC and Black Sun, 2014, p. 15)
- Integrated thinking is normalized ("Integrated thinking starts to become embedded," IIRC and Black Sun, 2015, p. 8)
- Measurable improvements in decision-making ("Our research found that a large majority of organisations experienced improvements in decision-making. In this case, significant improvements were seen at every stage of the reporting journey," IIRC, 2014, p. 24).

The third group of benefits from implementing integrated reporting concerning reporting practices seems to be very important and covers:

- Holistic discussion of performance over purely financial performance ("The true goal, however, is to move the needle and shift the default from talking solely about financial performance to a more holistic discussion on performance," IIRC and Black Sun, 2015)
- Increase in meaningful disclosures of value-relevant information to investors and stakeholders ("[...] we expect those on the Integrated Reporting journey to move away from boilerplate information driven by compliance to more meaningful disclosures that give stakeholders a clearer picture of the business," IIRC and Black Sun, 2012, p. 16, including "[...] journey many businesses have embarked upon towards communicating more coherent, value-relevant information to investors and other stakeholders", IIRC, 2012, p. 1)
- More cohesive and efficient corporate reporting ("[IR] promotes a more cohesive and efficient approach to corporate reporting that draws on different reporting strands," IIRC, 2013a,b,c)
- More relevant KPIs and integrated indicators linked to material issues ("Refinement of KPIs which are linked to material issues helps to improve performance management," IIRC and Black Sun, 2015, p. 8, "the ability to measure and manage non-financial information with implications for financial capital is a key challenge. [...] organizations reported that creating integrated indicators, capturing the interconnections, was an important objective," IIRC and Black Sun, 2014, p. 11).

In the <IR> framework, IIRC promotes integrated thinking, defined as "the active consideration by an organization of the relationships between its various operating and functional units and the capitals that the organization uses or affects" (IIRC, 2021, p. 3). Integrated thinking fundamentally changes the functioning of enterprises (Tweedie and Martinov-Bennie, 2015; Velte and Stawinoga, 2016; Feng et al., 2017). Further studies are needed to confirm this. The IIRC (2015) described integrated thinking as a requirement to ensure long-term value creation by enterprises building a connection between organizations, breaking internal barriers, and improving decision-making (p. 22).

Integrated reporting entails a significant change in corporate behavior because it requires a more holistic view of financial, natural, and human resource allocation decisions and the interrelationships therein (Eccles and Krzus, 2010a, p. 1). The expected changes also include how organizations react to the wider interests of stakeholders. Integrated reporting introduced in South Africa – based on King Committee (2001, 2009) and corporate governance – was part of wider reforms to eliminate corporate governance and social exclusion weaknesses, suggesting significant changes in organizational and social practices.

Analyses of early IR adopters of integrated reporting show that many initial fears remain unresolved. Moreover, some researchers have stated that instead of stimulating integrated thinking via integrated reporting, it is necessary to change how to think before the company can start considering integrated reporting (Al-Htaybat and von Alberti-Alhtaybat, 2018). Others find that the flexibility associated with integrated reporting allows for adapting it to the organization's strategies (Gibassier et al., 2018). However, this flexibility means the effects required and the effects of changes are too ambiguous (Vesty et al., 2018). This flexibility may limit the scope of the implementation of wider ideas. Others note that integrated reporting is becoming standardized as a tick-box, compliance-oriented exercise accepted for use because it has become fashionable (Gunarathne and Senaratne, 2017; McNally et al., 2017) instead of stimulating the systematic evolution of the way of thinking and understanding of value creation by managers.

Integrated reporting also induces a change in the established way of thinking and the company's approach to value creation. Different ways of thinking about how organizations create value are among the most important motives to initiate integrated reporting. In addition, an integrated report should reflect an integrated approach to creating value for an organization.

According to Higgins et al. (2019), the implementation of integrated reporting yields

- Better internal collaboration across organizations, understood as the breaking down of organizational silos, more productive environments, and more efficient operations
- Ongoing changes to management information and systems
- Concurrent improvements in the use of capital, creation of value, and business model (value chain mapping, showing how to create value in the company, presentation of stakeholder impacts)
- Change in a firm's mindset and approach to value creation – different ways of thinking about how a firm creates value is one of the most important motives for implementing integrated reporting
- Improved insight into business activity
- Integrated thinking is normalized
- Measurable improvements in decision-making – a more holistic discussion of performance and changes in approach to value creation
- Reporting practice changes – organizations are taking ideas from the <IR> framework rather than using it as a reporting template; for instance, companies are developing KPIs
- Holistic discussion of performance over purely financial performance
- More meaningful disclosures of value-relevant information to investors and stakeholders
- More cohesive and efficient corporate reporting – a single report
- More relevant KPIs and integrated indicators linked to material issues

In summary, integrated reporting introduces many benefits to the organization but also poses challenges. An in-depth understanding of the assumptions and goals of integrated reporting will affect how to think about the organization and performance measures and will influence the consideration of factors determining value creation.

2.5 Overview of research on integrated reporting

The dynamic development of integrated reporting worldwide has resulted in a rapid increase in integrated reporting research, which can generally be divided into two main groups: studies on the concept and practice of integrated reporting, respectively. Concept studies explored the following:

- Analysis of factors influencing the development of integrated reporting
- Analysis of the relationships between integrated reporting and sustainability reports and CSR reports
- The problem of verifying non-financial information presented in the integrated report
- Analysis of the costs and benefits of implementing integrated reporting
- Information base for integrated reporting
- Tools facilitating preparing an integrated report
- Quality of integrated reporting disclosures

Research on integrated reporting practice focuses on the following (Table 2.2):

- Analysis of the content of integrated reports
- Comparison of the structure of integrated reports with the <IR> framework
- Determining the benefits of implementing integrated reporting in organizations

The integrated report shows the connections between financial and non-financial data, which are more understandable and transparent to stakeholders; it presents risks, opportunities, and challenges in business activities in the form of narrative information. This report also reduces the pressure on the management board from the perspective of stakeholder prioritization because it captures all relevant information on sustainable development, corporate governance, ecology, and social and financial matters. Moreover, the integrated report provides financial and non-financial information to investors that is not presented in sustainability reports or any other report. The information addressed to stakeholders and the integrated reporting system will make the company's management board more transparent and trustworthy for investors.

Notably, integrated reporting is not synonymous with CSR reporting. Indeed, though the beginnings of integrated reporting are closely related to

Table 2.2 Research on non-financial disclosures in integrated reports

Research problem	*Authors*	*Research description*	*Outcomes*
Application of integrated reporting in non-profit units	Adams and Simnett (2011)	Research on the application of the principles of integrated reporting and the possibilities of its implementation in the Not-for-Profit sector in Australia	It is possible to use the concept of integrated reporting in the Not-for-Profit sector
	Veltri and Silvestri (2015)	The research explored the integrated report of a South African public university by comparing it with the International Integrated Reporting Council (IIRC) <IR> framework	The examined report does not follow the <IR> framework: the data do not have an outlook orientation, the information is not interconnected, the stakeholder relationships are not highlighted, and the organizational ability to create value is not disclosed
Factors affecting the development of integrated reporting	Jensen and Berg (2012)	Research on the factors that influence the decision to prepare integrated reports. The authors explained the decision to adopt integrated reports regarding institutional factors	Important factors influencing the implementation of integrated reporting into practice include the level of investor protection and the status of economic development
	García-Sánchez, Rodríguez-Ariza Frías-Aceituno (2013a)	Research on the impact of the Hofstede national cultural system, representative of the values of local stakeholders, on integrated reporting, relative to various unrelated documents on corporate performance. The study employed a sample of companies from 20 countries (2008–2010), with 3,042 observations from 1,590 companies	Companies in societies with stronger collectivist and feminist values are in the vanguard of information integration
	Dragu and Tudor-Tiron (2013)	Analysis of the impact of political, economic, and cultural factors on integrated reporting practices	There are positive and negative correlations between integrated reporting and political, economic, and cultural conditions

(*Continued*)

Table 2.2 (Continued)

Research problem	*Authors*	*Research description*	*Outcomes*
	Sierra-Garcia, Zorio-Grima, Garcia-Benau (2013)	Research on why companies are producing integrated reporting, paying special attention to the links with the assurance of the corporate social responsibility (CSR) report. The analysis covered the 2009–2011 period, with 7,144 worldwide observations	The likelihood of disclosing an integrated report is positively associated with having the CSR report assured, year, size, and supplement industry
	Frias-Aceituno et al., (2013b)	Research on the role of the management board in the dissemination of integrated social corporate reporting	Growth opportunities, the size of a company and its management bodies, and gender diversity are the most important factors in the integrated dissemination of information
Analysis of the quality of disclosure	Pistoni et al. (2018)	Research on the quality of integrated reports issued by firms, proposing a scoring model and an integrated reporting scoreboard, which were applied to analyze 116 integrated reports issued in 2013 and 2014	The quality of integrated reports is low
	Kiliç and Kuzey (2018)	The study examined the nature and scope of forward-looking disclosures in early examples of integrated reporting and investigated the determinants of those disclosures. The sample for research involved 55 non-financial companies whose reports are available in the integrated reporting examples database for 2014. The study employed content analysis to investigate the quantitative and qualitative forward-looking disclosures among early adopters of integrated reporting	Most of the entities tended to provide qualitative rather than quantitative forward-looking disclosures; gender diversity and firm size are positively related to forward-looking disclosures, whereas leverage is negatively related to forward-looking disclosures; there was no significant impact created by board size, board composition, profitability, or industry on forward-looking disclosures

(*Continued*)

Table 2.2 (Continued)

Research problem	*Authors*	*Research description*	*Outcomes*
Integrated reporting case studies	Eccles and Serafeim (2014)	The study discusses, through a series of case studies, what constitutes an effective integrated report (Coca-Cola Hellenic Bottling Company) and the role of regulation in integrated reporting (Anglo-American)	The study presented the two primary functions of corporate reporting (information and transformation) and why currently isolated financial and sustainability reporting are not likely to perform effectively those functions
	Eccles and Krzus (2014)	The study analyzed English-language integrated reports of 124 companies around the world for 2012 and assessed the quality of disclosure	The study provides insight into opportunities and challenges in integrated reporting
	Eccles, Krzus, Ribot (2015)	The study reviewed the integrated reports of 25 multinational companies that participated in the IIRC's Pilot Programme Business Network. It provides a summary of the best reporting practices, assuming three main distinguishing features of a truly integrated report: an explanation of a company's value-creation strategy and how it uses and affects the IIRC's concept of "six capitals," a clear and detailed explanation of the relationships between financial and non-financial performance, and the materiality of information	The study showed the compliance of the content of the analyzed reports with the integrated reporting framework, transparent presentation of the organization's business model, and presentation of social and environmental activities
	Chersan (2015)	The latest integrated reporting practices were presented by analyzing annual reports published on the IIRC website (all for 2014). The content analysis allowed for describing and explaining the identified tendencies and extracted inferences	The results of the study were used to identify features of integrated reports and positive and negative tendencies regarding their content and shape. The number of organizational reports considered representative of integrated reporting constantly increases, and the quality of disclosed information is also increasing. Unfortunately, the complexity also increases

(*Continued*)

Table 2.2 (Continued)

Research problem	*Authors*	*Research description*	*Outcomes*
	Jinga and Dumitru (2015b)	This study furnishes insight into the reporting practices of an experienced preparer of integrated reports on the example of Takeda Pharmaceutical Company	The experience in the field of integrated reporting supported the company's assimilation of the integrated reporting framework guidelines for organizational legitimacy
	Bek-Gaik and Rymkiewicz (2015a)	Research on integrated reports published by companies included in the WIG30 index of the Warsaw Stock Exchange for 2013	Key findings include the following: • Large volumes of integrated reports • Information presented is often reproduced from other published reports • Challenge in assessing the quality and credibility of the presented non-financial information • Lack of clear links between non-financial and financial data • Small number of performance indicators, which significantly reduces the credibility of published information • Information on the business model is dispersed in different parts of the report
	Garstecki (2015a)	Analysis of integrated reports of selected Polish companies	The study draws attention to the need for the unification of integrated reports, primarily the financial part. Although integrated reporting does not focus mainly on financial information, its appropriate selection and presentation may increase the usability of the integrated report
	Garstecki (2015b)	Research on the financial data disclosure integrated reports of Polish companies. The study analyzed five integrated reports from 2013	The study indicates the lack of standardization of integrated reporting in the financial part and the area of other financial information

(Continued)

Table 2.2 (Continued)

Research problem	*Authors*	*Research description*	*Outcomes*
	Walińska et al. (2015)	Analysis of disclosure methods of non-financial information by selected public companies included in the WIG20 index of WSE	The publication of many different types of reports hinders the analysis of a firm's performance; information is repeated in different reports
	Bek-Gaik and Rymkiewicz (2016)	The study was conducted on the sample of 60 companies included in the WIG20 and mWIG40 of WSE indexes, analyzing 337 corporate reports for the 2013–2014 period	Integrated reports are mainly prepared by companies that are leaders in their industries, the structure of reports is very diverse, and the quality of disclosure varies
Internal integrated reporting implementation mechanisms	Stubbs and Higgins (2014)	The study verifies the internal mechanisms of implementation of integrated reporting in Australian companies and finds the answer to the question of whether integrated reporting stimulates innovative mechanisms of information disclosure. A study was conducted on a sample of 23 managers responsible for company sustainability, communication, and finances, representing 15 organizations	Organizations producing some form of an integrated report are changing their processes and structures; their adoption of integrated reporting has not necessarily stimulated new innovations in disclosure mechanisms or reporting processes beyond incremental changes to processes and structures that previously supported sustainability reporting
	Lai et al., (2016)	The study seeks to ascertain whether the decision to adopt integrated reporting is an element of the legitimacy strategy to improve the negative image of the company regarding its sustainability. The study sample comprises enterprises that participate in the IIRC Pilot Program	Enterprise involvement in integrated reporting is not a matter of strategic legitimacy

(*Continued*)

Table 2.2 (Continued)

Research problem	*Authors*	*Research description*	*Outcomes*
	Lai, Melloni, Stacchezzini (2018)	The study analyzed how the preparers' mode of cognition influences the patterns of accountability associated with integrated reporting. It conducted in-depth interviews with the integrated reporting preparers of a global insurer that has used integrated reporting since 2013 were conducted	The preparers' narrative mode of cognition facilitates dialogue with users of integrated reports
	Higgins et al., (2019)	The study employs Morgan's analysis of the role of metaphors in understanding and managing organizations to assess in what respects organizations using integrated reporting are on a "journey" of organizational change. The study analyzed the integrated reporting practitioner literature and used in-depth interviews to assess the extent to which this metaphor captures how six early adopter organizations in Australia implement integrated reporting, and what changes resulted over 4 years	The journey metaphor implies substantive and holistic organizational change. By contrast, organizations use integrated reporting in contextual, instrumental, and piecemeal ways. The study proposed a "toolbox" metaphor to help present how organizations adapt their reporting to fit decisions already made and challenges presented through ordinary and ongoing strategic management
Integrated reporting tools	Haller and van Staden (2014)	The study discussed the concept of integrated reporting and proposed a practical and useful instrument that could help to apply the integrated reporting concept in corporate practice, a structured presentation of the traditional measure of "value-added" in a so-called "value-added statement"	The study proposed the structure of value-added statements to meet the guiding principles and concepts developed in the integrated reporting framework and help report on the monetary effects of different types of capital included in integrated reporting

(*Continued*)

Table 2.2 (Continued)

Research problem	*Authors*	*Research description*	*Outcomes*
	van Bommel (2014)	This study examines the multiplicity of views on integrated reporting to consider the possibility of gaining legitimacy through a compromise. The authors applied Boltanski and Thévenot's sociology of worth framework to analyze integrated reporting in the Dutch reporting field	Integrated reporting requires a compromise of common interests, avoidance of clarification, and maintenance of ambiguity to become a legitimate practice
Relationship between integrated reporting and CSR	Churet and Eccles (2014)	Using the database of over 2,000 companies surveyed during its annual Corporate Sustainability Assessment, the study discussed the extent and recent growth of integrated reporting and its likely effects on important indicators of ESG quality of management and financial performance	The relationship between integrated reporting and financial performance is significant for two sectors: healthcare and information technologies
	Lueg, Lueg, Andersen, Dancianu (2016)	The study shows how standards and guidelines for CSR can help a company in its integrated reporting. It probes the motivations of diverse stakeholders in fostering the adoption of CSR standards and guidelines after integrated reporting became mandatory in Denmark	Strategy, in which CSR is an essential value driver, fostered integrated reporting with guidelines and standards for CSR
Theoretical considerations and criticism of integrated reporting	Flower (2015)	Theoretical discussion. On its foundation, the IIRC's principal objective was the promotion of sustainability accounting. However, in the proposed <IR> framework, the IIRC has abandoned sustainability accounting	The IIRC's proposals have little impact on corporate reporting practices because of their lack of force

(*Continued*)

Table 2.2 (Continued)

Research problem	*Authors*	*Research description*	*Outcomes*
	Krasodomska (2012)	Analysis of the assumptions of integrated reporting – theoretical considerations. The study presents the reasons for modifying the current reporting solutions and the basic assumptions of integrated reporting	It presents the reasons for modifying the current reporting solutions and the basic assumptions of integrated reporting
	Sobczyk (2013)	Analysis of the theoretical basis of the concept of integrated reporting	An attempt to present the theoretical basis of the concept of integrated reporting, using the analysis of the literature on the subject and the method of deduction
	Gregorczyk (2015)	The study presents the role of integrated reporting in creating shared value, which is implementing economic objectives while meeting social needs	The study describes the role of the state as a regulator to create shared value, particularly in the development of reporting requirements, and the role of integrated reporting as a crucial factor in creating shared value
	Zyznarska-Dworczak (2015)	Analysis of the reliability of integrated reporting in the light of the strategic-information paradigm of accounting	The study suggested increasing the reliability of integrated reporting by including social responsibility management accounting in the implementation of a CSR policy, which promotes the transparent communication of information on the current and future economic, environmental, and social performance of the enterprise
	Walińska (2015)	This study identifies the relationship between the integrated report and financial statements	The proper solution is the coexistence of both forms of company reporting, and their integration should not be understood as only a combination of financial and non-financial data in one report. The effect of integration should be a value report that should show linked information

(*Continued*)

Table 2.2 (Continued)

Research problem	*Authors*	*Research description*	*Outcomes*
	Bek-Gaik (2015)	The study aims to present the views and opinions on the business model disclosure in the organization's financial and non-financial reporting	The study indicated the potential benefits and problems regarding implementing integrated reporting. Key problems include the following: • Credibility of the presented data, mainly of a non-financial and forward-looking nature • No uniform structure of integrated reporting • Lack of an appropriate database for integrated reporting • Too much information • Lack of defined key performance indicators
	Świderska and Bek-Gaik (2016)	Analysis of the pros and cons of integrated reporting. The study ascertains whether the current integrated can replace present reporting and improve its imperfections	Indicated problems: data reliability, lack of consistency and substantive links of presented data, impact of the involvement and cooperation of stakeholders on the scope of the report, and completeness of the issues covered in the report
	Remlein (2016)	Research on the costs and benefits of implementing and using integrated reporting	The study noted the following benefits: • Better satisfaction of the information needs of long-term investors • Showing links between factors inside and outside the entity and the impact of the entity on other members of the supply chain • Higher level of trust of key stakeholders • Better resource allocation decisions • Lower reputational risk • Easier access to capital

(*Continued*)

Table 2.2 (Continued)

Research problem	*Authors*	*Research description*	*Outcomes*
Perception of integrated reporting by the management	Perego, Kennedy, Whiteman (2016)	Research on the perception of integrated reporting by the management staff. Interviews were conducted with three key experts influencing integrated reporting practices at a global level	Experts perceive integrated reporting as fragmented and believe most companies currently have a weak understanding of the business value of integrated reporting
	Feng et al., Cummings, Tweedie (2017)	The study explores how integrated reporting stakeholders in Australia interpret integrated thinking, and how pilot organizations put integrated thinking into practice	The study suggests a lack of understanding of integrated thinking by practitioners and the need to accurately present the potential contribution of integrated reporting into organizational practice
Future research directions	Caraiani, Lungu, Bratu, Dascălu (2018)	The study investigated the perspectives of integrated reporting as an emerging field in mainstream academic literature. The current state of research and its development were explored using the structured literature review method on publications indexed in Clarivate Analytics' Web of Science	The findings suggest an evolution of integrated reporting research from the phase of spreading awareness regarding the new reporting paradigm toward an impact analysis phase. The accounting and audit journals have greatly contributed to the shift in the integrated reporting literature toward studying integrated reporting as a reporting practice and the need to discuss possible links between integrated reporting, governance, and integrated thinking

Source: Own elaboration.

the social and environmental aspects of enterprises, in its current form, integrated reporting has different priorities. Analysis of the IIRC publication shows that the idea of sustainable development, guiding integrated reporting from the beginning, stems from its foundation, and creating value for investors is central to integrated reporting.

Integrated reporting is primarily a process for companies to develop internal awareness of the mechanisms of value creation and sharing them with external stakeholders through documents that include information traditionally contained in financial statements and sustainability (or social) reports. In this sense, integrated reporting aims to provide transparent and integrated disclosure along with a strategic communication perspective.

Companies preparing integrated reports should define their own approach to disclosing non-financial information, with particular emphasis on the appropriate presentation of performance measurement. The role of KPIs in supporting the narrative explanation of organizational strategy should be emphasized.

Notes

1 (see Adams and Simnett, 2010; Eccles and Krzus, 2010b; Eccles and Saltzman, 2011; Berg and Jensen, 2012; Maroun and Solomon, 2012; Radley Yeldar, 2012; Dragu and Tudor-Tiron, 2013; Frías-Aceituno et al., 2013a,b; García-Sánchez et al., 2013; Sierra-Garcia et al., 2013; Bilolo et al., 2014; Eccles et al., 2014a; Eccles and Krzus, 2014; Eccles and Serafeim, 2014; Haller and van Staden, 2014; Rensburg and Botha, 2014; Stubbs and Higgins, 2014; van Bommel, 2014; Bek-Gaik and Rymkiewicz, 2015a; Bek-Gaik and Rymkiewicz, 2015b; Chersan, 2015; Eccles et al., 2015; Jinga and Dumitru, 2015a; Veltri and Silvestri, 2015; Velte and Stawinoga, 2016; de Villiers and Maroun, 2017; de Villiers et al., 2017, Dumay et al., 2017; Feng et al., 2017; Wen et al., 2017; Maroun, 2017; Albertini, 2019; Eccles and Klimenko, 2019; Malola and Maroun, 2019; Bek-Gaik and Surowiec, 2020b; Yousef, 2020).

2 IIRC is a global coalition of regulatory bodies, investors, business units, entities establishing standards, accounting professions, and non-governmental organizations. This coalition shares the view that communication on the creation of value by enterprises should be the next step in the evolution of corporate reporting (International Integrated Reporting Framework; IIRC, 2013d). IIRC was founded on the initiative of two leading organizations operating in the area of accounting for sustainable development: The Prince's Accounting for Sustainability Project-A4S and GRI. The first action by IIRC was the publication of the Discussion Paper: Towards Integrated Reporting – Communicating Value in the 21st Century Paper (IIRC, 2011). It considered the rationale for Integrated Reporting, offering initial proposals for the development of an International Integrated Reporting Framework and outlining the next steps towards its creation and adoption.

3 The discussion paper (IIRC 2011) also indicates that the disclosure of the strategy and business model should be clearly distinguished; they must be separate elements of disclosure. The company's strategy sets the appropriate objectives (a set of outputs), enabling the desired effects that will be significant for customers and other stakeholders. The business model aims to use this strategy to obtain the desired results (outcomes), which can be assessed based on KPIs.

4 In the relevant literature, it has been emphasized that such a huge interest in the business model as a reporting element is the reflection of the view that it is a key starting point for analysis by investors, for which reason IASB launched a new initiative together with the International Integrated Reporting Council to promote business model disclosure through integrated report. The integrated report is a transparent and concise representation of how an organization creates and maintains value, while its business model is a fundamental issue of disclosure.

5 The information in an integrated report should be presented on a basis that is consistent over time and in a way that enables comparison with other organizations to the extent that it is material to the organization's own ability to create value over time (IIRC, 2021).

3 Performance measurement systems from the perspective of integrated reporting

3.1 Essence of performance measurement

Performance measurement is currently among the most dynamically developed management concepts. It integrates the elements of management accounting and strategic management (Waśniewski, 2015, p. 317), enabling the assessment of the implementation of the strategy and objectives of the economic entity. The literature on the subject emphasizes that one of its basic goals is to provide reliable and credible information that supports decision-making (Waśniewski, 2016, p. 164). Performance measurement can be defined as the process of quantifying the efficiency and effectiveness of an action (Neely et al., 2005).

Undoubtedly, performance measurement systems (PMSs) can support the creation of integrated or non-financial reports. First, Waśniewski (2015, p. 317) assesses the implementation of the strategy and the objectives of the organization. For external stakeholders, these systems provide important information regarding key performance indicators (KPIs). De Villiers and Sharma (2020) emphasize that International Integrated Reporting Council (IIRC) does not require reporting any specific KPIs; Dumay et al. (2017) note that such flexibility and lack of normativeness in the scope of the disclosure and the lack of measures may promote the implementation of integrated reporting per the new European Union (EU) directive on non-financial disclosures (2014/95/EU). However, the importance of KPIs is widely recognized in intellectual capital reporting: IIRC plans to identify important and related measures and basic methodologies to facilitate the comparison of strategy, corporate governance, performance, and perspectives. Moreover, the World Intellectual Capital/Assets Initiative (WICI, 2016) notes the role of KPIs in complementing the narrative explanation of organizational strategy. This function is consistent with intellectual capital performance management and measurement, where indicators can play a fundamental role in legitimacy, learning, and mobilizing (Catasús and Gröjer, 2006) internal processes and resources aimed at understanding the relationship between intangible values and value creation (García-Meca and Martinez, 2007; Vergauwen et al., 2007).

DOI: 10.4324/9781003336068-4

Financial analysts also use the non-financial information presented in an integrated report to estimate a company's value and future performance. Companies publishing a greater amount of non-financial information allow financial analysts to present more detailed profit estimates and less distributed profit forecasts. Evidence based on surveys and analysis of analyst reports also indicates an increasing scope of the use of non-financial information by financial analysts (Luo et al., 2014). Financial analysts serve as intermediaries between companies and investors by collecting and providing information (Lang and Lundholm, 1996; Barker, 1998; Ivković and Jegadeesh, 2004; Chen et al., 2010). Analysts support investors and transform information into recommendations and profit forecasts regarding the shares that investors use to make investment decisions (Elgers et al., 2001; Chen et al., 2014; Chen et al., 2017). In particular, regarding non-financial information, financial analysts translate much non-financial information disclosed by companies into comprehensive information useful for investors. Although investors' demand for non-financial information increases over time, they have difficulty interpreting and translating non-financial disclosures on profits (Maines et al., 2002; Hoff and Wood, 2008). Moreover, there is no uniform reporting format for non-financial disclosures, which causes differences in the presentation of this information by various companies (Simpson, 2010; Eccles et al., 2011), thus increasing the complexity of non-financial information analysis. The lack of investors' knowledge about the impact of non-financial information on valuation increases incentives for financial analysts to explain how this information affects the assessment of the company's performance and value.

3.1.1 Essence of performance and performance measurement

Wettstein and Kueng (2002) define a company's performance as the degree of stakeholder satisfaction. Grüning (2002) defines it as the ability of a company to achieve goals or meet expectations; however, it emphasizes some special, multidimensional features of the company's performance, manifested in the integration of strategic and operational aspects.

Most definitions presented in the literature on the subject indicate the importance of performance as a degree of achievement of goals (e.g., the European Foundation for Quality Management, 2003).[1] Moreover, performance is closely related to the company's stakeholders because they expect the enterprise to achieve its goals. Lohman et al. (2004) defined performance measurement as the act of measuring performance using performance indicators applied to quantify the efficiency and effectiveness of organizational actions as part of or in all processes or systems regarding a given standard or objective.

Neely et al. (1995) define measurement (1995, p. 80) from the perspective of PMSs as "the process of quantifying something [that] leads to performance." Nita (2014b, pp. 37–52) defines four areas of performance measurement: functional (logistics, marketing, finance, production, and research and development), managerial (the enterprise, organizational units, and work positions), resource transformation (inputs, processes, and effects), and stakeholders (customers, suppliers, competitors, employees, and the public). Nita (2014a, p. 38) notes that performance measurement should be considered in the context of the most important strategic goals regarding value creation. At the same time, the performance measurement may concern many different areas, which can be divided into: functional area (covering, among others, logistics, marketing, finance, and production, i.e., individual areas of the company's activities), area related to the level of management (referring to the entire company or its organizational units or even individual workstations), area related to the transformation of resources (related to inputs, processes, and outcomes), and area related to individual stakeholder groups (according to the needs of customers, suppliers, employees, local communities, etc.) (Nita, 2014a, p. 40). The presented classification seems to be adequate for the performance measurement of a socially responsible enterprise because, given the scope of the corporate social responsibility (CSR) concept, all these areas must be considered.

Performance can be measured from different perspectives. From an operational perspective, a PMS is a "set of metrics used to quantify both the efficiency and effectiveness of actions" (Neely et al., 1995). It is also a reporting process that provides feedback on the outcome of actions (Bititci et al., 1997). From a strategic perspective, a PMS allows an organization to cascade down its business performance measures and provides it with the information necessary to challenge the content and validity of the strategy (Ittner et al., 2003). According to Lohman et al. (2004, p. 268), "performance measurement systems are systems (software, databases, and procedures) to execute performance measurement in a consistent and complete way." From a management accounting perspective, business performance measurement (BPM) is synonymous with management planning and budgeting (Otley, 1999).

Performance measurement cannot be performed without providing an adequate measuring system (PMS). The relevant literature presents a high level of differentiation of definitions. Kowalewski (2015, p. 28) defines performance measurement as a company's multidimensional information system, focusing on generating and reporting useful information for management, which enables permanent control of the most important areas of a company's functioning. Lohman et al. (2004) also define the PMS as a sustainable and dynamic system; that is, an organized set of mutually related databases, software, and procedures to enforce measuring performance in a complete and organized manner.[2] This system provides access to information that enables measurement of the performance and efficiency of management decisions (and their monitoring and correction), given (external and internal) changes in the enterprise. Thus, to properly measure performance, modern tools should be used to measure non-financial activities. The use of financial meters alone is currently insufficient and does not allow for full insight into the company's situation.

Michalak (2008, pp. 458–459) indicates that the development of the PMS should involve six consecutive stages: determining the subject of the measurement, determining the measurement unit and scale, selecting or constructing the measurement system, determining the base or pattern for comparison, making a real measurement, and comparing the obtained measurement results with the pattern. Notably, the elements of the PMS presented by Michalak coincide with those proposed by Ijiri, although they are more analytical.

The quality and effectiveness of performance measurement are also extremely important. They depend on the selection of the right and precise purpose of performance measurement, which should not be too general, and on determining procedures regarding obtaining and gathering information and determining the appropriate measures and measurement units, results analysis, proper communication, and motivating employees.

3.2 Financial and non-financial performance measures

Parmenter (2015, pp. 3–14) defined four groups of measures of organizational performance comprising financial and non-financial indicators:

- KPIs: measures that provide information on the functioning of the organization in the most important areas. Given permanent monitoring and management, the organization can improve its performance by undertaking proper corrective actions. The indicators include customer complaints that have not been addressed within a specified time or the number of innovations planned for implementation within a specified time (e.g., a month). Per the Pareto principle, the indicators should constitute 80% of all indicators within a PMS (Niemiec, 2017, p. 267).
- Performance indicators: complementing indicators that are not key to the business. Performance indicators help align teams' actions with the organization's strategy. They include the number of late deliveries to key customers, percentage increase in sales with the top 10% of customers, number of employees' suggestions implemented in the last 30 days, and number of internal and external training planned in the future.
- Key result indicators: measures providing general information on the result of many actions, showing whether the company is heading in the right direction. They cover a longer period than KPIs and include customer satisfaction, net profit before tax, customer profitability, employee satisfaction, and return on capital. Per the Pareto principle, they should constitute the remaining 20% of all indicators within the PMS (Niemiec, 2017, p. 267).
- Result indicators: measures that summarize activity and all financial performance measures. They show the managers the cooperation of individual teams in achieving the assumed results and help managers to fully understand what to increase or decrease by focusing on activities that

created the sales (result). These indicators include net profit on key product lines, sales made yesterday, customer complaints from key customers, and hospital bed utilization in the week.

Czerska and Gołębiewski (2017, p. 52) divided performance measures into four types assigned to two groups: efficiency (performance) and result. Within each group, two types of measures were indicated, divided into key and detailing measures, as follow:

- Performance indicators:
  - KPIs, of non-monetary nature, relate to individual teams, and are used by department managers
  - Performance indicators, of non-monetary nature, relate to individual teams, and are used by operational staff
- Result indicators:
  - Key result indicators, of non-monetary and monetary nature, relate to many divisions and departments, and are used by management board
  - Result indicators, of non-monetary and monetary nature, relate to many divisions and departments, and are used by department managers

Beyond the classification of indicators, literature on the subject complements the description by identifying their characteristics. Based on an analysis covering most organization types in the public and private sectors, Parmenter (2015) defined seven characteristics of KPIs: non-financial measures, measured frequently, acted on by the CEO and senior management team, clearly indicate what action required by staff, tie responsibility down to a team, have a significant impact (e.g., affect one or more of the critical success factors and more than one BSC perspective), and encourage appropriate action.

3.3 Performance measurement systems and capitals

The KPIs are a set of indicators that focus on those aspects of the company's operations that are most important for its success now and in the future (Parmenter, 2015). The role KPIs can play within integrated reporting is associated with the fact that integrated reporting aims to provide an effective and concise description of the company's ability to create current and future sustainable value by presenting information normally reported in several separate documents in a coherent whole. In this context, the role of KPIs involves measuring a company's ability to create value by increasing or transforming its tangible and intangible capital.

The KPIs are measures of the entity's progress in striving to achieve success in economic and socio-environmental areas, and their disclosure is recommended by the regulations. KPIs can be financial and non-financial. Financial KPIs are mainly used in financial analyses and for other financial statement data. Non-financial KPIs are often used to quantify things that are challenging to measure and should be treated more as "indicators" than as concrete measures. KPIs, by measuring the ability of the company to create sustainable value, can potentially play an important role in the preparation of an integrated report and, therefore, should be useful for report preparers. Given that the concept of the six capitals is a key concept in integrated reporting, the assessment of the effectiveness of their use is crucial and informative, hence the need to use KPIs in integrated reporting.[3]

The concept of "capital" is also related to the idea of "value," which is interpreted regarding the functions of variations in financial capital and as a "measure of the positive and negative effects generated across all of these capitals." It implies a relevant change in BPM and shifts the perspective of analysis from the short to the medium-long term (Busco et al., 2013). Thus, KPIs can be pivotal. Given KPIs, economic, environmental, and social-related factors can be measured and monitored. While managers use KPIs to assess their businesses, analysts and investors can make greater use of them in the future (Busco et al., 2013). Furthermore, KPIs can enhance the comparability of company results within the industry if they reflect widely accepted metrics.

Thus, to be useful, KPIs should possess important characteristics. First, they should be included in PMSs set up for internal purposes. According to recent national and international regulations, corporate reporting must align externally reported information with information reported to management for decision purposes. Hence, a large part of the information used by managers to run the business and evaluate the achievement of the company's strategy coincides with the capital providers' and other stakeholders' requirements for efficient decision-making (Bartolini et al., 2013).

Second, KPIs should be clear and understandable (IIRC, 2013b, Section 4.31). Integrated reporting must, thus, provide information that enables stakeholders to clearly understand each KPI disclosed. In particular, the following should be included for each KPI: its definition and calculation method, its purpose and the reason it is "key," and the source of underlying data and any assumptions.

Third, KPIs should be comparable (IIRC, 2013b, Section 4.31) over time and between organizations (at least within the same industry). Thus, comparability should be provided at two different levels: inter-firm comparability (PricewaterhouseCoopers, 2007) and inter-period consistency.

The integrated PMS framework, presented by Bartolini et al. (2013, p. 137), highlights four different value-creation dimensions (competitors and best practice, the entire value chain, innovation and knowledge, and internal processes) companies should include in their integrated performance management system to assess their ability to create value. Each dimension can be observed and managed from three perspectives: economic, environmental, and social (i.e., the triple bottom line). Moreover, each dimension involves all the various forms of capital (human, social, relationship, natural, intellectual, manufactured, and financial) on which the organization depends.

Bartolini et al. (2013, pp. 141–142) presented examples of KPIs for each dimension of the integrated PMS from a triple-bottom-line perspective:

1 Economic perspective covering:

- Financial capital:
    - Revenues by customers, market, etc.
    - Percentage of revenues by new products or services
    - Market share
    - Profitability ratios
    - Liquidity and financial position ratios
    - Value-adding operating costs
    - Payments to providers of capital (e.g., return on equity, earnings per share)
    - Timely payments to suppliers
    - New markets penetration rate
- Manufactured capital:
    - Investment in new technologies
- Intellectual capital:
    - Investment in new brands development
    - Number and value of new patents or copyrights
    - etc.

2 Environmental perspective covering:

- Natural capital:
    - Hazardous waste treated
    - Number of suppliers identified as having significant actual and potential negative environmental impacts
    - Percentage of new suppliers or customers that were screened using environmental criteria
    - Total weight of waste disposed of by reuse, recycling, composting, incineration, etc.
    - Waste reduction over the period
    - Volume of sills by categories (e.g., oil, fuel, and chemicals)
    - Total weight
    - Amount of significant air emissions
- Financial capital:
    - Total monetary value of fines for non-compliance with environmental laws and regulations
    - Prevention and environmental management costs
    - etc.

3 Social perspective covering:

- Financial capital:
  - Cost of actions taken manage risks or opportunities
- Human capital:
  - Number or percentage of new employee hires during the reporting period, by age group, gender, region, etc.
  - Employee turnover rate during the reporting period
  - Injury rate
  - Occupational diseases rate
  - Number of incidents of non-compliance with regulations
- Intellectual capital:
  - Average hours of training by categories
- Social and relationship capital:
  - Number of ethical or legal violations
  - Number of suppliers or customers subject to impact assessments for labor practices
  - Percentage of suppliers covered by ethical procurement
  - Negative impacts for labor practices identified in the supply chain
  - Percentage of new suppliers or customers screened using human rights criteria
  - Number of community complaints
  - Customer satisfaction
  - etc.

The authors correlated the listed indicators with four dimensions: value chain, internal processes innovation, knowledge competitors, and best practice.

Integrated reporting aims to report on outcomes, defined as the "internal and external consequences (positive and negative) on the capitals," rather than outputs. According to the framework, the integrated report should answer the question: "To what extent has the organization achieved its strategic objectives and what are its outcomes in terms of effects on the capitals?" Even though the IIRC aims to disclose outcomes, the KPIs proposed by the <IR> framework do not measure outcomes, and integrated reports cannot present the stocks for the six capitals and their flows. The outcomes are much more challenging to measure, which may further evolve as among the main challenges of integrated reporting. The integrated report considers the measurement (stock and flow) of capital, focusing less on reporting on the impacts of the company's activities and, thus, differs from sustainability or CSR reports.

3.4 Performance measurement systems

The development of the concept of performance measurement has led to the creation of an extensive catalog of tools, methods, and measurement systems. The literature on the subject includes three phases of development of the concept of performance measurement: using individual financial meters, using financial indicators, and the introduction of multi-criteria measurement of performance using diversified measures (with the distinction of three streams: maximization of value for shareholders, maximization of value for stakeholders, and maximization of intellectual capital) (Michalak, 2008, pp. 75–76; Kędzierska, 2012, p. 109). The first phase focuses on the use of individual financial measures within the control system (i.e., return on investment, profitability, and profit), which are insufficient in modern economic reality. Examples of measurement methods in this phase include revenue, financial results, return on equity (ROE), and return on assets. The second phase supplements financial measures with operational parameters that have a strong connection with the expected future performance of the organization. In this phase, we can distinguish such measurement methods as the Du Pont pyramid or discrimination models (e.g., the Altman model).

The last phase balances financial and non-financial measures, which allows for the balancing of short- and long-term goals and translates the mission and vision of the organization into its operations. A wide catalog of measurement methods developed in this phase includes economic value added (EVA), real asset value enhancer (RAVE), Tableu de Bord, BSC Performance Pyramid, Skandia navigator, and many others. The most important concepts of performance measurement presented in the literature on the subject and used in economic practice are as follows:

1 BSC
2 RAVE
3 Total performance scorecard (TPS)
4 Tableau de Bord
5 Performance Pyramid
6 Business Management Window
7 European Federation of Quality Management (EFQM) performance measurement model
8 Performance Prism

3.4.1 Balanced scorecard

Balanced Scorecard[4] (BSC) is one of the most commonly used concepts for performance measurement in economic practice.[5] The BSC, developed by Kaplan and Norton (1998), is a comprehensive solution to show managers a complex picture of the effects of their business[6] and is one of the most important tools for assessing the implementation of the strategy in individual periods.

The concept of a BSC is a response to the imperfection of original concepts, considering only short-term measures and financial analyses in the process of formulating and assessing the implementation of objectives and ignoring issues relevant to the organization (i.e., innovations, building relationships with customers, and organizational changes) (Pierścionek, 2011, p. 178). The main task of a BSC indicated in the literature is the measurement, assessment, and communication of performance to translate the strategy into activities via various meters grouped for four basic perspectives (Michalak, 2008, pp. 112–113) relevant from the operational and strategic management perspective: financial perspectives (determining financial goals and financial indicators, such as operational result, rate of return on capital, and EVA), customer (determining customers, market segments, and efficiency measures), internal processes (constructing an internal value chain, e.g., innovations, operational and after-sales service processes),[7] and learning and growth perspective (identification of resources and skills to develop). Individual perspectives should answer four questions (Kaplan and Norton, 1998, p. 188):

- To achieve our vision, how should we appear to our customers? (customer perspective)
- To satisfy our stakeholders and customers, what business processes must we excel at? (internal business processes perspective)
- To achieve our vision, how will we sustain our ability to change and improve? (learning and growth perspective)
- To succeed financially, how should we appear to our stakeholders? (financial perspective)

In order to answer the specific question for each BSC perspective, we can determine objectives and related measures, targets, and initiatives (Kaplan and Norton, 1998, p. 188).

All the perspectives are interrelated. The perspective of internal processes seems to be essential because the design, control, and improvement of internal processes lead to meeting customer needs (customer perspective) and, thus, achieving financial goals (financial perspective), and the company's intangible values determine achieving the goals of individual perspectives (development perspective) (Świderska, 2010, pp. 535–536).

According to the authors of this concept, the idea of BSC is to be an innovative management system enabling the translation of mission and strategy into objectives and measures to communicate the strategy of the business and help align individual, organizational, and cross-departmental initiatives to achieve a common goal. Thus, to visualize the corporate objectives within the four perspectives of BSC, Kaplan and Norton (2000) introduced strategy maps as tools to chart how intangible assets are converted into tangible outcomes (Figure 3.1). They noted that the strategy map shows a company's critical objectives and the crucial relationship among them that drives

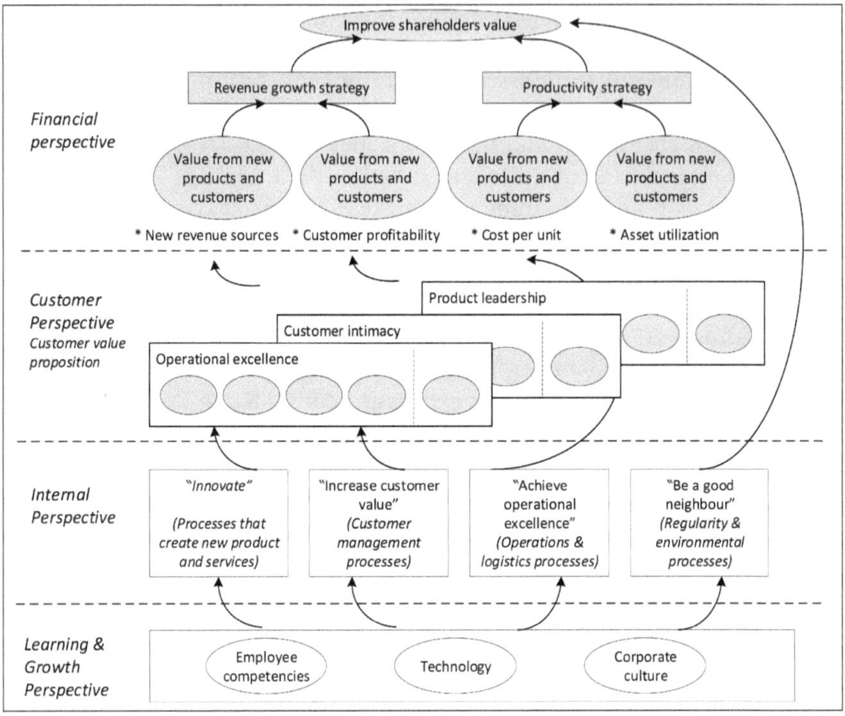

Figure 3.1 Strategy map based on balanced scorecard perspectives

Source: Neely et al. (2003, p. 130)

organizational performance. The strategy map illustrates how the interconnectivity of a company's resources, especially between the intangible assets, contributes to creating value.

The BSC has an advantage over the traditional measurement system only when three conditions are met:

- All measures (financial and non-financial) are developed based on the vision and strategy adopted by the company
- Measures should be combined with a cause-and-effect assessment to describe the strategy
- The cause-and-effect chain pervades all four perspectives of a BSC

The BSC helps to properly document, communicate, and measure progress in the implementation of the strategy, as well as to answer the following questions: how can we proceed to achieve the best results from each of the four perspectives? Moreover, the BSC draws attention to activities that bring current profits to the company and gives it a chance for success in the future. What distinguishes the BSC from other PMSs is the linking of goals with financial and non-financial performance indicators.

The BSC supports management in the formulation and implementation of this strategy. This concept serves throughout the enterprise as an instrument of communication and management, allowing for permanent control of objectives in all areas of activity, such as the production area that should be focused on the process of creating value. The new requirements set by the environment prompted many enterprises to critically analyze the information management system and revise it. Traditionally used indicators of profitability and productivity are insufficient to ensure future success, even if they provide early warning signals.

The BSC focuses on factors that create long-term value. Traditional financial reports show the past without presenting a perspective on future value creation. The BSC determines the factors that create long-term value in an organization:

- Customer orientation: satisfy, preserve, and acquire customers in the target segments
- Economic processes: provide value to target customers, innovative products and services, flexible and effective high-quality operational processes, better after-sales service
- Development of organization: develop talented motivated employees, provide access to strategic information, and align individual and group goals with the company's objectives

The close connection between qualitative and quantitative productivity measures, optimal use of internal and external information, systematic expansion of the information system, and consistent use of employees' knowledge are the basis of the company's long-term success.

The BSC is a universal tool that can be implemented by many enterprises. Considering that this tool effectively links vision, strategy, objectives, and measures, especially in strategic planning, the BSC is an instrument of comprehensive business management.

As part of a BSC, we can distinguish two groups of measures: lagging and leading indicators. The former regards the measure of the implementation of objectives and illustrates a company's situation. This group of measures includes most of the financial indicators belonging to the financial perspective (e.g., company value, share price, and value for shareholders) and indicators belonging to the customer's perspective (e.g., price, delivery time, and quality). Leading measures, also called predictive measures of future performance, encompass measures included in the customer's perspective (e.g., customer loyalty and customer profitability), the internal processes perspective (e.g., availability and readiness of the staff and duration of the production cycle), and the learning perspective (e.g., improving staff skills) (Michalak, 2008, p. 113).

3.4.1.1 Balanced scorecard perspectives

The financial perspective encompasses the most important financial goals of an organization. Examples of these measures include operating profit, return on investment, and profitability. This perspective should also consider long-term indicators, such as product development and the individual phases of the product life cycle, and adapt the indicators:

- Focus on sales growth in the introduction phase
- Strive to reduce costs in the growth phase
- Increase product profitability in the maturity phase

The main measures of the financial perspective may relate to different objectives:

- Survive – cash flow
- Succeed – quarterly sales growth and increase in operating income by independent units
- Prosper – increased market share and ROE, free cash flow, and EVA

The customer perspective encompasses the most important market goals of a firm and determines the achievement of financial goals. Examples of these measures are market share, sales growth, customer turnover indicators, and customer satisfaction levels. There are two groups of indicators. The first group is market share, number of customers acquired, and level of customer satisfaction and loyalty, which can be used by most enterprises. The second group describes aspects related to their specific needs that are especially important for clients of a given industry.

Currently, many companies focus their missions on their customers. However, it is the company's behavior from the customer's perspective that has now become the priority of all managers. Once articulated in the mission, the BSC requires management to focus on good customer service in specific measures that reflect matters that relate to customers' concerns.

Customer concerns can be classified into four categories: time, quality, performance, service, and cost. Lead time is the time required to meet customer needs. For existing products, lead time can be measured as the time the company receives an order until the goods or services are delivered to the consumer. For new products, it can represent the time from the development of the product idea to its final shipment (e.g., loading it into a container).

The measure of quality can be the number of products or defects returned by consumers. It can also be expressed in delivery-on-time or the accuracy of the forecasted delivery dates. The combination of meeting expectations and customer service measures how products or services contribute to creating value for customers.

One of the advantages of the BSC is that the company relies on internal measures dependent on the company's specificity but listens and examines how the environment or customers see and react to its proposition by, for example, conducting a survey.

Companies sometimes engage third parties by ordering independent institutions to conduct research for information about customer preferences and the effectiveness of customer service. This should ensure full transparency and help avoid subjectivism by the company. As noted earlier, it allows for considering the customer's perspective. The main performance indicators from the customer perspective may relate to different objectives:

- New products – percent of sales from new products; percentage share of patent-protected products in sales revenues
- Responsive supply – on-time delivery (defined by the customer)
- Preferred supplier – share of key accounts' purchases
- Customer partnership – number of cooperative engineering efforts
- Customer performance – customer acquisition, customer retention, and customer satisfaction

The internal business process perspective allows for monitoring the effectiveness of key processes for achieving the goals expressed from the customer and financial perspectives, that is, those on which the company's success depends. Examples of these measures are customer service time, product quality, and production cycle efficiency. These indicators may indicate the need to reduce the time to market (shorten the time needed to design, manufacture, and deliver a product that satisfies customer expectations). Considering all the important operational measures, the BSC allows managers to see which areas require improvement. The internal business process perspective may include measures that relate to different objectives:

- Technology capability – manufacturing geometry versus competition
- Manufacturing excellence – cycle time, unit cost, and yield
- Design productivity – material efficiency and engineering efficiency
- New products introduction – actual implementation schedule versus plan

The learning and growth perspective allows managers to monitor key factors to achieve future success, such as investing in the professional development of employees. These factors often improve the effectiveness of the processes specified from the perspective of internal processes. Examples of measures include key employee turnover, expenditure on training, and research and development expenses.

The purpose of managing the area of knowledge and innovation is to increase the potential of employees and recognize the necessary resources, which will provide the company with a stable future and secure its competitive position in the market. It is also important to create an information system that provides lagging indicators about the environment (e.g., based on accounting data) and early warning indicators. The learning and growth perspective uses measures that relate to such objectives as:

- Technology leadership – time to develop the next generation of product
- Manufacturing learning – process time to maturity

- Products focus – percent of products that equal 80% of the sales
- Time to market – new product introduction versus competition

Therefore, the BSC allows for a simple and logical description of the cause-and-effect relationships between individual strategic goals. Given the BSC, it is possible to maintain the right balance between short-term results (financial perspective) and investing in future development and success (customer, internal processes, and learning and growth perspectives). This balance forms the foundation of a company's long-term success. All the perspectives of the BSC are interrelated. Kaplan and Norton (1996, p. 31) presented the cause-and-effect relationships of the BSC perspectives. The learning and growth perspective expressed as employee skills affects internal business process perspective measures, such as process quality and process cycle time. Internal business process influences customer perspective, measured by on-time delivery and customer loyalty. And finally the customer perspective measures determine the financial perspective expressed by return on capital employed or EVA.

Adoption of the company's mission, precise specification of strategic goals, and identification of key success factors allow for determining basic measures from the four perspectives of the BSC. Measures and indicators included in the BSC should be selected to maintain a balance in the four dimensions:

1 Between external indicators related to the satisfaction of shareholders and customers and internal indicators regarding the company's economic processes and their ability to learn and develop
2 Between the indicators regarding the main strategic goals and those describing the key success factors (i.e., factors determining the implementation of strategic goals)
3 Between financial indicators and non-financial indicators
4 Between indicators describing long-term goals and indicators referring to short-term targets (milestones)

Thus, the properly constructed BSC describes the organization's strategy. It should clearly show:

- Cause-and-effect relationships – each goal should be part of the cause-and-effect chain describing the organization's strategy
- Link to the financial perspective – ultimately, there should be a reference to the company's financial performance for each goal and measure
- Factors for future success – the BSC should contain measures of performance (e.g., financial measures) and measures that indicate factors determining future success and improvement of efficiency
- Change-inducing measures – the BSC should contain measures that induce the organization to change its behavior and processes

Achieving cohesion and balancing goals, activities, and results from four perspectives allows for implementing the company's strategy. A well-constructed BSC should be a combination of indicators defining future desired results (strategic goal performance measures) and the key factors (strategic goal achievement determinants):

1. A comprehensive approach to financial and market goals in the field of internal, learning, and growth processes
2. Striving for a balance between short-term and long-term goals
3. Striving for a balance between financial and non-financial goals, that is, improvement of internal and learning and growth processes
4. Striving for a balance between internal and external measures (Pierścionek 2011, pp. 177–178)
5. Enables managers to continuously monitor the company's performance
6. Enables communication between the main and operational goals (Buczkowska, 2012, p. 14)
7. The ability to adapt to the individual needs of an entity (Murby and Gould, 2005, p. 3)

3.4.2 *Real asset value enhancer*

The RAVE concept is a performance measurement concept that considers four dimensions of the company's operations: economic (capital-driven), customer (customer-driven business), employee (employee-driven business), and supplier (supplier-driven business). Individual dimensions show how shareholder value is shaped by factors regarding individual stakeholder groups, such as employees, customers, and suppliers.

The economic dimension is assessed using the EVA, which shows residual income, defined as income exceeding the cost of capital, as determined by the capital markets. The economic value-added formula is expressed as the difference between the return on invested capital and the weighted average cost of capital multiplied by invested capital:

$$EVA = (ROIC - WACC) * IC$$

- ROIC – return on invested capital (which is profit divided by invested capital)
- WACC – weighted average cost of capital
- IC – invested capital

The second dimension regards employee factors. In this case, the value-added indicator is expressed as the product of the number of employees, the difference between the value added to the employee, and the average cost of the employee.

The third dimension includes customer-related factors. The value-added indicator for this dimension is calculated as the product of the number of customers and the difference between the value added per customer and the average customer cost.

The last dimension includes factors regarding suppliers that affect the creation of value for shareholders. The value added is calculated for this dimension as a difference in value added by the system of relationships with suppliers (*VAS*) and the product of the cost of relationships with customers (*CSR*) and weighted risk (*VAR*).

3.4.3 *Total performance scorecard*

The TPS, according to Rampersad (2005, p. 75), is the systematic process of continuous, gradual, and routine improvement, development, and learning, focusing on a sustainable increase in personal and organizational performance. The concept of the TPS helps companies translate their strategies into concrete and definable goals and metrics. Consequently, enterprises can obtain a transparent and comprehensive picture of their situation.

The TPS supports management in formulating and implementing a strategy. This concept serves as a company-wide communication and management instrument that allows for the permanent control of objectives in all areas of the company. Optimizing a company's productivity should focus on the value-creation process. New requirements imposed by the environment have prompted many enterprises to critically analyze their information management systems and, in many cases, revise them. Traditionally used performance and efficiency measures are no longer sufficient to ensure future success, even if they generate early warning signals.

The TPS focuses on the factors that create long-term value. Traditional retrospective financial reports present only past information (costs incurred and revenues generated) and do not measure the creation of future value. The TPS determines the factors that create long-term value in an organization:

- Customer orientation: satisfy, preserve, and acquire customers in target segments
- Economic processes: provide value to target customers:
    - Innovative products and services
    - Flexible and high-quality operational processes
    - Perfect after-sales service
- Organization development:
    - Develop capable and motivated employees
    - Provide access to strategic information
    - Align individual and group objectives to the goals of the company

The interrelated parts of the TPS concept according to Rampersad (2005, p. 78) comprise:

- Organizational Balanced Scorecard
- Personal Balanced Scorecard
- Total quality management
- Competence management

The close interrelation of qualitative and quantitative productivity measures, optimal use of internal and external information, systematic development of the information system, and consistent use of employees' knowledge are the basis of the company's long-term success.

TPS "encompasses the personal and organizational mission, vision, key roles, core values, critical success factors, objectives, performance measures, targets, and improvement actions, as well as the resulting process of continuous improvement, development, and learning" (Rampersad, 2005, p. 75). Therefore, it is an instrument that is used for comprehensive business management.

3.4.4 Tableau de Bord

Tableau de Bord is a method of measuring performance focused on stakeholders, developed in France by process engineers looking for ways to improve the production process. Its structure resembles a dashboard (as illustrated by its name) for controlling the company. The main goal of engineers was to develop a tool to observe relationships between individual activities included in the process and the result of this process (Żak, 2006, p. 231).

The main advantage of Tableau de Bord over traditional concepts of performance measurement is the use of non-financial measures. Examples of indicators include production time, employee morale, efficiency, and failure elimination time (Michalak, 2008, p. 112). Tableau de Bord, a concept that uses non-financial measures, can be an interesting solution for measuring the performance of socially responsible enterprises. It is possible to consider indicators such as accidents, employee absence, product safety, and the size of greenhouse gas emissions.

Developing Tableau de Bord comprises translating the mission and vision of the company into objectives, objectives into key success factors, and key success factors into KPIs (Epstein, Manzoni, 1997, p. 4). Tableau de Bord can measure a company's overall performance and the performance of individual units. The most important advantages of Tableau de Bord are as follows:

1 Providing concise information on an entity's performance, thus facilitating decision-making by managers
2 Informing on the performance of individual organizational units of the company

3 Inducing individual organizational units to position themselves within the context of the firm's overall strategy and responsibilities of other units
4 Forcing individual organizational units to identify key success factors and KPIs
5 Contributing to structuring management's agenda and directing managerial focus and discussions

3.4.5 Performance pyramid

The performance pyramid (also called the strategic management and reporting technique) was proposed by Cross and Lynch (1992). It is the concept of performance measurement based on a hierarchy. It presents the company's long-term intent from activities (pyramid base) to vision (top of the pyramid), allowing for considering financial and non-financial data. The structure of the performance pyramid encompasses external and internal effectiveness measures. Both internal and external effectiveness measures are distinguished according to business units, business operating systems, and departments and work centers.

The external effectiveness measures include:

- For business units – market measures
- For business operating systems – customer satisfaction and company's flexibility
- For departments and work centers – measures related to quality and delivery

The internal effectiveness measures include:

- For business units – financial measures
- For business operating systems – company's productivity and flexibility
- For departments and work centers – measures related to waste and process time

The performance pyramid translates the mission and vision of the organization into individual activities to achieve adequate internal and external efficiency, which leads to creating value. The individual levels of the performance pyramid illustrate measures of performance for individual organizational levels, from departments and work centers to strategic business units. The goal of the performance pyramid is to link the company's strategy with its operations through the hierarchy by translating objectives from the top down and measures from the bottom up (Tangen, 2004, p. 731).

The performance pyramid represents stakeholder views from different perspectives. The left-hand side takes the customer view (from corporate vision through market objectives) to customer satisfaction priorities, considering two main elements of that perspective: quality and delivery. The right-hand side is the shareholder's view regarding the corporate vision, financial objectives, production resources and activities, and the main internal elements of cycle time and waste. The bottom side of the pyramid represents the employees' perspective with the four criteria of quality, delivery, cycle time, and waste (Kippenberger, 1996, pp. 10–11). The following advantages of this concept are mentioned in the literature on the subject:

1 Transferring the objectives developed by the top management to all management levels
2 Fast transmission of information relevant to the management of the organization at individual levels
3 Communication and reporting of internal recipients' information on performance (considering their financial and non-financial goals) (Michalak, 2008, pp. 118–119)
4 Level of measures that determine the goals should be determined by the participation of stakeholders
5 Flexibility and the possibility of adapting to the needs of the organization
6 Use of strategy and vision as an evaluation criterion
7 Complexity of the company's operations picture (Michalak, 2008, pp. 118–120, Buczkowska, 2012, p. 15).

3.4.6 *Business management window*

The business management window is a development of the concept of a BSC (a combination of the BSC concept with the concept of a business cycle) aimed at linking strategic financial aspects. This concept can be strongly related to CSR because one of its basic elements is to consider the interests of important groups of stakeholders, including society. Appropriate financial measures are assigned for each stage of the cycle, considering the interests (Michalak, 2008, p. 121).

3.4.7 *European Federation of quality management performance measurement concept*

The EFQM focuses on improving the quality of enterprises based on the assumptions of the philosophy of total quality management (Michalak, 2008, p. 122).

The EFQM concept allows for assessing all the most important areas of a company's activities. It assumes the role of determining the purpose and requirements, which serves as a pattern for an organization to achieve and sustain outstanding results that meet or exceed stakeholder expectations (Kacała and Kołaczyk, 2013, pp. 158–159). The foundation for achieving and sustaining excellence is following these rules:

1 The primacy of the customer
2 The need to take a long-term, stakeholder-centric view
3 Understanding the cause-and-effect linkages between why an organization does something, how it does it, and what it achieves as a consequence of its actions[8]

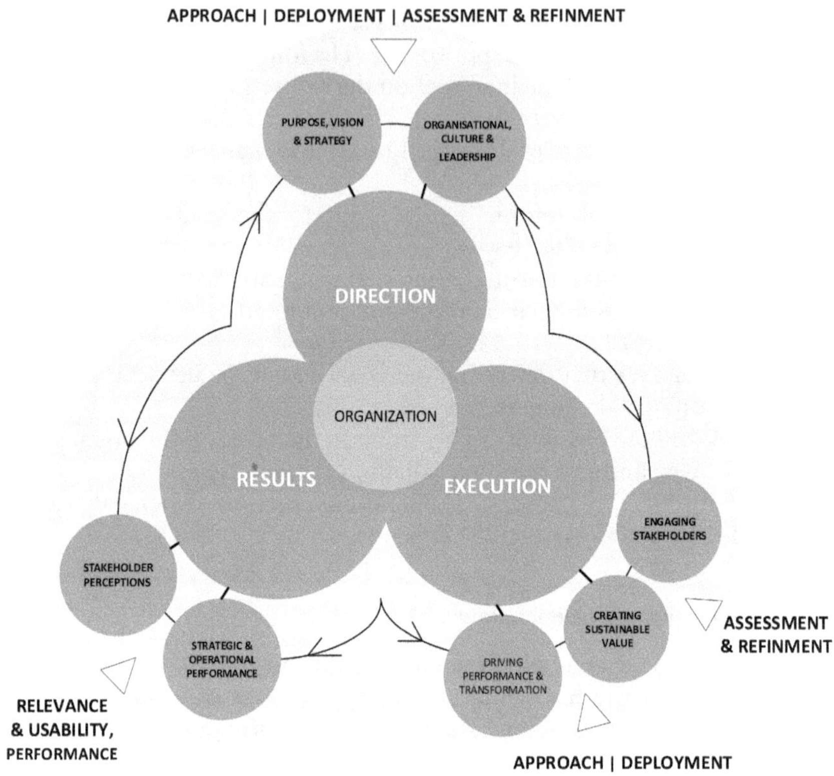

Figure 3.2 Guiding principles of the European Federation of Quality Management model
Source: https://efqm.org/the-efqm-model/; © EFQM 2023

The EFQM model is focusing on operational performance and has a results orientation (Figure 3.2), showing the guiding principles of performance measurement.

The key elements of the EFQM concept are results, approach, deployment, assessment, and refinement (RADAR), constituting a tool to help organizations manage change and improve performance (Figure 3.3). At its highest level, RADAR logic states that an organization must

- Determine the Results it is aiming to achieve as part of its strategy
- Have an Approach that will deliver the required result now and in the future
- Deploy this approach appropriately
- Assess and Refine the deployed approach to learn and improve

The most important advantages of the EFQM concept presented in the literature are as follows:

1 Possibility of assessment and achieving recognition
2 Ability to identify strengths and weaknesses of the organization

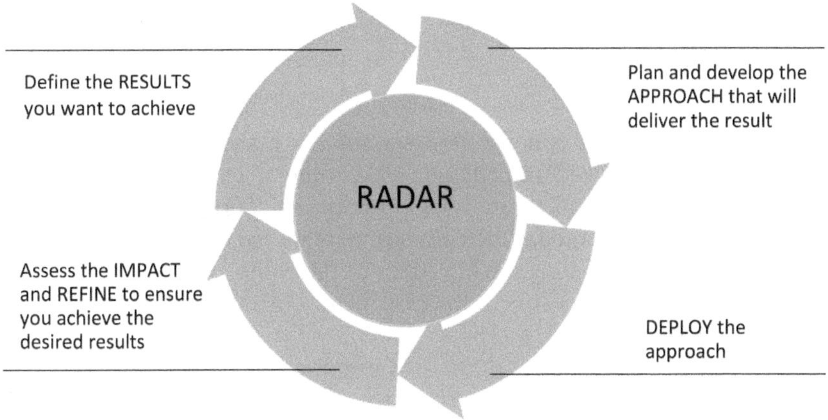

Figure 3.3 RADAR of the European Federation of Quality Management model
Source: https://efqm.org/the-efqm-model/; © EFQM 2023

3 Understanding organizational maturity and managing risks – building resilience
4 Driving transformation programs and managing corporate actions
5 Possibility of performance benchmarking
6 Increasing employees' involvement in organizational improvement
7 Sensing and responding to the impact of market disruption
8 Building organizational capability for improvement

The EFQM concept can also be an interesting solution for measuring the performance of socially responsible enterprises, as it includes the creation of value for the organization and other stakeholder groups, such as employees, customers, and society (stakeholder perception – criteria related to results in the EFQM model).

3.4.8 *Performance prism*

The performance prism concept is based on five interrelated perspectives: satisfaction of stakeholders (determining stakeholders, their needs, and expectations), strategy (determining a strategy that will meet the needs and expectations of stakeholders), processes (determining processes enabling the implementation of the strategy), capabilities (material and intangible resources that enable execution of the organization's business processes, such as combination of people, practices, technology, and infrastructure), and stakeholder contribution (a relationship with stakeholders that should involve the stakeholders contributing to the organization). The five facets of the Performance Prism include (Neely et al., p. 12):

- Stakeholder satisfaction
- Strategies

- Processes
- Capabilities
- Stakeholder contribution

The performance prism concept assumes success is more often achieved by organizations that have identified their stakeholders, needs, and expectations and by knowing what stakeholders can offer organizations. The concept also draws maps of success and failure (sometimes maps for various stakeholders), which allow for determining the key areas of the company and determine the factors affecting the success or failure of the organization (Michalak, 2008, p. 125; Buczkowska, 2012, p. 16).

The PMSs are extremely helpful and important for integrated reporting practice. First, they provide opportunities to measure the efficiency of the resources on which the organization operates, as well as constant monitoring of results. In this way, they also affect the credibility of the data presented in integrated reports – indicators are well developed and monitored and allow for an assessment of the effectiveness of the business model. This is extremely important because every business model adopted by an organization requires measurement of effectiveness, and if it is ineffective, it requires renewal or complete change. For example, to assess the effectiveness of the business model presented in integrated report, it is necessary to show the effectiveness of individual capitals as well as the entire organization – and this certainly enables BSC.

According to Ittner and Larcker (2003, pp. 88–95), as well as Kaplan and Norton (2004), the key task of managers and management accounting specialists is to measure the actual relationships of business model elements presented in integrated report, using performance metrics. In case when managers do not test these dependencies, they condemn themselves to measuring variables that have a moderate impact (or no impact) on achieving organizational success. Therefore, according to the researchers mentioned, testing business models should serve to verify the correctness of the selection of elements and metrics used to describe the business model, whether they are related to each other and whether they lead together to improve organizational results.

Michalak et al. (2018, p. 32) proposed the following tools for examining the effectiveness of the business model:

- Customer segmentation and customer relationships: profitability analysis of customer segments (multi-block and multi-segment costing); analysis of customer value throughout the relationship cycle (customer lifetime value)
- Distribution channels: profitability analysis of distribution channels
- Value proposition: target costing along with value for customers analysis
- Key processes: activity-based costing; value stream costing, product features, and characteristics costing
- Resources: resource consumption costing, strategic, capital and operational budgeting

- Key partners: open book accounting, interorganizational accounting
- Revenue and cost streams: variable costing, cost-volume-profit analysis, cost allocation methods, kaizen costing, and operational budgeting

Furthermore, companies integrate sustainability strategies with business strategy and also want to have related information. Organizations need operational, environmental, social, and employee indicators. In the case of voluntary non-financial disclosures in the form of KPIs, pressures from various stakeholder groups will lead to the progressive integration of non-financial information that is reported externally with internal PMSs used in enterprises. Subsequently, KPIs used in decision-making and control processes in the enterprise will be included in its reporting system to better match the reporting process to stakeholder expectations (Arvidsson, 2011; Lisi, 2018).

Performance measurement is an extremely complex and multi-threaded issue. At the same time, performance measurement is most effective when it is tailored to such elements as business strategy, organizational culture, and the external environment of a given organization. The literature clearly emphasizes that an effective PMS, containing a list of KPIs, should also identify relationships between these indicators, as well as their impact on the entire organization. The literature emphasizes that PMSs should be multidimensional, have a strategic focus, and should be cascading, i.e., measuring performance at various levels of the organizational structure in order to cascade the goals from strategic to operational and tactical levels. The PMS should also be linked to the motivational system (cf. Buhovac and Groff 2012).

Notes

1 The extensive review of the definition of "performance" was presented in Niemiec (ed.) (2016).

2 Niemiec (red.) (2016), p. 43, quote from Lohman et al. (2004), op. cit., s. 268.

3 The <IR> Framework (IIRC, 2021) does not prescribe specific key performance indicators, measurement methods, or the disclosure of individual matters. KPIs that combine financial measures with other components (e.g., the ratio of greenhouse gas emissions to sales) or narrative that explains the financial implications of significant effects on other capitals and other causal relationships (e.g., expected revenue growth resulting from efforts to enhance human capital) may be used to demonstrate the connectivity of financial performance with performance regarding other capitals. In some cases, it may also include monetizing certain effects on the capitals (e.g., carbon emissions and water use).

4 Kaplan and Norton developed the concept in the early 1990s; it has since been modified many times for the needs of individual enterprises (see Murby and Gould, 2005).

5 The concept of the BSC has evolved since its introduction. The relevant literature notes three stages of BSC development. The first version of the BSC was defined as a holistic approach to performance measurement that provides managers with useful information on financial performance, internal processes, customer perspectives, and internal learning and development (i.e., the four BSC perspectives). Within the first generation of BSC, financial and non-financial measures

of performance are used in the short and long terms, considering internal and external perspectives. However, the original version of the BSC could not provide adequate information to other stakeholders of the company. The so-called stakeholder scorecard was, thus, developed. The second generation of BSC allows for understanding the business model through value propositions and the causal relationships between objectives. The third generation of BSC allows for testing business models by providing better transparency between sought-after non-financial drivers of performance and cash flows.

6 See Buczkowska (2012, p. 12).

7 The model was presented by Kaplan and Norton.

8 https://efqm.org/the-efqm-model/

4 Disclosure practice in integrated reports of Polish companies (2013–2020)

4.1 Applied research methodology

This chapter examines the integrated reporting practice of Polish companies in the 2013–2020 period to provide useful insight into the current state. It presents the results of quantitative and qualitative assessments of integrated reporting. It employs content analysis using a weighted disclosure index (Likert scale) and a case study analysis to examine the quality of integrated reports. The quality of disclosures was assessed based on 120 integrated reports published by 27 capital groups during the period under consideration. A case study analysis was conducted based on the Integrated Report of the PGNiG Group, published in 2020.

The study aimed to assess compliance with the formal requirements of integrated reporting, forms of non-financial information presentation, quality of disclosures, and use of performance measurement tools for preparing reports. Only some companies in Poland have published integrated reports. A total of 120 reports, considered integrated reports, were published during the examined period (Table 4.1). Relative to 2013, the number of companies publishing integrated reports has gradually increased, stabilizing at around 20 since 2018. Table 4.1 presents the number of reports for each year.

The research process included identifying companies preparing integrated reports, quantitative and qualitative assessment of disclosures, and assessing whether non-financial information in integrated reports is presented using performance measurement systems (PMSs). The study analyzed the form of integrated reports, changes in the content and quality of individual disclosures in integrated reports, and the scope of use of PMSs in presenting non-financial information. For this study, a list of elements subject to assessment was defined. The analysis followed Pistoni et al. (2018), modified for tthis study. This study evaluated the following areas:

1 Background
2 Assurance and reliability
3 Form
4 Content
5 Use of PMSs

DOI: 10.4324/9781003336068-5

Table 4.1 Integrated reports published by Polish companies (2013–2020)

No.	*Company*	*2013*	*2014*	*2015*	*2016*	*2017*	*2018*	*2019*	*2020*
	WIG20								
1	JSW						+	+	+
2	KGHM	+	+	+	+	+	+	+	+
3	LOTOS	+	+	+	+	+	+	+	+
4	LPP					+	+	+	+
5	ORANGEPL				+	+	+	+	+
6	PGE			+	+	+	+	+	+
7	PGNIG					+	+	+	+
8	PKNORLEN		+	+	+	+	+	+	+
9	PZU						+	+	+
10	TAURONPE			+	+	+	+	+	+
	WIG30								
11	GRUPA AZOTY	+	+	+	+	+	+	+	*
12	MBANK					+	+	+	+
	mWIG40								
15	BUDIMEX				+	+	+	+	+
12	INGBSK				+	+	+	+	+
13	PKPCARGO					+	+		
	sWIG80								
27	BNP Paribas							+	+
14	BOGDANKA		+	+	+	+	+	+	+
18	ERBUD				+	+	+	+	+
16	PEKABEX						+	+	+
17	ŚNIEŻKA				+				
25	TIM						+	+	+
	Other – not listed								
19	ANG	+	+	+	+	+	+		
20	GAZ-SYSTEM	+	+	+	+	+			
21	GRUPA GPEC			+	+				
22	PELION	+	+	+	+				
23	PSE				+	+	+	+	*
26	Totalizator Sportowy								+
	Total	6	8	11	17	18	21	20	19

Source: Own elaboration.

Notes:

+ integrated report.

* Report in preparation.

For each area identified, the authors proposed specific variables and attributes. In the area of background, the authors adopted the following variables:

- Motivations underlying the choice of adopting integrated reporting
- Objectives pursued by integrated reporting
- Beneficiaries of the document
- Manager in charge of the integrated reporting process

- CEO's commitment
- Title of the report
- Consistency of integrated reporting with generally applied disclosure standards

The attributes of background quality assessment were: adoption of reporting guidelines and standards, and clear statement of vision from the CEO.

The next examined area of integrated reports was assurance and reliability. In this area, the following variables were identified:

- Internal audit
- Third-party verification
- Acknowledgments and awards for integrated reporting

In turn, attributes of quality assessment of assurance and reliability were: third-party verification and achievement of awards and accolades.

Another area examined was the form of integrated reports. The variables used were:

- Financial report included
- Traditional publishing (paper, digital)
- Interactive online publishing

The attribute of quality assessment of integrated reports form was wide access to the document.

The following variables were distinguished in the content area:

- Organizational overview and external environment
- Business model
- Risks and opportunities
- Strategy and resource allocation
- Governance
- Performance
- Outlook
- Basis of presentation
- Capitals
- Value-creation process

and following attributes of quality assessment:

- Quantitative disclosure
- Establishment of, and reporting against (appropriate) targets
- Ability to accurately assess performance from disclosures
- Good coverage of significant issues
- Reporting of normalized data

The last areas of assessment were the PMSs and other management tools used. Variables analyzed were:

- Balanced scorecard
- Evaluation of investment performance
- Environmental performance measurement
- Operational budgets
- Capital budgets
- Segmented income statements
- Customer costing
- Life cycle costing
- Value chain analysis

Attributes associated with quality assessment of PMSs used for the purpose of preparing integrated reports were:

- Performance
- Risks and opportunities
- Short- and long-term strategic goals
- Customers
- Indicators of various capitals
- Business activities
- Financial goals
- Capital expenditure

Regarding a quantitative assessment of the background, assurance and reliability, form, and use of PMSs, the presence or absence of each proposed variable was assessed. A score of 0 (1) was given in the absence (presence) of a particular element in the report. To assess the quality of future disclosures, a six-point Likert scale was adopted, where 5 is the highest rating and 0 means the element is absent in the content of the report.

4.2 Analysis of the quality of integrated reports and their compliance with the <IR> Framework

The qualitative assessment of integrated reports comprises several steps. In the first stage of the analysis, the entire sample of 120 reports was assessed to obtain a general level of advancement regarding the area of background, assurance, reliability, and form of presentation. The analysis results indicated that most reports included defined elements. Table 4.2 presents the level of the variables characterizing the examined integrated reports in the overall sample (26 firms, 120 firm-year observations). From the results, all surveyed companies indicate the recipients of the report, the involvement of managers indicates 98% of the surveyed entities, and the same part of the reports has an "integrated report" in the title. Most reports (94%) were prepared based on Global

Table 4.2 Presence of variables of the background, assurance and reliability, and form areas in the overall sample

	Yes	*%*	*No*	*%*	*Total*	*%*
Variables						
Background						
Motivations underlying the choice of adopting integrated reporting	92	77%	28	23%	120	100%
Objectives pursued by the integrated report	108	90%	12	10%	120	100%
Beneficiaries of the document	120	100%	0	0%	120	100%
Manager in charge of the integrated reporting process	77	64%	43	36%	120	100%
CEO's commitment	118	98%	2	2%	120	100%
Title of the report	117	98%	3	3%	120	100%
Consistency of integrated reporting with IIRC standard	92	77%	28	23%	120	100%
Consistency of integrated reporting with Global Reporting Initiative Guidelines	113	94%	7	6%	120	100%
Assurance and reliability						
Internal audit	105	88%	15	13%	120	100%
Third-party verification	41	34%	79	66%	120	100%
Acknowledgments and awards for integrated reporting	11	9%	109	91%	120	100%
Form						
Financial report included	80	67%	40	33%	120	100%
Traditional publishing (paper, digital)	83	69%	37	31%	120	100%
Interactive online publishing	94	78%	26	22%	120	100%

Source: Own elaboration.

Reporting Initiative (GRI) guidelines; the International Integrated Reporting Council (IIRC) standard as the basis for preparing reports was indicated by 91% of companies. The results under background indicate that the reporting entities do not pay much attention to disclosure regarding the persons responsible for preparing the report (only 64%) and the reasons for publishing the report (77%). However, more reports included information regarding the purpose of publishing the report (90%). Regarding credibility and reliability, most of the reports were the subject of an internal audit (88%) and much fewer (34%) were external audits. A small number of reports (9%) achieved awards or accolades for quality. Under form, the interactive online version of reports prevails (78%), slightly less (69%) are reports available in the traditional version (in the form of a PDF document), and about 67% of reports contain a full financial statement.

The next section evaluated the presence of variables characterizing the area of background, assurance and reliability, and form of presentation in respective years (Table 4.3). The comparison of the presence of individual variables of reports over time is challenging because of the different number of published reports, which is why the survey is illustrative and the relative values expressed by the structure ratios have been compared.

Table 4.3 Presence of variables, characterizing the area of background, assurance and reliability, and form of presentation in respective years

Variables	*2013 6 reports*		*2014 8 reports*		*2014/2013 (%)*	*2015 11 reports*		*2015/2014 (%)*	*2016 17 reports*		*2016/2015 (%)*	*2017 18 reports*		*2017/2016 (%)*	*2018 21 reports*		*2018/2017 (%)*	*2019 20 reports*		*2019/2018 (%)*	*2020 19 reports*		*2020/2019 (%)*
	No.	%	No.	%		No.	%		No.	%		No.	%		No.	%		No.	%		No.	%	
Background																							
Motivations underlying the choice of adopting integrated reporting	2	33	6	75	200	8	73	33	10	59	25	15	83	50	17	81	13	17	85	0	17	89	0
Objectives pursued by the integrated report	6	100	8	100	33	9	82	13	13	76	44	17	94	31	19	90	12	18	90	–5	18	95	0
Beneficiaries of the document	6	100	8	100	33	11	100	38	17	100	55	18	100	6	21	100	17	20	100	–5	19	100	–5
Manager in charge of the integrated reporting process	3	50	5	63	67	6	55	20	11	65	83	12	67	9	14	67	17	13	65	–7	13	68	0
CEO's commitment	6	100	6	75	0	11	100	83	17	100	55	18	100	6	21	100	17	20	100	–5	19	100	–5
Title of the report	6	100	8	100	33	11	100	38	17	100	55	18	100	6	19	90	6	19	95	0	19	100	0
Consistency of integrated reporting with IIRC standard	5	83	7	88	40	9	82	29	13	76	44	14	78	8	17	81	21	14	70	–18	13	68	–7
Consistency of integrated reporting with GRI Guidelines	6	100	8	100	33	10	91	25	14	82	40	17	94	21	20	95	18	19	95	–5	19	100	0
Assurance and reliability																							
Internal audit	6	100	7	88	17	10	91	43	16	94	60	17	94	6	19	90	12	16	80	–16	14	74	–13
Third-party verification	3	50	5	63	67	5	45	0	4	24	–20	7	39	75	6	29	–14	6	30	0	5	26	–17
Acknowledgments and awards for integrated reporting	2	33	2	25	0	0	0	–100	3	18		2	11	–33	0	0	–100	2	10		0	0	–100
Form																							
Financial report included	2	33	3	38	50	7	64	133	12	71	71	12	67	0	16	76	33	14	70	–13	14	74	0
Traditional publishing (paper, digital)	6	100	7	88	17	8	73	14	11	65	38	12	67	9	13	62	8	12	60	–8	14	74	17
Interactive online publishing	4	67	6	75	50	9	82	50	14	82	56	15	83	7	17	81	13	14	70	–18	15	79	7

Source: Own elaboration.

Information characterizing the beneficiaries of the report, the manager in charge of the integrated reporting process, and the name "integrated report" in the title are revealed in most reports, more often than in other elements (Table 4.3). According to the integrated approach, preparers of reports follow the materiality principle to ensure good coverage of significant issues and accurately indicate the recipients of integrated reports. A high level of implementation of integrated reporting guidelines regarding disclosure for stakeholders may indicate that organizations recognize the significance of stakeholders' engagement in determining organizational strategy. Most reports are not subjected to an external audit and do not contain information on the persons responsible for preparing the report.

The scores under assurance and reliability show a high share of reports subjected to internal audits, which indicates the use of good practices resulting from the IIRC guidelines. In some cases, the growing interest in reports translated into awarding prizes for quality. When assessing formal features, the number of reports published in interactive form, containing links to related information, is increasing. Therefore, the share of reports published in the traditional form, as uniform reports with a specific structure, decreases.

In the next section, the content elements of the integrated report occurring in the analyzed reports are assessed (Table 4.4) in terms of quality per the proposed scoring system. The results of the qualitative analysis of the assessed variables may be more subjective than those of the quantitative assessment because of the wider scale of scoring.

The content area showed significant diversity in quality; only one of the assessed variables achieved an average score higher than 4. The performance is described in the reports in the most detailed and comprehensive manner. The organization's profile and environment achieve a score close to four, and the associated key quantitative information is presented in the best way. The outlook (average score of 3.14) and business model regarding capital (average score of 3.22) are presented to the smallest extent. Although the description of the strategy is assessed relatively well (3.88), the disclosure of such strategic elements as financial strategic goals (average score of 2.65) and the structure of capital expenditure (Table 4.4) is much worse explained.

From the obtained results, the quality of disclosures under content is not satisfactory, especially regarding forward-looking disclosures and business models. There was also a broad diversity of scores between individual items in the content area. Particularly, the low quality indicates innovative elements of reports introduced in the IIRC guidelines.

The average assessment of disclosures in the content area (Table 4.5) indicates that the scores for most items were higher in 2020 than in 2013.

The quality of information on the business model (increase in average scores by 65%) and strategy (increase by 30%) has improved during the analysis period. Significant growth can be observed, especially regarding environmental disclosures (92%), intellectual capital (84%), and financial strategic goals (83%). However, stability is visible in corporate governance, the

Table 4.4 Frequency of scores* in the overall sample for the items in the content area

Content area	*Frequency of scores*						*Mean*	*Median*	*Total*
	0	*1*	*2*	*3*	*4*	*5*			
Organizational overview and external environment	*0%*	*0%*	*3%*	*18%*	*59%*	*20%*	*3.97*	*4*	*120*
Key quantitative information	0%	0%	3%	10%	69%	18%	4.01	4	120
Mission	0%	2%	5%	42%	48%	4%	3.48	4	120
Vision	5%	8%	20%	25%	38%	4%	2.97	3	120
Core markets	0%	0%	1%	21%	64%	14%	3.92	4	120
Customers	0%	2%	2%	44%	46%	7%	3.54	4	120
Competitors	0%	3%	23%	39%	33%	3%	3.08	3	120
Stakeholders	0%	4%	8%	25%	53%	10%	3.56	4	120
Governance	**0%**	**2%**	**9%**	**43%**	**35%**	**12%**	**3.46**	**3**	**120**
Group structure	0%	4%	13%	18%	48%	17%	3.60	4	120
Management board	0%	3%	14%	41%	35%	8%	3.31	3	120
Board of directors	0%	8%	20%	27%	39%	7%	3.18	3	120
Corporate governance	0%	5%	8%	25%	48%	13%	3.57	4	120
Business model	**0%**	**4%**	**18%**	**42%**	**37%**	**0%**	**3.11**	**3**	**120**
Capitals	2%	8%	25%	16%	30%	19%	3.22	3	120
Financial capital	2%	7%	27%	19%	33%	13%	3.13	3	120
Manufactured capital	8%	5%	17%	22%	32%	18%	3.18	3	120
Human capital	3%	5%	20%	25%	37%	10%	3.17	3	120
Intellectual capital	2%	18%	21%	17%	30%	13%	2.93	3	120
Social capital	2%	12%	25%	17%	31%	14%	3.06	3	120
Natural capital	4%	18%	18%	18%	28%	15%	2.93	3	120
Business activities	0%	0%	5%	21%	71%	3%	3.73	4	120
Business activities	0%	0%	6%	16%	62%	17%	3.89	4	120
Social responsibility activities	0%	0%	17%	58%	23%	3%	3.13	3	120
Environmental activities	0%	6%	18%	33%	43%	2%	3.17	3	120
Activities in favor of employees	0%	0%	13%	48%	33%	6%	3.31	3	120
Outputs	0%	0%	3%	19%	69%	8%	3.83	4	120
Products and services	16%	0%	3%	13%	61%	8%	3.26	4	120
By-products	70%	14%	13%	3%	0%	0%	0.49	0	120
Outcomes	0%	0%	3%	30%	53%	13%	3.78	4	120
Value-creation process	0%	9%	15%	12%	49%	15%	3.46	4	120
Risks and opportunities	**0%**	**3%**	**13%**	**23%**	**42%**	**19%**	**3.60**	4	**120**
Risks map	1%	6%	11%	26%	38%	18%	3.50	4	120
Strategy and resource allocation	**0%**	**0%**	**5%**	**26%**	**45%**	**24%**	**3.88**	4	**120**
Short-, medium-, and long-term strategic goals	0%	0%	9%	32%	43%	17%	3.67	4	120
Strategy	0%	0%	6%	32%	59%	3%	3.60	4	120
Financial strategic goals	0%	10%	33%	39%	17%	1%	2.65	3	120
Capital expenditure	3%	16%	23%	30%	25%	3%	2.68	3	120
Performance	**0%**	**0%**	**0%**	**12%**	**56%**	**33%**	**4.21**	**4**	**120**
Outlook	**0%**	**3%**	**25%**	**36%**	**29%**	**8%**	**3.14**	**3**	**120**
Basis of presentation	**3%**	**0%**	**4%**	**16%**	**57%**	**21%**	**3.87**	4	**120**

Source: Own elaboration.

Notes:

* The detailed scoring system is as follows:

0 – element not present in the content.

1 – element present, but poor description.

2 – element present; description based on some quantitative information.

3 – element present; balanced description of contents; average quantity of information.

4 – element present; good and detailed description.

5 – element included in the content; excellent description.

Bold values – Frequency - how many reports (the percentage of reports) scored the particular grade (0, 1, 2, 3, 4 or 5)

Table 4.5 Average scores of disclosures in the content area in respective years

	2013	*2014*	*2015*	*2016*	*2017*	*2018*	*2019*	*2020*	*2020/2013%*
Content area									
Organizational overview and external environment	4.00	3.75	3.64	4.00	4.39	4.19	3.75	3.79	-5%
Key quantitative information	3.50	3.50	3.73	3.88	4.17	4.24	4.15	4.11	17%
Mission	3.33	3.63	3.27	3.41	3.56	3.62	3.45	3.42	3%
Vision	2.17	2.25	2.45	2.88	3.33	3.33	3.05	3.05	41%
Core markets	3.83	4.00	3.73	3.82	4.06	4.10	3.90	3.79	-1%
Customers	3.33	3.38	3.09	3.47	3.89	3.71	3.55	3.47	4%
Competitors	3.00	2.75	2.82	3.00	3.44	3.33	3.05	2.89	-4%
Stakeholders	3.67	3.25	2.91	3.35	4.00	3.86	3.60	3.42	-7%
Governance	3.50	3.25	3.27	3.06	3.56	3.67	3.55	3.58	2%
Group structure	3.67	3.50	3.18	3.12	3.61	3.86	3.80	3.79	3%
Management board	3.00	3.00	2.91	2.82	3.61	3.57	3.45	3.47	16%
Board of directors	3.17	2.75	2.64	2.65	3.28	3.43	3.40	3.53	11%
Corporate governance	3.33	3.63	3.09	3.35	3.61	3.71	3.60	3.84	15%
Business model	2.50	2.25	2.55	3.00	3.28	3.24	3.45	3.42	37%
Capitals	2.17	1.63	2.64	3.06	3.56	3.67	3.50	3.58	65%
Financial capital	2.17	1.88	2.55	2.82	3.44	3.67	3.40	3.42	58%
Manufactured capital	3.00	2.13	2.64	2.94	3.39	3.62	3.30	3.37	12%
Human capital	2.67	2.00	2.64	2.94	3.44	3.62	3.35	3.37	26%
Intellectual capital	1.83	1.25	2.09	2.88	3.33	3.43	3.10	3.37	84%
Social capital	2.00	1.50	2.27	2.88	3.56	3.62	3.30	3.32	66%
Natural capital	1.83	1.25	2.09	2.59	3.28	3.38	3.35	3.53	92%
Business activities	3.17	3.50	3.45	3.76	3.89	4.05	3.70	3.63	15%
Business activities	3.17	3.50	3.64	4.00	4.11	4.10	3.90	3.89	23%
Social responsibility activities	2.83	2.88	3.00	3.24	3.33	3.24	3.05	3.05	8%
Environmental activities	3.17	2.88	2.82	3.18	3.28	3.14	3.30	3.26	3%
Activities in favor of employees	3.00	3.00	3.09	3.18	3.44	3.52	3.40	3.32	11%
Outputs	3.50	3.63	3.36	3.88	4.00	3.95	3.95	3.79	8%
Products and services	2.50	2.88	2.91	3.06	2.89	3.14	3.95	3.79	52%
By-products	0.33	0.38	0.18	0.18	0.17	0.38	1.05	0.89	168%
Outcomes	3.17	3.25	3.36	3.65	4.00	4.05	3.95	3.89	23%
Value-creation process	3.00	2.63	2.64	3.35	3.78	3.71	3.70	3.68	23%
Risks and opportunities	3.00	3.38	3.64	3.53	3.89	3.76	3.55	3.53	18%
Risks map	2.50	2.63	3.09	3.41	3.67	3.86	3.75	3.68	47%
Strategy and resource allocation	3.00	3.38	3.64	3.82	4.39	4.10	3.85	3.89	30%
Short-, medium-, and long-term strategic goals	3.00	3.38	3.45	3.47	3.94	3.90	3.60	3.84	28%
Strategy	2.83	3.00	3.09	3.47	3.72	3.90	3.80	3.84	36%
Financial strategic goals	1.67	1.75	2.18	2.53	2.72	2.95	2.90	3.05	83%
Capital expenditure	2.17	2.50	2.18	2.41	2.94	2.76	2.95	2.79	29%
Performance	3.83	4.38	4.09	4.18	4.39	4.24	4.15	4.21	10%
Outlook	2.83	2.88	2.82	2.94	3.56	3.43	3.00	3.16	11%
Basis of presentation	3.67	3.75	3.45	3.53	4.11	4.14	3.95	3.89	6%

Source: Own elaboration.

organizational overview, and external environment disclosure, which probably results from the fact that companies prepare such information given other formal requirements, such as preparing CSR reports. A significant increase in the disclosure quality regarding opportunities and risks can also be observed. Notably, in recent years, the quality of separate forward-looking information has improved (although only in some reports). Information on the process of creating value has also been systematically enriched.

4.3 Analysis of the use of the key performance indicators in integrated reports

All integrated reports published between 2013 and 2020 were analyzed regarding the use of information generated by PMSs (Table 4.6). The reports were analyzed regarding the use of the following performance measurement tools: BSC, investment efficiency measures, operating and capital budgets, segmented income statements, customer costing, life cycle costing, value chain analysis, investment performance evaluation, and environmental performance measurement. Table 4.6 presents the scope of the use of PMSs for integrated reporting.

From the results, the most frequently used information while preparing reports was generated with the help of popular PMSs. Table 4.6 presents the scope of the use of individual performance measurement tools in presenting information contained in integrated reports in the overall sample. Based on the results, during the entire period considered, all analyzed reports most often used information provided by a BSC, which provided information characterizing the business model and data for describing the strategy used.

The PMS, also often used for integrated reporting, is value chain analysis, which is used primarily in the presentation of the value-creation process. Approximately, 77% of reports used this tool. The environmental performance measures were used to a similar extent (75%) in integrated reports. A fairly common range of use of information provided by PMSs is associated with the fact that, according to IIRC recommendations, the organization should disclose qualitative and quantitative financial and non-financial results and their impact in a separate part of the report referred to as performance.

Information from operational budgets was used in 59% of the examined reports to present information on individual forms of capital. To a lesser extent, data provided in capital budgeting were used; 34% of reports were

Table 4.6 Use of performance measurement and management tools for integrated reporting in the overall sample

Performance measurement systems	*Yes*	%	*No*	%	*Total*	%
Balanced scorecard	100	100%	0	0%	120	100%
Operational budgets	59	49%	61	51%	120	100%
Capital budgets	34	28%	86	72%	120	100%
Segmented income statements	20	17%	100	83%	120	100%
Customer costing	8	7%	112	93%	120	100%
Life cycle costing	10	8%	110	92%	120	100%
Value chain analysis	77	64%	43	36%	120	100%
Evaluation of investment performance	21	18%	99	83%	120	100%
Environmental performance measurement	75	63%	45	38%	120	100%

Source: Own elaboration.

based on data from capital budgets, which was primarily information about planned capital expenditures, presented as an element of strategy description.

The results of the analysis of the use of PMSs in the preparation of integrated reports indicate that the report preparers, to a small extent, use such tools as customer costing (only 7%), life cycle costing (8%), and segmented income statements (17%).

The next stage of the study analyzed the structure of the use of PMSs in integrated reports in the respective years (Table 4.7). The comparison of the presence of individual variables over time in analyzed reports is challenging because of the increasing number of integrated reports, which is why the study is illustrative, and the relative values, expressed by structure indicators, have been compared.

Indeed, 2016 saw the largest increase in the use of management accounting tools for the construction of integrated reports, which is associated with the current significant increase in reports relative to earlier years. In 2015, the number of reports was 11. In 2016, 17 companies published integrated reports. The largest increase in use concerned such tools as capital budgets (300% in 2016), environmental performance measures (300% in 2015), segmented income statements (150% in 2026), and value chain analysis (125% in 2016). The following years saw no such significant increases in the use of management accounting tools, which resulted from the stable number of reports published in 2017 and 2018, oscillating within 20 years, and a similar level of implementation of integrated reporting guidelines in these years.

From the analysis of the content of the reports, most PMSs are useful in presenting the business model in integrated reports. The analysis of the value chain is used in the presentation of the input elements of the business model and in presenting the process of creating value. Operational budgets are used for the presentation of expenditure regarding key capital, which the organization utilizes for operations, and are important for creating value over time and business model sustainability.

Environmental performance measures are primarily used to describe natural and social capital. Segmented income statements are used to present the output elements of the business model. The characteristics of business model outcomes may be based on variance analysis. The BSC tool is used in the presentation of various elements of an integrated report. It is used for presenting a business model (where the perspective of internal processes can help present business activities), some information on corporate governance (mission and vision), and risks and opportunities. The key performance indicators (KPIs) are used in several elements of integrated reports to present the business model outcomes and describe performance, strategy, and resource allocation. Budgeting systems, particularly flexible budgets, are used to present future prospects (outlook). Further, an internal PMS can be used to describe the risks and opportunities.

Given that the most frequently used PMS is the BSC, the study analyzes the most commonly used measure of the BSC perspectives. Table 4.8 and Figures 4.1–4.4 present the results of the analysis.

Table 4.7 Use of performance measurement and management tools for integrated reporting in individual years

	2013 *6 reports*		*2014* *8 reports*		2014/2013 %	*2015* *11 reports*		2015/2014%	*2016* *17 reports*		2016/2015 %	*2017* *18 reports*		2017/2016 %	*2018* *21 reports*		2018/2017 %	*2019* *20 reports*		2019/2018 %	*2020* *19 reports*		2020/2019 %
	No.	%	No.	%		No.	%		No.	%		No.	%		No.	%		No.	%		No.	%	
Balanced scorecard*	6	100	8	100	100	11	100	100	17	100	100	18	100	100	21	100	100	20	100	100	19	100	100
Operational budgets	1	17	0	0	–100	4	36		6	35	50	11	61	83	12	57	9	12	60	0	13	68	8
Capital budgets	0	0	2	25		1	9	–50	4	24	300	7	39	75	7	33	0	7	35	0	6	32	–14
Segmented income statements	0	0	0	0		2	18		5	29	150	3	17	–40	4	19	33	3	15	–25	3	16	0
Customer costing	0	0	1	13		1	9	0	1	6	0	2	11	100	1	5	–50	1	5	0	1	5	0
Life cycle costing	0	0	0	0		0	0		3	18		2	11	–33	2	10	0	2	10	0	1	5	–50
Value chain analysis	3	50	3	38	0	4	36	33	9	53	125	13	72	44	14	67	8	16	80	14	15	79	–6
Evaluation of investment performance	0	0	0	0		0	0		2	12		4	22	100	6	29	50	4	20	–33	5	26	25
Environmental performance measurement	1	17	1	13	0	4	36	300	9	53	125	12	67	33	16	76	33	17	85	6	15	79	–12

Source: Own elaboration.

Note:

* If any balanced scorecard key performance indicator is used, the report is considered to use the balanced scorecard.

Table 4.8 Use of balanced scorecard key performance indicators in integrated reporting in individual years

Year	*2013*	*2014*	*2015*	*2016*	*2017*	*2018*	*2019*	*2020*
Total number of reports	*6 reports*	*8 reports*	*11 reports*	*17 reports*	*18 reports*	*21 reports*	*20 reports*	*19 reports*
	%	%	%	%	%	%	%	%
Financial perspective								
Revenues by customers, market …	100	100	100	100	100	100	100	100
Percentage of revenues by new products or services	67	63	82	76	83	76	80	84
Market share	33	38	45	41	50	43	50	53
Profitability ratios	83	88	91	100	83	86	95	100
Liquidity and financial position ratios	83	88	91	94	83	86	90	95
Operating costs	83	88	91	94	94	95	95	95
Payments to providers of capital (e.g., return on equity and earnings per share)	100	100	100	94	100	100	100	100
Earnings before interest, taxes, depreciation, and amortization	33	38	45	47	44	52	55	53
Learning and growth perspective								
Investment in new technologies	17	25	18	24	22	24	25	21
Investment in new brands development	17	25	27	24	0	0	0	0
Number and value of new patents or copyrights	17	25	18	18	22	24	20	26
Average hours of training	67	75	73	76	72	81	80	79
R&D expense	83	88	91	94	89	95	95	100
Internal business process perspective								
Production volume	100	100	100	100	94	100	100	100
Number of new innovations	67	63	73	71	72	67	70	74
Total weight of waste disposed of (including hazardous waste) by reuse, recycling, composting, incineration	67	63	73	65	56	57	60	53
Waste reduction over the period	50	63	73	71	78	76	80	79
Amount of significant air emissions	67	63	73	53	50	62	50	58

(*Continued*)

Table 4.8 (Continued)

Year	*2013*	*2014*	*2015*	*2016*	*2017*	*2018*	*2019*	*2020*
Total number of reports	*6 reports*	*8 reports*	*11 reports*	*17 reports*	*18 reports*	*21 reports*	*20 reports*	*19 reports*
	%	%	%	%	%	%	%	%
Total monetary value of fines for non-compliance with environmental laws and regulations	17	13	9	18	11	14	10	11
Prevention and environmental management costs	67	75	82	82	94	95	100	100
Employee turnover rate during the reporting period	100	100	100	100	100	100	100	100
Number of employees	100	100	100	100	100	100	100	100
Employment structure	100	100	100	100	100	100	100	100
Accident rate	83	88	91	94	94	95	95	95
Customer perspective								
Customer satisfaction	17	13	9	12	11	10	15	11
Number of individual and business customers	83	100	100	100	94	100	100	100
Annual sales (annual sales/customers)	100	100	100	100	100	100	100	100
Marketing expenses	17	13	18	18	11	14	15	16
Number of customer complaints	17	13	9	12	17	14	15	16

Source: Own elaboration.

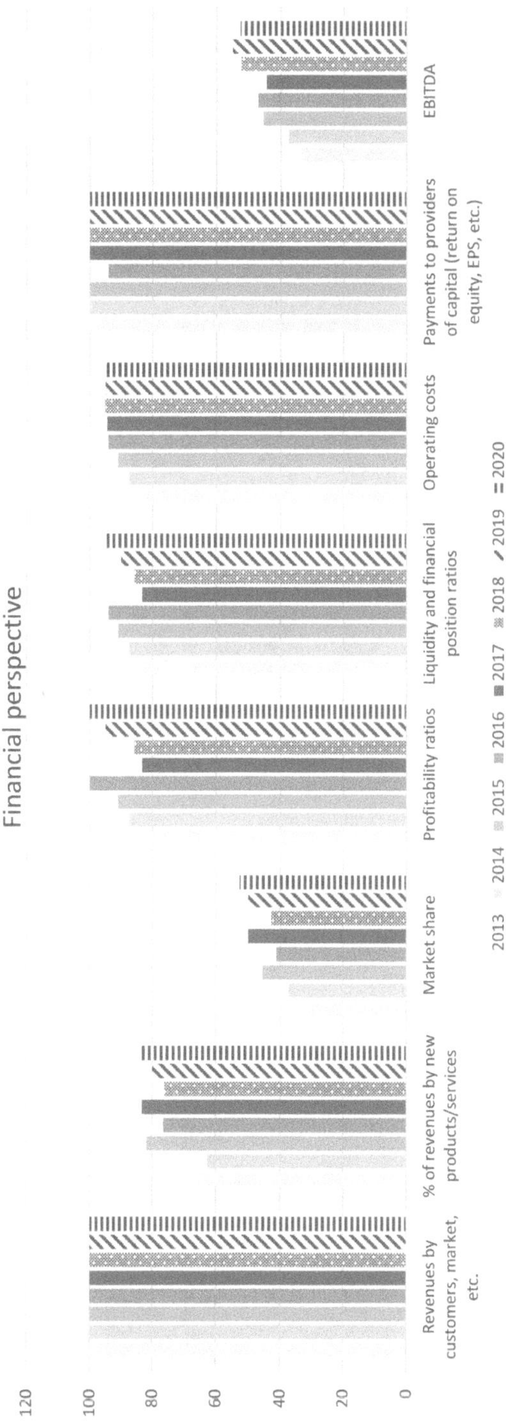

Figure 4.1 Use of a balanced scorecard's financial perspective key performance indicators in integrated reporting

Source: Own elaboration

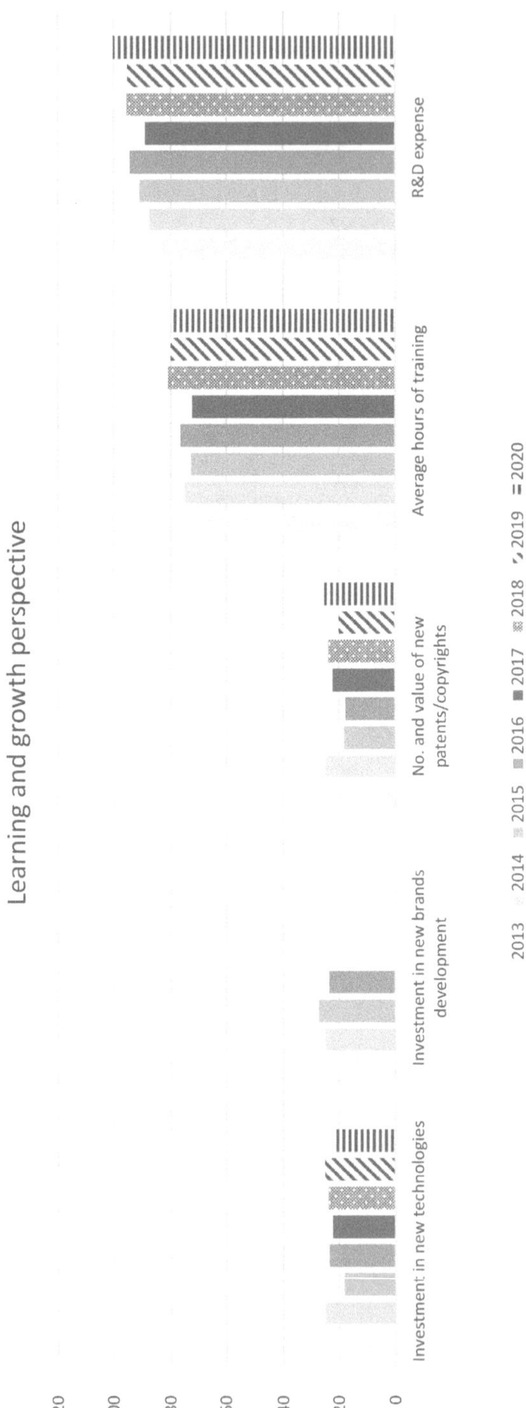

Figure 4.2 Use of a balanced scorecard's learning and growth perspective key performance indicators in integrated reporting

Source: Own elaboration

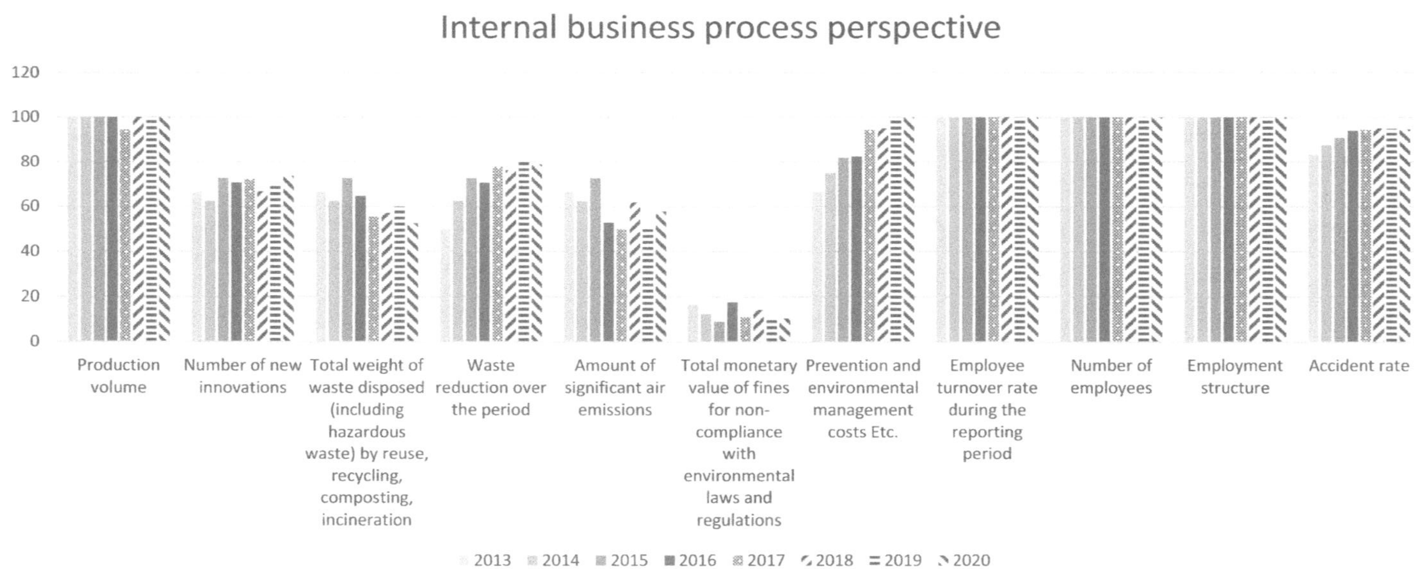

Figure 4.3 Use of a balanced scorecard's internal business process perspective key performance indicators in integrated reporting

Source: Own elaboration

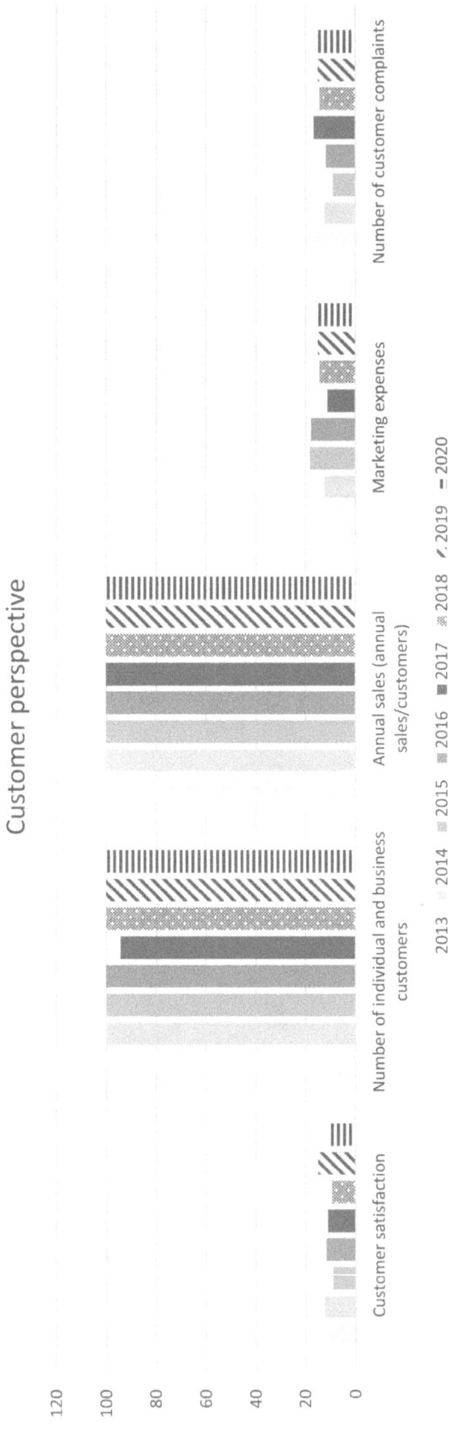

Figure 4.4 Use of a balanced scorecard's customer perspective key performance indicators in integrated reporting

Source: Own elaboration

Analyzing the use of information generated by a BSC reveals that, for integrated reporting, indicators belonging to the internal processes and financial perspectives are used primarily. Almost all reports present indicators such as production volume, number of employees, employment structure, employee turnover rate, revenues, ROE, number of customers, and sales to customer groups. The analysis period reveals a significant increase in the use of indicators such as market share and earnings before interest, taxes, depreciation, and amortization and indicators belonging to the learning and growth perspective (R&D expense, average hours of training). Customer perspective indicators, such as customer satisfaction, marketing expenses, and the number of customer complaints, are used to the smallest extent.

Relative to financial reporting, where information systems and organizational processes have been developed and refined for many years, the systems and processes for preparing an integrated report and disseminating its content remain in the development phase. Undoubtedly, various PMSs are vital in creating useful and practical frameworks for integrated reporting. The existing measurement tools can provide relevant information for preparing integrated reports.

Senior managers must be aware of the growing demand of investors for reliable, non-financial reporting on company sustainability and, at the same time, know the guiding principles regarding the preparation of an integrated report. Hence, companies can provide relevant information to be presented in an integrated report.

4.4 Use of performance measurement systems' information – Case study

The Integrated Annual Report 2020 was the fourth integrated report by the PGNiG Group. The information contained in the report regards the period from January 1, 2020, to December 31, 2020, and describes the status at the end of 2020, unless otherwise stated in the content of the report. Reporting was conducted annually and the last report was published in August 2020.

The integrated report was prepared based on the International GRI Standards 2016, with 2018 updates developed by the GRI. Moreover, this report reflects the recommendations contained in the International Petroleum Industry Environmental Conservation Association's (IPIECA's) Sustainability Reporting Guidance for the Oil and Gas industry. The reported indicators include the "core" GRI indicators, the selected "core" and "additional" indicators taken from IPIECA's guidelines, and the PGNiG Group's indicators. This report also reflects the selected guidance contained in the communication from the commission – Supplement on reporting climate-related Information (2019/C 209/01) and recommendations published by the Task Force on Climate-related Financial Disclosures on environmental reporting.

The activities presented in the report are often a response to the challenges defined in the 2030 Agenda of the Sustainable Development Goals, as announced by the UN in September 2015. We implement these goals through long-term programs to develop employees at all levels and care for the social and market environment.

The KPIs are presented in terms of capital (Table 4.9). Financial capital is key to providing funding for the PGNiG Group's day-to-day operations and delivering ambitious strategic goals. The funding sources are equity, debt, and funds generated from business activities. The overriding goal of the current strategy is to drive value growth and ensure the financial stability of the PGNiG Group. We aspire to achieve a cumulative of PLN 33.7 billion in the 2017–2022 period. Thus, the Group must continue its efforts to solidify its competitive position while promoting the growth of the gas market and further expanding the gas network in Poland.

The PGNiG Group defines manufacturing capital as the property, plant, and equipment it uses to conduct its business. The key items are buildings and structures, plants, and equipment, which are mainly associated with exploring and producing natural gas and crude oil and with gas trading, storage, and distribution.

Human capital is important because the PGNiG Group is one of Poland's largest employers. The workforce comprises highly qualified professionals with extensive experience. Meanwhile, it is frequently the first employer of many young people. Proper application of employee skills and competencies allows the organization to offer products that meet customer expectations and ensure Poland's energy security. Employee commitment to ensuring the growth of the PGNiG Group guarantees the delivery of strategic plans and the achievement of ambitious goals that contribute to building stable market leadership. A strong and recognizable brand can attract specialists and qualified professionals who are ready to work as a team to leverage their potential and contribute to its growth. A key aspect of the group's operations is providing employees with stable employment and rewarding career opportunities in a safe and friendly working environment.

The PGNiG Group defines innovation capital as a knowledge-based intangible asset. Investments in innovation and advanced solutions drive operational efficiency, contribute to the growth of the PGNiG Group's business potential, and help address new challenges associated with environmental impacts and climate. The PGNiG Group aims to foster collaborative partnerships with the scientific community and support and spur the growth of small and medium-sized enterprises, particularly start-ups.

PGNiG defines social capital as the ability to share, build strong relationships, and cooperate with stakeholders.

Given the strategic importance of the group's products, the group is particularly vital to the everyday lives of local communities. The nature, operational scale, and presence of infrastructure for hydrocarbon exploration, production, storage, and distribution make the PGNiG Group deeply committed to building partnership relations with local communities and governments, suppliers, and contractors, with the ultimate goal of pursuing joint

Table 4.9 Capitals and BSC perspectives in PGNiG Group

Categories of capitals	*Key performance indicators*	*2020*	*Balanced scorecard perspectives*
Financial capital	Market capitalization	32,023	Financial
Financial capital	Equity	44,125	Financial
Financial capital	Total assets	62,871	Financial
Financial capital	Debt ratio (liabilities to assets ratio) (%)	30.0%	Financial
Financial capital	Debt to equity ratio (financial leverage) (%)	42.8%	Financial
Financial capital	Available funding sources: lines of credit and bond programs	15,236	Financial
Financial capital	Net cash from operating activities	14,118	Financial
Financial capital	Net cash from investing activities	–6,254	Financial
Financial capital	Return on equity	16,6%	Financial
Financial capital	Return on assets	11,5%	Internal business process
Financial capital	Current ratio	3.0	Financial
Financial capital	Quick ratio	2.6	Financial
Human capital	Total employment at the end of 2020	24,608	Internal business process
Human capital	Employment at the end of the period by segments – 2020: exploration and production	6,534	Internal business process
Human capital	Employment at the end of the period by segments – 2020: trade and storage	3,026	Internal business process
Human capital	Employment at the end of the period by segments – 2020: distribution	11,517	Internal business process
Human capital	Employment at the end of the period by segments – 2020: generation	1,817	Internal business process
Human capital	Employment at the end of the period by segments – 2020: other activities	1,714	Internal business process
Human capital	Annual retention rate for PGNiG employees who were still employed 12 months after returning from parenting-related leave	89%	Internal business process
Human capital	New hires as a percentage of the total workforce	5.32%	Internal business process
Human capital	Leavers as a percentage of the total workforce	5.56%	Internal business process
Human capital	Employees on parenting-related leave	2.15%	Internal business process
Human capital	Average number of training hours per the PGNiG Group employees in 2019	14	Learning and growth
Natural capital	The PGNiG Group's direct GHG emissions (Scope 1)	7.18 mln	Internal business process
Natural capital	The PGNiG Group's electricity consumption	1,122 GWh	Internal business process

(Continued)

Table 4.9 (Continued)

Categories of capitals	*Key performance indicators*	*2020*	*Balanced scorecard perspectives*
Natural capital	The PGNiG Group's water consumption	144.6 mln m^3	Internal business process
Natural capital	Total volumes of wasted water generated by the PGNiG Group	144.6 mln m^3	Internal business process
Social capital	Estimated number of beneficiaries of social programs by PGNiG Group including PGNiG Foundation is a result of a specific year in which all of the activities were devoted to fighting against the pandemic	20 m people	Customer perspective
Social capital	Participants of the "Rachunek wdzięczności PGNiG" program supporting veterans fighting in the Warsaw Uprising or veterans of the Defence War in 1929	408	Customer perspective
Social capital	Initiatives received support from Group companies and the PGNiG Foundation	550	Customer perspective
Innovation capital	Innovation projects implemented in 2020 with the participation of the PGNiG Group	150	Internal business process
Innovation capital	Budget earmarked for innovation projects in 2019	515 ca. PLN m	Internal business process
Innovation capital	New patent decisions obtained in 2020 for applications resulting from ongoing R&D projects	4	Internal business process
Natural capital	PGNiG Group's direct GHG emissions (scope 1) in 2020 (7.18 million Mt eCO_2 in 2019, 7.15 million Mt eCO_2 in 2018)	6.8 m Mt eCO_2	Internal business process
Natural capital	PGNiG Group's electricity consumption in 2020	1099.7 GWh	Internal business process
Natural capital	PGNiG Group's water consumption in 2020 (144.6 million cubic meters in 2019, 160.6 million cubic meters in 2018)	154.8 mcm	Internal business process
Manufacturing capital	Number of oil and gas extraction facilities in Poland (2019: 54)	53	Internal business process
Manufacturing capital	Number of production licenses in Poland (2019: 190)	189	Learning and growth
Manufacturing capital	Number of production wells (2019: over 2,000)	>2,000	Internal business process
Manufacturing capital	Number of licenses for exploration for and appraisal of mineral deposits in Poland (2019:47)	47	Learning and growth
Manufacturing capital	Natural gas sales by volume (including transactions on the Polish Power Exchange) (2019: 29.8 bcm)	30.7 bcm	Internal business process

(Continued)

Table 4.9 (Continued)

Categories of capitals	*Key performance indicators*	*2020*	*Balanced scorecard perspectives*
Manufacturing capital	Natural gas imports by volume (2019: 14.9 bcm)	14.8 bcm	Internal business process
Manufacturing capital	Distributed gas by volume (2019: 11.5 bcm)	11.6 bcm	Internal business process
Manufacturing capital	Estimated volume of gas fuel transmitted over the network, according to GAZ System (2019: 18.9 bcm)	18.1 bcm	Internal business process
Manufacturing capital	Number of customers (2019: 7.1 mln)	7.3 mln	Customer perspective
Manufacturing capital	Exploration and production Capital expenditure on property, plant, and equipment in 2020 (2019: PLN 2,508 m)	2,557 m	Internal business process
Manufacturing capital	Exploration and production Capital expenditure on property, plant, and equipment abroad in 2020 (2019: PLN 1,554 m)	1,707 m	Internal business process
Manufacturing capital	Trade and storage Capital expenditure on property, plant, and equipment in 2020 (2019: PLN 159m)	90 mln PLN	Internal business process
Manufacturing capital	Distribution Capital expenditure on property, plant, and equipment in 2019, including spending on gas network expansion and upgrade projects (2019: PLN 2,278 m)	PLN 2,945 m	Internal business process
Manufacturing capital	Generation: Capital expenditure on property, plant, and equipment in 2020, including PLN 500 m of CO_2-related spending (2019: PLN 493 m)	PLN 1,076 m	Internal business process
Manufacturing capital	Quality of offered products		Customer perspective

Source: Own elaboration based on PGNIG IR 2020.

objectives. PGNiG Group creates opportunities for cooperation and builds an understanding of mutual relations and interdependencies with individual stakeholder groups.

The value-creation process for PGNiG Group[1] presents inputs (six capitals), business segments (comprising the exploration for and production of natural gas and crude oil, import, storage, sale and distribution of gas and liquid fuels, as well as heat and electricity generation and distribution), and outputs according to individual capital (informing of key metrics, performance/outcomes, approach to results/performance management, and how does individual capital affect other types of capital).

In summary, the obligation to report non-financial information forced organizations to identify and analyze the performance of the company not only in the financial sphere but also in the non-financial sphere. Due to this fact, non-financial reporting must be the result of the entire process related to the strategic analysis of the organization and should meet the expectations of all stakeholders. PMSs can be a source of significant information for non-financial reports, and their use is associated with identifying KPIs. Taking into account the key role that integrated reporting is supposed to play is informing about the value creation process, and lack of detailed IIRC guidelines on how integrated reports should be presented, the practice shows that companies use their own individual solutions in this area.

Note

1 https://pgnig2020.pl/en/pgnig-group/value-creation-process/

5 Use of performance measurement systems' information in integrated reporting

Questionnaire survey

5.1 Applied research methodology and characteristics of the research sample

This study aimed to assess the level of knowledge about integrated reporting, factors determining the implementation of this type of reporting, scope, and the possibility of using performance measurement systems (PMSs) for preparing integrated reports.

The analysis of the data aimed to diagnose the views of management accountants, controlling specialists, and financial managers in the focal organizations on the aim and usefulness of integrated reporting, factors determining its implementation, and practical aspects of integrated reporting.

The implementation of integrated reporting requires the engagement of certain resources. Hence, one of the objectives of the analysis was to determine the respondents' perceptions of the possibilities of using a company's information and PMSs to prepare integrated reports.

This study was conducted using a survey method. The structured questionnaire, comprising a set of questions, was developed based on a study conducted by MIA-ACCA (2016) and modified to determine the level of knowledge about integrated reporting and the perception of the role of PMSs in the preparation of integrated reports.

The results of the analysis will help answer the question: what is the level of knowledge about integrated reporting among managerial staff and financial and accounting specialists? Particularly,

1 What is the general state of knowledge about integrated reporting?

- What are the primary recipients of integrated reports?
- What types of information are presented in integrated reports?
- Does the information presented in the integrated reports comply with the International Integrated Reporting Council (IIRC) <IR> framework requirements?
- What are the forms of presentation of non-financial information in integrated reports?

DOI: 10.4324/9781003336068-6

2 What are the barriers and challenges in implementing integrated reporting?

- Cost of integrated report preparation?
- Increasing resource involvement?
- Need to create interdisciplinary teams dealing with collecting information for integrated reports?

3 What changes are required to adapt existing information systems for integrated reporting?
4 What are the company's benefits, if any, of implementing integrated reporting?

- Improving the image of the company?
- Legitimization of activities?
- Increase in a company's market share?
- Increasing the interest of potential investors?
- Improving intra-organizational communication?

5 What are the benefits of integrated reporting for external stakeholders?
6 To what extent do knowledge and experience in PMSs contribute to integrated reporting?

Thus, to answer these research questions, the survey was conducted among preparers of corporate reports and other stakeholders, such as analysts, investors, and auditors to examine the views of various groups on integrated reporting issues.

The empirical data analysis included:

1 Analysis of the characteristics of entities represented by respondents
2 Identification of the current scope of reporting
3 Analysis of the scale of application of PMSs
4 Diagnosis of respondents' perceptions of the challenges and benefits of integrated reporting for the company
5 Diagnosis of respondents' perception of the benefits of integrated reporting for various stakeholders
6 Determining the possibility of PMSs in the practice of integrated reporting

Empirical data were analyzed using descriptive statistics of the frequency of individual variables.

Empirical research was conducted based on anonymous data received from the respondents. To determine the benefits and challenges of integrated reporting and the possibility of using PMSs in the preparation of integrated reports, a survey was conducted among postgraduate students in the field of accounting and control in Lesser Poland Voivodeship in 2021. The survey captured current observations and opinions regarding integrated reporting. The total number of surveys carried out was 148, of which 31 were considered incomplete and omitted from the analysis; 117 completed questionnaires were analyzed.

The target respondents represented companies whose organizational structure included departments of management accounting or control.

The survey questionnaire comprised questions grouped into five thematic blocks concerning:

- Entities represented by respondents and professional functions held by respondents
- Level and sources of knowledge of respondents on integrated reporting
- Usefulness of integrated reports for external stakeholders and perceived benefits of integrated reporting for reporting entities
- Perceived challenges related to the implementation of integrated reporting
- Possibilities of supporting the process of integrated reporting development

Because there were corporate report preparers and non-reporters among the respondents, the survey was prepared in a version enabling the selection of questions depending on the respondent's profile. One goal of this study was to verify the knowledge and perception of integrated reporting. As part of the survey, respondents were asked to answer questions on a scale from 1 to 5. The answers allowed for identifying the level of knowledge and views on integrated reporting, despite being subjective assessments. Subjective measures of qualitative phenomena are widely accepted in organizational research (Powell, 1995); however, they have result generalization limitations.

The criterion for selecting respondents participating in the study was their engagement in the practice of management accounting or control and employment in the reporting department, management accounting or control department, or planning department. The selected respondents represented small-, medium-, and large-scale enterprises; 54 responses were from medium-sized enterprises; 48 were from small and micro enterprises; and 15 were from large enterprises.

The structure of entities represented by respondents, from the perspective of the financial situation, is dominated by companies declaring the average financial situation (constituting over 86% of the studied population). Enterprises whose situation was assessed as very good (less than 10%) and very bad (less than 4%) have a smaller share in the research sample. Figure 5.1 presents the distribution of respondents, considering the size and status of their entities (listed or unlisted companies).

Most companies (83.0%) were not listed on the stock exchange and 17% were listed companies. The entities represented in the study operate in many different sectors, particularly in the production industry, construction, real estate, and services. Four respondents (3.4%) indicated that they represent entities co-owned or wholly owned by the State Treasury. The analysis of the population of the respondents surveyed showed that the largest groups are individuals whose professional function involves participating in the preparation of corporate reports (over 64% of all respondents). Respondents engaged in preparing corporate reports include accountants, management

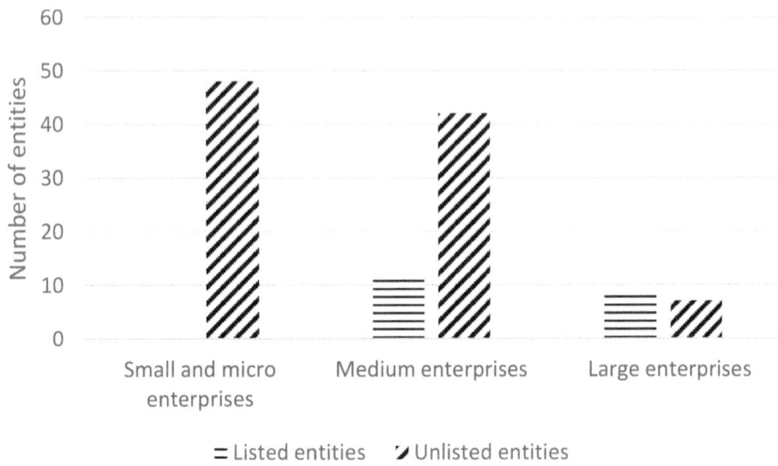

Figure 5.1 Size and status of the examined entities

Source: Own elaboration

accountants, internal auditors, financial managers, board members, and independent directors. The next group comprises respondents who served as financial analysts (approximately 14%). This function is most often performed within large enterprises in the examined sample. Investors (12%), consultants, and others (less than 10%) (Table 5.1) were the smallest group in the studied population.

Most respondents (64.96%) prepare financial statements. Individuals who do not practice corporate reporting represent nearly 35% of all respondents. This sample structure allowed for conducting the study from two perspectives.

5.2 Level of knowledge on integrated reporting

The respondents' current level of knowledge on integrated reporting was examined relative to the sources and scope of information; they were interested in learning more about integrated reporting. Respondents rated their level of

Table 5.1 Characteristics of the respondents' profile

Respondents' profile	*Quantity*	%
Corporate report preparers, including	76	64.96%
• Independent directors and board members	4	3.42%
• Chief Financial Officer (CFO), internal auditors	6	5.13%
• Accountants and management accountants	66	56.41%
Financial analysts	16	13.68%
Marketing and public relations specialists	14	11.97%
Consultants and other	11	9.40%

Source: Own elaboration.

Table 5.2 Respondents' level of knowledge of integrated reporting

Level of knowledge	*Corporate report preparers*	%	*Non-reporters*	%
5 – in-depth knowledge	7	9.21%	2	4.88%
4 – good knowledge	8	10.53%	7	17.07%
3 – average knowledge	34	44.74%	17	41.46%
2 – limited knowledge	18	23.68%	9	21.95%
1 – lack of knowledge	9	11.84%	6	14.63%
Total	76	100.00%	41	100.00%

Source: Own elaboration.

knowledge on a scale from 1 (lack of knowledge) to 5 (in-depth knowledge). In general, most respondents declared familiarity with this form of reporting. However, the level of knowledge about integrated reports among respondents was low, which suggests that most respondents did not have practical knowledge (Table 5.2 and Figure 5.2).

The largest part of the respondents (66%) indicated a score of 3 or 4, describing themselves as having an average or poor level of knowledge. Thus, they assess their level of knowledge about integrated reporting as low. Only 8% were in the highest category of scores, describing themselves as having a higher-than-average level of knowledge about integrated reports, while about 13% declared that they do not know about integrated reporting. Respondents preparing corporate reports more often claim that they have average knowledge (approximately 45%) than users of corporate reports (41.0%). Thus, people not involved in corporate reporting more often (17%) than respondents preparing corporate reports (11%) declare that they have good knowledge.

The average level of knowledge of preparers of corporate reports is 2.82, and that of non-preparers is 2.76. Thus, the difference in the average

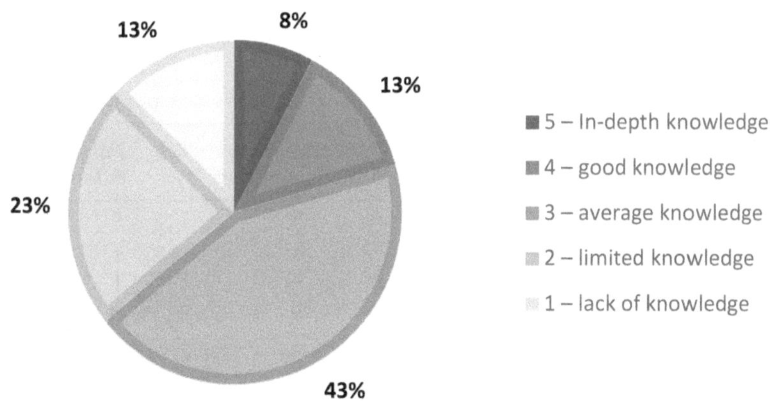

Figure 5.2 Respondents' level of knowledge of integrated reporting

Source: Own elaboration

Table 5.3 Level of knowledge of integrated reporting among corporate report preparers

Level of knowledge	*Small and micro enterprises*	%*	*Medium enterprises*	%*	*Large enterprises*	%*
5 – in-depth knowledge	-	-	5	7%	2	3%
4 – good knowledge	2	3%	2	3%	4	5%
3 – average knowledge	8	11%	23	30%	3	4%
2 – limited knowledge	11	14%	4	5%	3	4%
1 – lack of knowledge	6	8%	2	3%	1	1%
Total	27	36%	36	47%	13	17%

Source: Own elaboration.

Note:

* Percentage share of the entire group of respondents participating in the preparation of corporate reports.

level of knowledge between the two groups is not significant. Less than 20% of preparers of corporate reports have good or in-depth knowledge of integrated reporting (Table 5.3), 2% less than users of corporate reports (22%). The low level of knowledge, as indicated by the survey findings, may result from the relatively low popularity of integrated reporting in Poland and the small group of entities publishing integrated reports in Poland (see also Table 5.4).

From Tables 5.3 and 5.4, micro and small enterprises have the largest share of respondents indicating very poor knowledge of integrated reporting among corporate report preparers (8%) and users (15%). However, medium-sized enterprises and small and microentities, respectively, saw the largest number of respondents declaring an average level of knowledge among corporate report preparers (23%) and users (29%).

From Figure 5.3, 80% (78%) of corporate report preparers (users) assess their level of knowledge on integrated reporting as average or lower than average. Further, 85% (81%) of corporate report preparers (users) rated themselves as having less than adequate knowledge of integrated reporting

Table 5.4 Level of knowledge of integrated reporting among corporate report users

Level of knowledge	*Small and micro enterprises*	%*	*Medium enterprises*	%*	*Large enterprises*	%*
5 – in-depth knowledge	-	-	2	5%	-	-
4 – good knowledge	2	5%	4	10%	1	2%
3 – average knowledge	12	29%	4	10%	1	2%
2 – limited knowledge	1	2%	8	20%	-	-
1 – lack of knowledge	6	15%		0%	-	-
Total	21	51%	18	44%	2	5%

Source: Own elaboration.

Note:

* Percentage share of the entire group of respondents participating in the preparation of corporate reports.

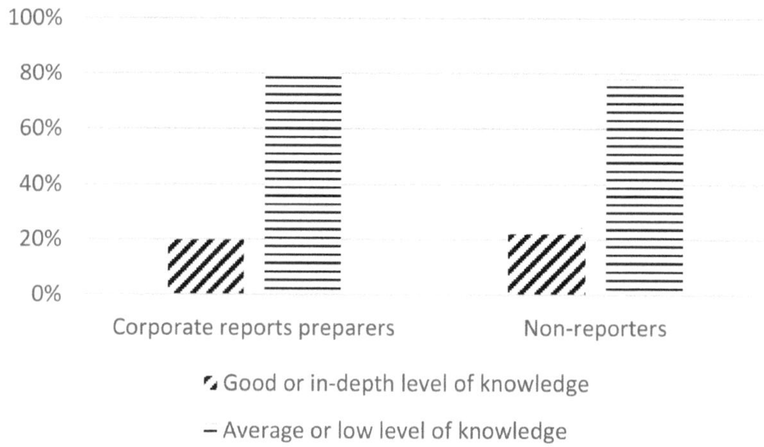

Figure 5.3 Declared level of knowledge of integrated reporting in the overall sample

Source: Own elaboration

and plan to learn more about integrated reporting (Figure 5.4). Thus, there is a high demand for further education on integrated reporting among the respondents. Meanwhile, in comments, the respondents indicated that they would like to take advantage of training, workshops, and publications for additional knowledge about integrated reporting. Overall, approximately 70% of all respondents answered that they wanted to learn more about integrated reporting. The analysis of respondents indicating an average or high level of knowledge about integrated reporting (scores 3 to 5) shows that over

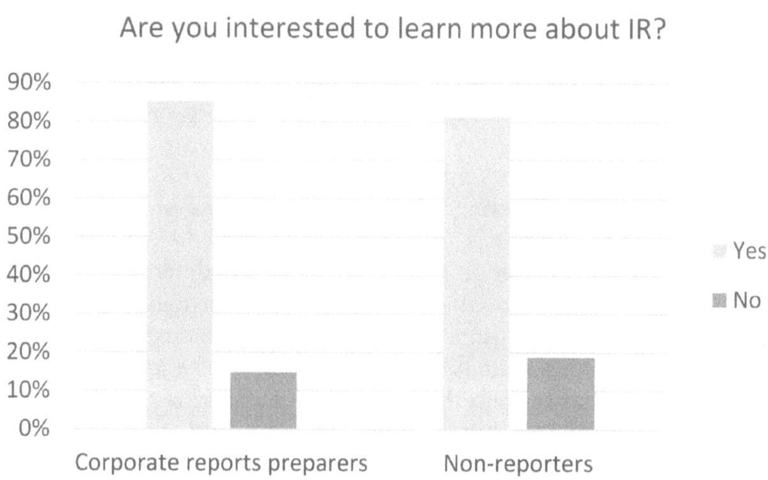

Figure 5.4 Respondents interested to learn more about integrated reporting

Source: Own elaboration

Table 5.5 Approach to integrated reporting among entities represented by respondents

Question	*Yes*	%	*No*	%
Has integrated reporting been discussed within the company?	22	19%	95	81%
Does the company prepare integrated reporting?	9	8%	108	92%
Would the company consider adopting integrated reporting?	15	14%	93	86%
Do you consider yourself a proponent of integrated reporting?	23	20%	94	80%

Source: Own elaboration.

65% of this group of respondents are individuals involved in the preparation of corporate reports.

Further analysis of the state of knowledge about integrated reporting concerned the approach of the entities to integrated reporting and examined whether the integrated report was discussed in the company and whether the company used or considered the possibility of implementing it (Table 5.5).

From Table 5.5, only 8% of respondents confirmed that the integrated report is an element of corporate reporting in their companies. Further, 19% declared that discussions on integrated reporting occurred in their companies, mainly at the board level. Regarding respondents representing entities where integrated reporting has not been implemented, only 14% would consider adopting integrated reporting. Assumedly, this result indicates the management board's approach to the integrated reporting initiative because it has the competence to decide on the implementation of a specific form of reporting in the company. It may also indicate the reluctance of chief financial officers (CFOs) and other decision-makers to implement this form of reporting. An explanation may also be the lack of knowledge of the differences between integrated reporting and other forms of reporting, such as sustainability, environmental, social, corporate governance, and other reports. The survey participants were asked about the differences between the integrated reports and corporate social responsibility (CSR) or sustainability reports (Figures 5.5 and 5.6).

There were differing views among respondents regarding the scope and purpose of integrated reporting relative to other types of reports, such as CSR and sustainability reports. Almost 20% of respondents admitted that they do not have an opinion on whether there is any difference. The largest percentage (36%) responded that sustainability reporting was a subset of integrated reporting. Only a small percentage of respondents perceived integrated reports and the sustainability or CSR reports as excellent substitutes (7%) or indicated that the sustainability or CSR report is sufficient without integrated reporting (10%). In fact, integrated reporting and CSR or sustainability reporting are not perfect substitutes, though they overlap; only 14% of the respondents reflected this answer. The answers to the analyzed issue do not differ much between the two main groups of respondents, that is, preparing corporate reports and non-reporters. The greatest disproportion is in the

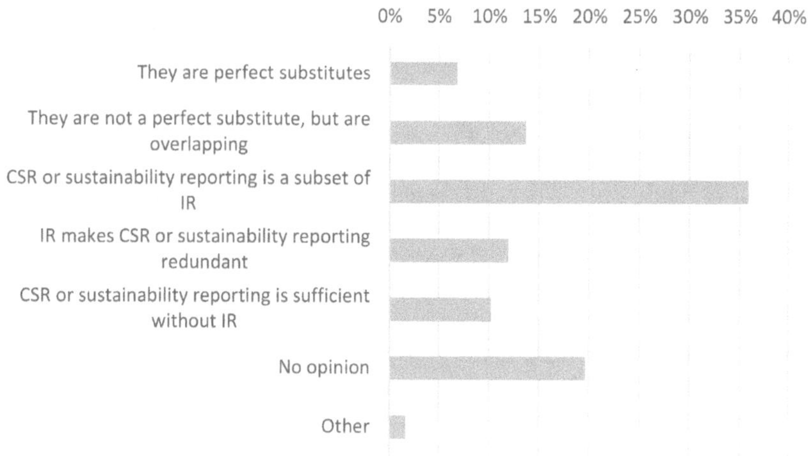

Figure 5.5 Perceived difference between integrated reports (IR) and corporate social responsibility (CSR) or sustainability reporting in the overall sample

Source: Own elaboration

option indicating that reporting on sustainability or CSR is sufficient without integrated reporting (Figure 5.6). Further, 6% more respondents among users of corporate reports indicated this option. The main sources of knowledge on the issue of integrated reporting are participation in training, workshops, and conferences, which are mostly theoretical knowledge.

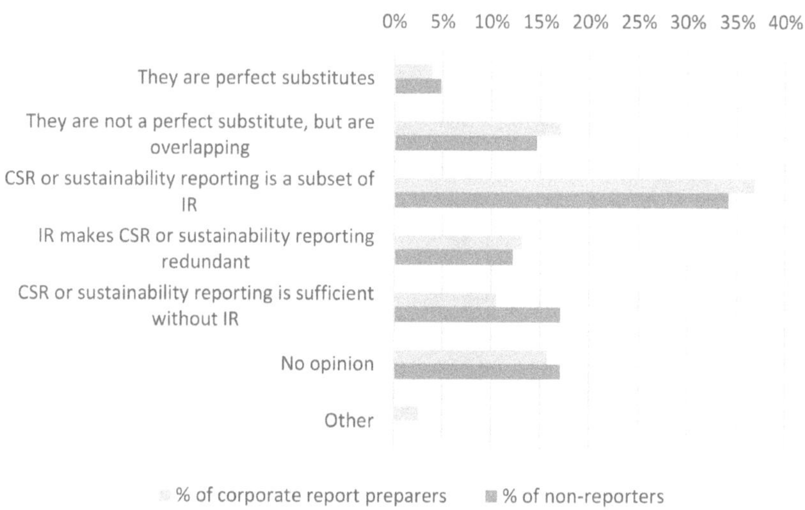

Figure 5.6 Perceived difference between integrated reports (IR) and corporate social responsibility (CSR) or sustainability reporting among corporate report preparers and non-reporters

Source: Own elaboration

5.3 Integrated reporting in the communication of value-creation process

Respondents fear that the cost of preparing integrated reports is a major challenge, and the benefits of implementing integrated reporting may not outweigh the costs. Hence, assumedly, the decision to implement integrated reporting is made only when the benefits of reporting exceed the potential costs. The scale of interest of various stakeholder groups is an important factor that may increase integrated reporting benefits. Therefore, the information presented in the integrated report must correspond to the information needs of the identified stakeholders. As part of the survey, respondents were asked to indicate the three main groups of recipients of the integrated report. Figure 5.7 shows how respondents perceived the importance of various stakeholders as target recipients of integrated reports.

According to respondents, current and potential investors and providers of capital are perceived as the main recipients of integrated reporting. Customers and analysts are also relatively important recipients of integrated reports. Therefore, the respondents believe that the integrated report provides essential information about the organization primarily to attract investors, creditors, and customers. As outlined in the <IR> Framework, the main purpose of the integrated report is to explain how financial capital providers create value over time to enable a more efficient allocation of capital. Therefore, survey respondents identify current and potential investors as the main recipients of integrated reports.

Research on the subject (Ernst and Young, 2015) shows that when making investment decisions, investors use information about the value-creation process presented using the capital approach, which is usually not presented

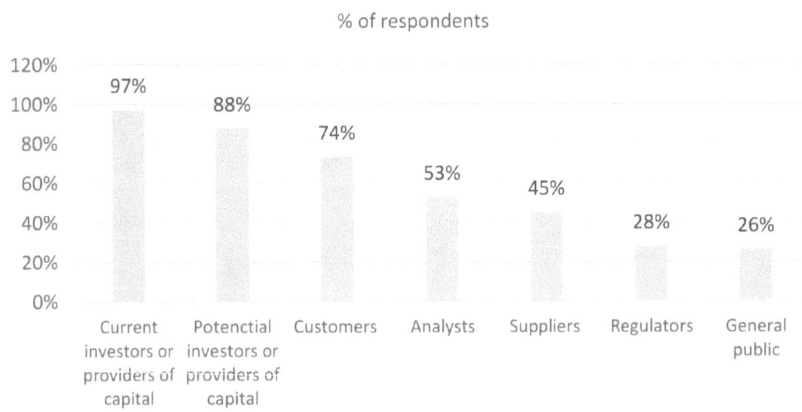

Figure 5.7 Main recipients of integrated reports

Source: Own elaboration

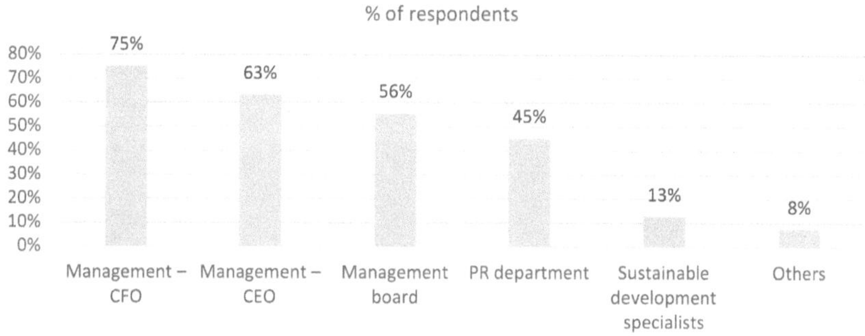

Figure 5.8 Parties responsible for preparing the integrated report

Source: Own elaboration

in traditional annual reports. Integrated reporting aims to fill this information gap by providing investors with information in a broader context, considering social aspects and future prospects to help understand the business model, strategy, and results. Therefore, it is important to include all the necessary information while preparing the report and ensuring its credibility. Figure 5.8 presents who, according to the respondents, should be responsible for preparing the integrated report.

There was a large diversity of responses. Most respondents indicated that CFOs were responsible for preparing the integrated report. However, as integrated reports are not limited to financial information, such responsibility may exceed the CFO's competence. Next was the chief executive officer, followed by the company's management board. Such responses seem more justified because integrated reports should provide the necessary information about the company's long-term perspectives and strategic objectives. Others indicated that external consultants were responsible for preparing the report.

The presentation of the company's business model and strategy in the annual report communicates to investors and other stakeholders how the company creates value for its stakeholders. However, the integrated reporting guidelines regarding consistency and connectivity of information helped provide a more coherent communication of information through one document. Therefore, the respondents were asked whether they believed the adopted <IR> Framework enables better communication of the value and potential of creation of value to investors and other stakeholders (Figure 5.9).

According to many of the respondents, integrated reporting does not contribute to communicating the value and the organization's potential to create value. The many negative answers may stem from the lack of a requirement to verify the information presented in integrated reports and, therefore, limited trust in published information.

Figure 5.9 Integrated reporting and the communication of value-creation process
Source: Own elaboration

5.4 Use of performance measurement systems' information in integrated reports

Presenting all necessary financial and non-financial information in integrated reports and the credibility of this information can significantly depend on using the right methods and tools. In particular, various PMSs in the reporting entity can facilitate the preparation of non-financial information. The need to use PMSs for companies' internal purposes stems from many years of experience functioning in a competitive environment. For PMSs to support an integrated reporting system, it is important to determine what information generated by various PMSs can be used in the preparation of individual elements of the integrated report.

Integrated reports are intended to communicate the organization's strategy, corporate governance, and the results of the unit's activities and forecasts in the context of creating value in the short, medium, and long term. The strategic orientation of an integrated report suggests the possibility of using specific PMSs in the reporting process. As part of the survey, a question was asked about the usefulness of such PMSs as investment effectiveness measures, segmented income statements, customer costing, life cycle costing, value chain analysis, and a BSC. Table 5.6 presents the opinions of respondents regarding the possibility of using information generated by various PMSs for integrated reporting.

According to most of the respondents (72%), BSC is a tool that can generate useful information to prepare integrated reports. The least number of respondents indicated the possibility of using various measures of value-added in integrated reporting. Respondents were then asked to indicate which of the PMSs could provide information to the individual elements of the integrated report. Table 5.7 and Figure 5.10 illustrate the answers provided by the respondents.

According to the respondents, most PMSs are useful for the preparation of information on the performance of the organization. Respondents indicated the possibility of using the information provided by such tools as a BSC, segmented

Table 5.6 Possibilities of using performance measurement and management tools for the preparation of <IR>

Performance measurement systems	*Possibilities of using for the preparation of <IR>*
Balanced scorecard	72%
Operational and capital budgets	48%
Segmented income statements	53%
Customer costing	38%
Life cycle costing	37%
Value chain analysis	31%
Evaluation of investment performance	36%
Value-added measurement (economic value added [EVA], market value added [MVA], free cash flow [FCF])	18%

Source: Own elaboration.

income statements, customer costing, and value-added measures. Moreover, in the presentation of the business model, respondents saw the possibility of using several tools, such as evaluation of investment performance, segmented income statements, customer costing, and value chain analysis. Only two PMSs, indicated by the largest number of respondents, were considered useful in the preparation of information on strategy and resource allocation. Hence, more than half of the respondents saw the opportunity to use BSC indicators and investment performance measures. The smallest number of respondents saw the possibility of using PMS information to prepare information on corporate governance. Table 5.8 presents a comparison of the answers provided by the study participants and the indications in the relevant literature.

According to the respondents, BSC is the most useful tool in preparing an integrated report and various management reports and evaluating investment performance. Although these tools were designed primarily for internal purposes, they can also be used for external reporting. Hence, the most useful PMS to prepare an integrated report seems to be the BSC. A BSC presents the results of the organization from four perspectives: financial, customer, internal business processes, and learning and development. It combines these measures with the company's strategy, considering cause-and-effect relationships; uses future-oriented measures; and simultaneously provides information for internal and external stakeholders. Integrated reporting should somewhat be based on information generated by the PMSs and other management tools and reports.

5.5 Benefits and challenges of integrated reporting

Generally, all respondents saw the benefits of this form of reporting but mainly for improving the company's image and enhancing general knowledge about the organization. However, they assess the usefulness of integrated reports for financial analysts to be quite low.

Table 5.7 Performance measurement and management tools and the elements of <IR>

Performance measurement systems <IR> elements	*Organizational overview and external environment*	*Governance*	*Business model*	*Risks and opportunities*	*Strategy and resource allocation*	*Performance*	*Outlook*
Balanced scorecard							
Customer perspective			42%	70%			
Internal process perspective		5%	63%		52%	63%	
Learning and growth perspective	7%			48%	45%		42%
Financial perspective			60%		44%	72%	55%
Operational and capital budgets			32%	21%	50%		
Segmented income statements			36%			38%	
Customer costing			15%			32%	
Life cycle costing	29%						14%
Value chain analysis			19%	14%			
Evaluation of investment performance						21%	21%
Value-added measurement (economic value added, market value added, and free cash flow)						18%	

Source: Own elaboration.

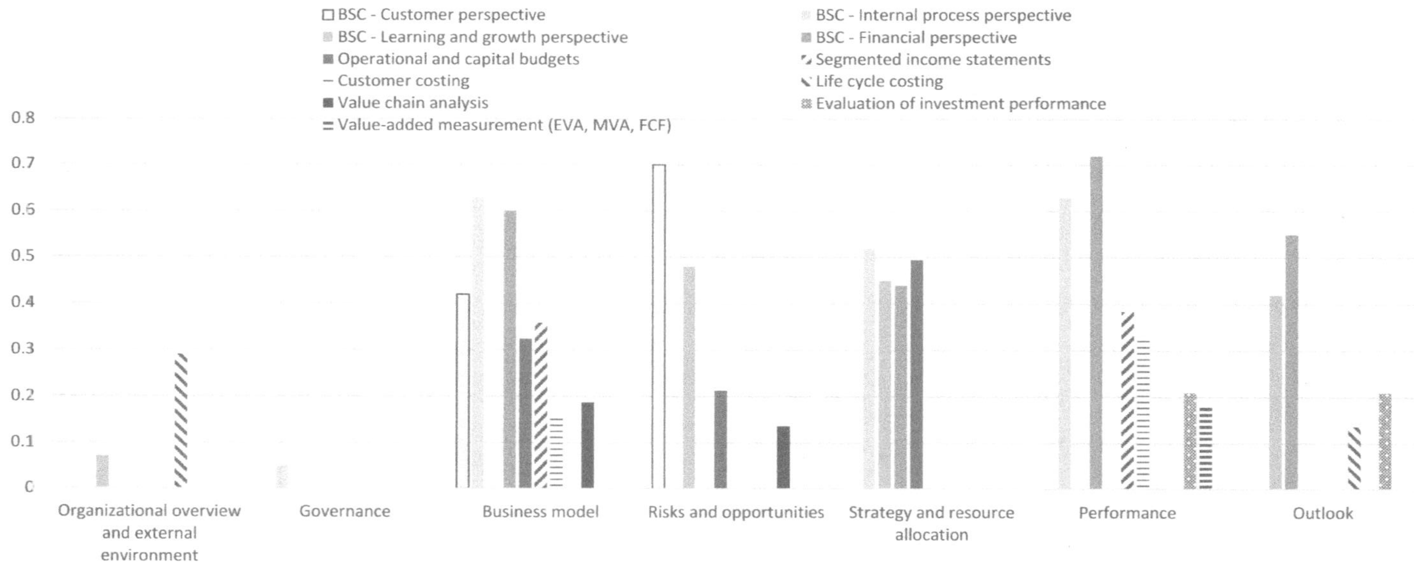

Figure 5.10 Performance measurement and management tools and the elements of <IR>

Source: Own elaboration

Table 5.8 Theory and practice of the use of performance measurement systems' information in integrated reports

<IR> elements	*Performance measurement and management tools indicated in the literature*	*Performance measurement and management tools indicated by respondents*
Organizational overview and external environment	• CSR reports • Environmental reports • Strengths, weaknesses, opportunities, threats (SWOT) analysis	• Life cycle costing • Balanced scorecard
Governance	• Management commentary	• Balanced scorecard
Business model	• Balanced scorecard • Management reports (e.g., Intellectual capital reports, human resource reports, and CSR reports) • Operational and capital budgets • Audit reports • Segmented income statements • Customer costing • Value Reporting	• Balanced scorecard • Evaluation of investment performance • Segmented income statements • Customer costing • Value chain analysis
Risks and opportunities	• Balanced scorecard • Strategic plans and SWOT analysis • Risk reports • Value chain analysis	• Operational and capital budgets • Value chain analysis
Strategy and resource allocation	• Operational and capital budgets • Strategic plans • Balanced scorecard	• Balanced scorecard • Operational and capital budgets
Performance	• Balanced scorecard • Key performance indicators • Financial ratios • Value-added measures (economic value added, market value added, and free cash flow) • Customer profitability reports	• Balanced scorecard • Segmented income statements • Customer costing • Evaluation of investment performance • Value-added measures (economic value added, market value added, and free cash flow)
Outlook	• Balanced scorecard • Segmented income statements • Value-added measures (economic value added, market value added, and free cash flow)	• Balanced scorecard • Life cycle costing • Evaluation of investment performance

Source: Own elaboration.

From the answers to the general question on the usefulness of integrated reporting in improving corporate reporting, 91% of respondents somewhat agreed with this position, and 89% agree it is useful for preparing corporate reports (Table 5.9).

Even though integrated reports contain financial information, they are still not treated entirely as reliable sources for conducting financial analyses or formulating forecasts.

Table 5.9 Perceived benefits of integrated reporting

Will integrated reporting contribute to improving corporate reporting?	*Total %*	*Corporate report preparers %*	*Users of corporate reports %*
Yes	48%	46%	51%
No	9%	11%	7%
Maybe	43%	43%	41%
Total	100%	100%	100%

Source: Own elaboration.

Some respondents found the integrated report to be an unnecessary document, stating that the annual report and management commentary are already sufficient reports containing financial and non-financial information. Some respondents also stated that it depended on the internal culture of the organization.

Respondents who perceive integrated reporting as a tool that will help improve current corporate reporting were asked to indicate the benefits of integrated reporting implementation in the enterprise. Table 5.10 presents the results.

The two main benefits of adopting integrated reporting, as indicated by the respondents, include improvement in communication with external stakeholders and improvement in transparency and reporting on corporate governance. Respondents see the benefits of reporting non-financial information when making decisions by investors, particularly socially responsible investors. They recognize non-financial information about the business model as particularly useful, provided that it was presented per the requirements of the IIRC and information on the risk and risk management system. Incidentally, other benefits specified in the question, such as easier access to capital, lower capital cost, and increase in stock price, were indicated; thus, such changes will probably not appear as the effect of integrated reporting implementation. However, given that integrated reporting improves communication with stakeholders, including capital providers, its use may facilitate access to equity capital in a competitive environment in the long term.

Table 5.10 Perceived benefits resulting from the implementation of integrated reporting

Perceived benefits of adopting the integrated reporting	*Percentage of respondents*
Improving communication with external stakeholders	81%
Improving transparency and reporting of corporate governance	72%
Promoting integrated thinking by exchanging information and cooperation in the organization	67%
Easier access to financial capital	21%
Lower cost of capital	5%
Increase in share prices	4%
Other	-

Source: Own elaboration.

Table 5.11 Expected costs, benefits, and workload of integrated reporting

Average for	*Benefits %*	*Costs %*	*Workload %*
Total	44	46	53
Corporate report preparers	26	46	53
Users of corporate reports	38	-	-

Source: Own elaboration.

Some respondents were convinced of the possibility of improving the organization's reporting given the implementation of integrated reporting, stating that enterprises can achieve synergy and reduction of reporting work by integrating external and internal reporting. For example, it applies to the use of some key performance indicators (KPIs), which have been presented in internal reporting and could also become an element of integrated reporting because they interest investors.

The concept of six capitals yielded much controversy among the respondents. Some noted that "the concept is useful for managers, while there is no direct translation into financial performance and usefulness for investors," and "the development of non-financial information caused significant chaos and did not gain much interest among investors." Respondents who believed integrated reporting can improve corporate reporting were asked to assess the costs and benefits of implementing it (Table 5.11). A total of 100 points for the present benefits of corporate reporting and the actual costs of preparing corporate reports were adopted as the base scores. For example, if the respondents decided that the benefits of reporting would increase by 10% because of integrated reporting adoption, they should grant a score of 110.

The responses show that adopting integrated reporting would significantly increase the cost of corporate reporting. They indicate that respondents believe integrated reporting will bring significant improvements in corporate reporting, generating an average increase of 44% in benefits. However, respondents also indicated an increase in reporting costs, on average 46% over the current level. While most preparers of corporate reports are convinced that integrated reporting can improve corporate reporting, they believe the effort and costs involved would outweigh the benefits. Respondents (53% on average) expressed concerns regarding the increase in workload associated with preparing the integrated reports relative to the current state. This concern may partly reflect limited knowledge of the integrated reporting process among some respondents and concerns about the need to share information between different departments within the organization.

Apart from the increase in costs and workload, integrated reporting implementation is associated with several other challenges that reporting entities must face. All respondents were asked about the main challenges related to integrated reporting implementation (Table 5.12).

The main perceived challenge in adopting IR is cost, followed by the lack of adequate IT systems to support integrated reporting creation. The lack of an appropriate information system is undoubtedly perceived from the perspective

Table 5.12 Perceived challenges of integrated reporting implementation

Perceived challenges of integrated reporting	*Percentage of respondents*
Costs of integrated reporting implementation	88%
Lack of an appropriate information technology (IT) system supporting the preparation of integrated reporting	85%
Fear of disclosing sensitive information	64%
Lack of information systems integration in the organization to enable access to the necessary data	61%
Fear of lawsuits given the uncertainty of forward-looking information	48%
Lack of support from the board and management	46%
Little interest from investors	37%
Resistance from the lower-level administration	36%
Other	1%

Source: Own elaboration.

of costs, as reporting entities incur significant costs and put a lot of effort into obtaining the necessary information. Information integrity can be problematic even when information is available. Thus, many respondents noted problems regarding the process of preparing integrated reports, as it requires the involvement of various company departments, especially regarding large companies. Challenges in extracting relevant financial information from accounting, financial, or controlling departments were also pointed out, especially because the information system is not adapted to the concept of six capitals. A respondent indicated, as an additional challenge, the need to establish a special team or unit that would only cater to the preparation of such a report to ensure compliance with IIRC requirements.

The structures of the answers of the two main respondent groups (Figure 5.11) differed significantly. The corporate report preparers' answers

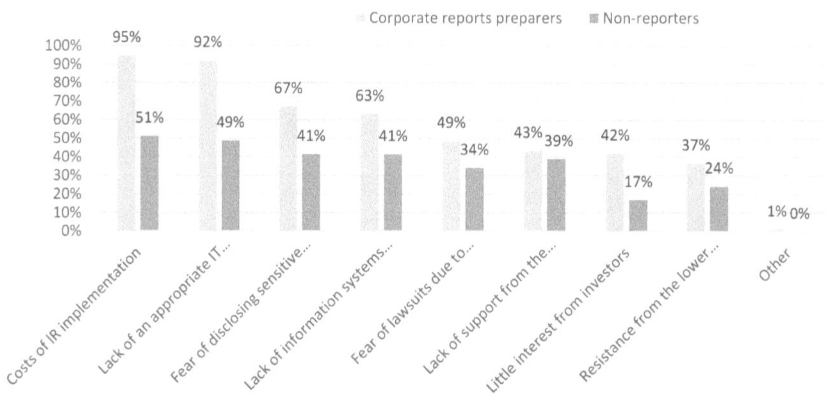

Figure 5.11 Perceived integrated reporting challenges among corporate report preparers and non-reporting respondents

Source: Own elaboration

reflected the overall results, and the same main challenges were noted. However, among non-reporting respondents, a smaller percentage (51%) considered costs to be a key challenge and 49% indicated the lack of an appropriate information technology (IT) system to support the preparation of the integrated report. The results of the study show that those preparing corporate reports and other stakeholders share the same views on the role of the board and management of the organization in the implementation of integrated reporting.

Summary

Corporate disclosures have changed significantly in recent years. Integrated reporting represents a relatively new approach and is probably the future of corporate reporting worldwide. Policymakers and standard setters are looking at this new way of reporting with interest and, given some limitations of annual reports and sustainability or corporate social responsibility (CSR) reports, with great hope as well.

Investors and other stakeholders must understand how an organization creates and sustains value over time. A description of the company's business model explains how resources (capital) are used and which activities add value and increase and transform capital. The business model presentation also provides insights into threats and opportunities resulting from external factors, such as economic, social, and environmental factors; competitive forces; and technological factors. Integrated reporting aims to ensure an effective and concise description of the company's ability to create current and future value by presenting a coherent form of information usually contained in several separate documents. Separate business reports that increase information complexity do not show critical interdependencies between strategic issues. An integrated report should highlight the importance of different capitals for the past and future performance of a company.

The concept of integrated reporting improves the consistency of reported information and provides a comprehensive image of the organization. Integrated reporting principles, such as linking information and materiality, help determine the information type that should be included in the report. Integrated reporting aims to communicate the value and the organization's potential to create value for investors and other stakeholders. In particular, the presentation of the business model and the company's strategy in the integrated report communicates the company's value-creation process to stakeholders.

Integrated reporting develops dynamically, which creates the demand for appropriate tools that could be helpful when preparing reports. It seems that integrated reporting information requirements may be met by performance measurement systems (PMSs) that can provide significant support when preparing integrated reports. These systems can be a source of data to assess the effectiveness of individual capital and provide financial and non-financial measures.

Most PMSs comprise several individual performance measures. There are various ways in which these performance measures can be categorized, ranging from Kaplan and Norton's (1992) balanced scorecard (BSC) to Parmenter's (2015) financial and non-financial indicators. The strength of PMSs lies in how they seek to integrate different dimensions of performance. One of the problems with the performance measurement literature is that it is diverse. It means that individual authors tend to focus on different aspects, such as quality, time, flexibility, cost, and value-added. However, some systems provide only criteria for PMS design, enabling, for example, the comparison of organizations that are in the same business. Such performance criteria should be selected through discussions with the stakeholders involved, should be directly related to the firm's strategy, and should consider that measures change as circumstances do. Moreover, one measure is not suitable for all departments or units. It is also important that the system be adapted to the individual needs of a given company and consider its specificity. The results of the authors' research showed that a helpful tool for an integrated report would undoubtedly be a BSC. Although it was developed for the internal needs of organizations, it can also be used for external reporting. BSCs offer a set of indicators to assess organizational performance from four perspectives: financial, customer, internal business processes, and learning and growth. These measures can be successfully used to assess the effectiveness of individual organizational capital.

At the current stage of integrated reporting practice, it is challenging to determine measurable benefits, but integrated reporting brings intangible benefits, including improving the internal process of preparing corporate reports, overcoming resistance against providing information to other departments in the organization in the process of preparing corporate reports, and better connectivity of information related to various content elements. The implementation of integrated reporting raises new challenges organizations must face. An important challenge is overcoming internal resistance to disclosing information or the pursuit of individual participants in the reporting process to present the content provided in a certain way. Hence, to overcome potential challenges, it is important to have support for such a project from higher-level management and good relations between management and preparers of reports. Knowledge about the essence of integrated reporting should be propagated among middle- and lower-level managers in the organization and should motivate and induce greater involvement of employees in social undertakings, creating values, and increasing awareness of the value-creation process.

An undoubted success factor is the promotion of integrated thinking among people preparing reports and creating multidisciplinary teams. Sharing information about the organization's business model and strategy helps reinforce the belief in the legitimacy of cooperation. Thinking about the organization in terms of six capitals allows for increasing long-term orientation and better decision-making; however, knowledge of the concept among the respondents is limited. It is important that the management board properly communicates the need to implement this report to employees and does not treat it as another marketing tool.

Integrated reporting requires the disclosure of the company's strategy and business model. Thus, the implementation of integrated reporting may be a response to the need to improve the quality of disclosure regarding the strategy and business model and improve the quality of information for the benefit of investors.

Ensuring the connectivity of information in the integrated report by having content guidelines for each section of the report and a holistic view of the presented content contributes to improving the quality of reporting. Involving external consultants can facilitate the reporting team's understanding of the principles and guidelines of integration and the process that must be undertaken to implement changes.

The framework of integrated reports was generally assessed positively. However, there was a lack of consistency in the presented information. Most of the respondents expressed the opinion that integrated reporting should not be mandatory. However, if the global market adopts this form of reporting, appropriate training programs at various levels of advancement should be implemented. Most respondents noted that non-financial reporting must be better organized given its significant growth in recent times.

Arguably, it is not possible to fully present information without information from various PMSs. Among the issues noted by respondents, the following stand out:

- In preparing integrated reports, the information provided by the BSC is used to a significant extent to present the performance of various areas of the company's activity.
- It is necessary to create teams to address the integration of financial and non-financial information.
- Duplication of information in the management commentary and the CSR report is visible.
- It is important to present information about the company's value over time.
- Presenting the scope of verifiability of forecast from previous reports.
- Introducing integrated reporting requires the adaptation of a company's information systems.
- Identifying cause-and-effect relationships and integrating information are the biggest challenges in implementing integrated reporting.

According to the respondents, the implementation of integrated reporting is associated with certain risks. There is a risk of focusing on non-financial indicators because many companies declare that they present them based on Global Reporting Initiative (GRI) guidelines, which mainly focus on sustainable development and the exclusion of other aspects. Challenges with a practical comparison of non-financial information in the reports of various entities have also been noted. Another significant impediment is the fear of sharing information, which has thus far been part of internal reporting. Integrated reporting is perceived as a management report, which should be a source of information regarding the value-creation process in an organization. The integrated report should also explain business relationships with stakeholders.

It was challenging for the respondents to indicate what International Integrated Reporting Council (IIRC) guidelines to focus on to promote the use of integrated reporting more widely. They highlighted specifying the rules for presenting individual information, focusing on the concept of six capitals, and determining a set of indicators enabling the comparability of reports.

Notably, the research bore the following limitations:

- Restrictions as to the use of the selected research method
- Credibility of non-financial reports resulting from striving to create a positive image
- Information overload and, thus, challenges in filtering out essential information
- Reliability of survey data
- Obtained answers can be characterized by high subjectivity, and interviewees may provide inaccurate information
- Subjectivism in carrying out content analysis to assess quality

The authors are aware that the conducted research is not perfect and has certain limitations associated with the adopted methods, including relatively small representativeness of the results, subjectivity of respondents' opinions, as well as difficulties in selecting representative sample. Nevertheless, the authors express the belief that the conducted research will contribute to the development of integrated reporting practices and will affect the broad use of PMSs in their preparation.

Further research can employ a triangulation of various scientific research methods to minimize the limitations. In summary, integrated reports promote integrated thinking and cause-and-effect relationships between strategic and operational goals throughout the value chain; hence, the use of various PMSs, including BSC, is fully justified. Additionally, integrated reporting can help managers build a more holistic image of the company.

References

Accounting Act of September 29, 1994, consolidated text (Journal of Laws of 2021, item. 217, as amended), https://polishtax.com/wp-content/uploads/2012/01/Polish-Accounting-Act.pdf

Adamek, J., Bąk, M., Kogut, J. (2018), Non-financial information in accounting – an opportunity or threat for enterprise, Conference Proceedings of 5th International Multidisciplinary Scientific Conference on Social Sciences & Arts SGEM 2018, Albena, Bulgaria, Vol. 5, No. 1.3, 257–268.

Adams, C. A. (2015), The international integrated reporting council: A call to action, Critical Perspectives on Accounting, Vol. 27, No. March, 23–28.

Adams, S., Simnett, R. (2011), Integrated reporting: An opportunity for Australia's not-for-profit sector, Australian Accounting Review, Vol. 21, No. 3, 292–301.

Agustia, D., Sriani, D., Wicaksono, H., Gani, L. (2020), Integrated reporting quality assessment, Journal of Security and Sustainability Issues, Vol. 10, No. 1, 47–59.

Albers, C., Günther, T. (2010), Disclose or not disclose: Determinants of social reporting for Stoxx Europe 600 firms, International Journal for Theoretical and Applied Statistics, Vol. 21, No. 3, 323–347.

Albertini, E. (2019), Integrated reporting: An exploratory study of French companies, Journal of Management and Governance, Vol. 23, 513–535.

Al-Htaybat, K., von Alberti-Alhtaybat, L. (2018), Integrated thinking leading to integrated reporting: Case study insights from a global player, Accounting, Auditing and Accountability Journal, Vol. 31, No. 5, 1435–1460.

Aljifri, K., Hussainey, K. (2007), The determinants of forward-looking information in annual reports of UAE companies, Managerial Auditing Journal, Vol. 22, No. 9, 881–894.

Anderson, J. C., Frankle, A. W. (1980), Voluntary social reporting: As iso-beta portfolio analysis, The Accounting Review, Vol. LV, No. 3, 468–479.

Artene, A., Bunget, O., Dumitrescu, A., Domil, A., Bogdan, O. (2020), Non-financial information disclosures and environmental protection – evidence from Romania and Greece, Forests, Vol. 11, No. 8, 814.

Arvidsson, S. (2011), Disclosure of non-financial information in the annual report: A management-team perspective, Journal of Intellectual Capital, Vol. 12, No. 2, 277–300.

Barker, R. (1998), The market for information-evidence from finance directors, analysts and fund managers, Accounting and Business Research, Vol. 29, No. 1, 3–20.

Bartolini, M., Santini, F, Silvi, R. (2013), Performance measurement and capitals, in: Busco, C., Frigo, M.L., Quattrone, P., Riccaboni, A. (2013), Integrated Reporting: Concepts and Cases That Redefine Corporate Accountability, Springer, Heidelberg, 127–146.

Beck, C., Dumay, J., Frost, G. (2017), In pursuit of a 'single source of truth': From threatened legitimacy to integrated reporting, Journal of Business Ethics, Vol. 141, No. 1, 191–205.

Bek-Gaik, B. (2015), Sprawozdawczość zintegrowana – wybrane problemy, Rachunkowość w zarządzaniu jednostkami gospodarczymi, Zeszyty Naukowe Uniwersytetu Szczecińskiego, Finanse, Rynki Finansowe, Ubezpieczenia No. 77, 479–491.

Bek-Gaik, B., Rymkiewicz, B. (2014), Społeczna odpowiedzialność przedsiębiorstw a finansowe miary dokonań, Zeszyty Naukowe Uniwersytetu Szczecińskiego No. 804, Finanse, Rynki Finansowe, Ubezpieczenia No. 67, 137–151.

Bek-Gaik, B., Rymkiewicz, B. (2015a), Sprawozdawczość Zintegrowana w Praktyce Polskich Spółek Giełdowych, in: Micherda B. (ed.), Sprawozdawczość i Rewizja Finansowa: Uwarunkowania Ekonomiczne, Społeczne i Regulacyjne, Wydawnictwo Uniwersytetu Ekonomicznego, Kraków, 60–83.

Bek-Gaik, B., Rymkiewicz, B. (2015b), Pozostałe Elementy Zintegrowanego Raportu Spółki, in: E. Walińska, B. Bek-Gaik, J. Gad, B. Rymkiewicz, Sprawozdawczość Przedsiębiorstwa Jako Narzędzie Komunikacji z Otoczeniem – Wymiar Finansowy i Niefinansowy, Wydawnictwo Uniwersytetu Łódzkiego, Łódź, 136–147.

Bek-Gaik, B., Rymkiewicz, B. (2016), Tendencje rozwoju sprawozdawczości zintegrowanej w praktyce polskich spółek giełdowych, Finanse, Rynki Finansowe, Ubezpieczenia, Vol. 1, No. 79, 767–783.

Bek-Gaik, B., Surowiec, A. (2019), Polityka informacyjna spółek giełdowych w dobie zrównoważonego rozwoju. Raportowanie zintegrowane, Wydawnictwo CeDeWu, Warszawa.

Bek-Gaik, B., Surowiec, A. (2020a), Forward-looking disclosures in integrated reporting of Polish companies, Conference proceedings, 35th IBIMA Conference, 1–2 April 2020, Seville, Spain.

Bek-Gaik, B., Surowiec, A. (2020b), Informacje Niefinansowe w Sprawozdawczości Organizacji, CeDeWu, Warszawa.

Bek-Gaik, B., Surowiec, A. (2020c), The business model as the subject of disclosures in integrated reporting on the example of selected Polish companies, Conference proceedings, 35th IBIMA Conference, 1–2 April 2020, Seville, Spain.

Belkaoui, A. (1976), The impact of the disclosure of the environmental effects of organizational behavior on the market, Financial Management, Vol. 5, No. 4, 26–31.

Belkaoui, A., Karpik, P. (1989), Determinants of the corporate decision to disclose social information, Accounting, Auditing and Accountability Journal, Vol. 2, No. 1, 36–51.

Berg, N., Jensen, J. C. (2012), Determinants of traditional sustainability reporting versus integrated reporting. An institutionalist approach, Business Strategy and the Environment, Vol. 21, No. 5, 299–316.

Berndt, T., Bilolo, C., Muller, L. (2014), The Future of Integrated Reporting, 4th Annual International Conference on Accounting and Finance, Phuket, Thailand, 195–206.

Bescos, P. L, Cauvin, E., Decock-Good, C., Westlund, A. H. (2007), Characteristics of performance measures for external reporting, Total Quality Management, Vol. 18, No. 10, 1055–1074.

Bilski, P., Zawadzki, B. (2020), Raportowanie w rachunkowości XXI wieku - ocena informacji, ujawnienia niefinansowe, Prace Naukowe, Uniwersytet Ekonomiczny w Katowicach, Rachunkowość XXI wieku, 40–49.

Bititci, U.S., Carrie, A.S., McDevitt, L. (1997), Integrated performance measurement systems: A development guide, International Journal of Operations and Production Management, Vol. 17, No. 5–6, 522–534.

Black Sun. (2012), Understanding transformation: Building the business case for integrated reporting, International Integrated Reporting Council, London, Bogner, http://integratedreporting.org/wp-content/uploads/2012/11/BUILDING-THE-BUSINESS-CASE-FOR-INTEGRATED-REPORTING.pdf

Bobitan, R., Petru, S. (2017), The non-financial reporting – the story behind the numbers, Annals - Economy Series, Constantin Brancusi University, Faculty of Economics, Vol. 3, 94–100.

Borys, G. (2005), Środowiskowe Aspekty Zawartości Rocznego Raportu i Rocznego Sprawozdania Finansowego Spółki, in: T. Kiziukiewicz (ed.), Rachunkowość w Zarządzaniu Jednostkami Gospodarczymi, Uniwersytet Szczeciński, Akademia Rolnicza, Szczecin.

Bowman, E., Haire, M. (1975), A strategic posture toward corporate social responsibility, California Management Review, Vol. 18, No. 2, 49–58. http://dx.doi.org/10.2307/41164638

Bravo, F. (2016), Forward-looking disclosure and corporate reputation as mechanisms to reduce stock return volatility, Spanish Accounting Review, Vol. 19, No. 1, 122–131.

Brine, M., Brown, R., Hackett, G. (2006), Corporate social responsibility and financial performance in the Australian context, Proceedings of the Economic Round-up, Issue Autumn 2007, 47–58.

Brown, J., Dillard, J. (2014), Integrated reporting: On the need for broadening out and opening up, Accounting, Auditing and Accountability Journal, Vol. 27, No. 7, 1120–1156.

Buczkowska, A. (2012), Cele przedsiębiorstwa a pomiar jego dokonań, Zeszyty Naukowe Uniwersytetu Szczecińskiego No. 684, Finanse, Rynki Finansowe, Ubezpieczenia No. 45, 5–19.

Buhovac, A.R., Groff, M.Z. (2012), Contemporary performance measurement systems in Central and Eastern Europe: A synthesis of the empirical literature, Journal of East European Management Studies, Vol. 17, No. 1, 68–103.

Busco, C., Frigo, M.L., Quattrone, P., Riccaboni, A. (2013), Integrated Reporting: Concepts and Cases That Redefine Corporate Accountability, Springer, Heidelberg.

Caraiani, C., Lungu, C., Bratu, A., Dascălu, C. (2018), Exploring the perspectives of integrated reporting for future research opportunities, Journal of Accounting and Management Information Systems, Faculty of Accounting and Management Information Systems, The Bucharest University of Economic Studies, Vol. 17, No. 4, 532–565.

Catasús, B., Gröjer, J. (2006), Indicators: On visualizing, classifying and dramatizing, Journal of Intellectual Capital, Vol. 7, No. 2, 187–203. https://doi.org/10.1108/14691930610661854

Celik, O., Ecer, A., Karabacak, H. (2006), Disclosure of forward looking information: Evidence from listed companies on Istanbul stock exchange (ISE), Investment Management and Financial Innovations, Vol. 3, No. 2, 197–216.

Cellier, A., Chollet, P. (2010), The impact of corporate social responsibility on stock prices: An event study of Vigeo rating announcement, 30.04.2010.

CFA Institute. (2007), A comprehensive business reporting model: Financial reporting for investors, codes, standards and position papers, Vol. 2007, No. 6.

Chen, J. J, Cheng, X., Gong, S. X., Tan, Y. (2014), Do higher value firms voluntarily disclose more information? Evidence from China, British Accounting Review, Vol. 46, No. 1, 18–32.

Chen, J. J., Cheng, X., Gong, S. X., Tan, Y. (2017), Voluntary non-financial disclosure, corporate governance, and investment efficiency, https://acfr.aut.ac.nz/__data/assets/pdf_file/0003/29910/486490-Voluntary-nonfinancial-disclosure.pdf

Chen, X., Cheng, Q., Lo, K. (2010), On the relationship between analyst reports and corporate disclosures: Exploring the roles of information discovery and interpretation, Journal of Accounting and Economics, Vol. 49, No. 3, 206–226.

Cheng, M., Green, W., Conradie, P., Konishi, N., Romi, A. (2014a), The international integrated reporting framework: Key issues and future research opportunities, Journal of International Financial Management and Accounting, Vol. 25, No. 1, 90–119.

Cheng, B., Ioannou, I., Serafeim, G. (2014b), Corporate social responsibility and access to finance, Strategic Management Journal, Vol. 35, No. 1, 1–23.

Chen, S., Zhang, D., Hao, M. (2019), A multidimensional analysis of the relationship between corporate social responsibility and firm's financial performance—based on the data of 78 listed companies in 10 years in Henan Province, China, Open Journal of Applied Sciences, Vol. 9, No. 3, 104–114, doi: 10.4236/ojapps.2019.93009

Chersan, C. (2015), Study on practices and tendencies in integrated reporting, Audit Financiar, Vol. 13, No. 129, 91–101.

Chojnacka, E., Jadanowska, E. (2020), Użyteczność i korzyści ujawniania informacji niefinansowych – Wyniki badania ankietowego przeprowadzonego wśród spółek notowanych na giełdzie papierów wartościowych w warszawie, Zeszyty Teoretyczne Rachunkowości, Vol. 106, No. 162, 45–65.

Churet, C., Eccles, R. G. (2014), Integrated reporting, quality of management, and financial performance, Journal of Applied Corporate Finance, Vol. 26, No. 1, 56–64.

Ciechan-Kujawa, M. (2013), Użyteczność raportów CSR w ocenie stopnia zaanagażowania przedsiębiorstw w odpowiedzialność społeczną, Prace Naukowe Uniwersytetu Ekonomicznego We Wrocławiu, No. 311, 32–44.

Cochran, P.L., Wood, R.A. (1984), Corporate social responsibility and financial performance, The Academy of Management Journal, Vol. 27, No. 1, 42–56.

Cohen, J., Holder-Webb, L., Nath, L., Wood, D. (2011), Retail investors' perceptions of the decision-usefulness of economic performance, governance, and corporate social responsibility disclosures, Behavioral Research in Accounting, Vol. 23, No. 1, 109–129.

Cohen, J. L. L., Holder-Webb, L. N., Wood, D. J. (2012), Corporate reporting on non-financial leading indicators of economic performance and sustainability, Accounting Horizons, Vol. 26, No. 1, 65–90.

Coram, P. J., Mock, T. J., Monroe, G. S. (2011), Financial analysts' evaluation of enhanced disclosure of non-financial performance indicators, The British Accounting Review, Vol. 43, No. 2, 87–101.

Coulson, A., Adams, C., Nugent, M., Haynes, K. (2015), Exploring metaphors of capitals and the framing of multiple capitals: Challenges and opportunities for IR, Sustainability Accounting, Management and Policy Journal, Vol. 6, No. 3, 290–314.

Cross, K.F., Lynch, R.L. (1992), For good measure, CMA Magazine, April, 20–23.

Czaja-Cieszyńska, H. (2018), Raportowanie informacji niefinansowych w organizacjach pozarządowych w polsce, Studia Prawno-Ekonomiczne, Vol. CIX, 189–204.

Czerska, J., Gołębiewski, Ł. (2017), Wykorzystanie wskaźników efektywności w doskonaleniu wyników przedsiębiorstwa, Finanse i Controlling, No 49, https://www.controlling-24.pl/autorzy/lukasz-golebiewski

de Villiers, C., Hsiao, P.-C. K., Maroun, W. (2017), Developing a conceptual model of influences around integrated reporting, new insights and directions for future research, Meditari Accountancy Research, Vol. 25, No. 4, 450–460.

de Villiers, C., Maroun, W. (ed.) (2017), Sustainability Accounting and Integrated Reporting, 1st Edition, Routledge, London.

de Villiers, C., Rinaldi, L., Unerman, J. (2014), Integrated reporting: Insights, gaps and an agenda for future research, Accounting, Auditing and Accountability Journal, Vol. 27, No. 7, 1042–1067.

De Villiers, C., Sharma, U. (2020), A critical reflection on the future of financial, intellectual capital, sustainability and integrated reporting, Critical Perspectives on Accounting, The University of Auckland Business School Research Paper, https://ssrn.com/abstract=3750445

de Villiers, C., van Staden, C. J. (2011), Where firms choose to disclose voluntary environmental information, Journal of Accounting and Public Policy, Vol. 30, No. 6, 504–525.

Deloitte (2012), Integrated Reporting Navigating your way to a truly Integrated, Report Deloitte, February.

Dhaliwal, D., Li, O., Tsang, A., Yang, Y. (2011), Voluntary nonfinancial disclosure and the cost of equity capital: The initiation of corporate social responsibility reporting, The Accounting Review, Vol. 86, No. 1, 59–100.

di Donato, F., Izzo, M.F. (2012), The relation between corporate social responsibility and stock prices: An analysis of the Italian listed companies, https://papers.ssrn.com/sol3/Delivery.cfm/SSRN_ID1986324_code907333.pdf?abstractid=1986324&mirid=1 (30.10.2017)

Directive 2014/95/EU of the European Parliament and of the Council of 22 October 2014 amending Directive 2013/34/EU as regards disclosure of non-financial and diversity information by certain large undertakings and groups.

Dissanayake, D. M., Ekanayake, E. M. (2018), Decision usefulness of corporate environmental reporting and firm performance: Evidence from Sri Lanka, The IUP Journal of Accounting Research and Audit Practices, Vol. XVII, No. 3, 7–23.

Dobrescu, D. (2013), The impact of corporate social responsibility on corporate value, The USV Annals of Economics and Public Administration, Vol. 13, No. 2, 91–101.

Dragu, I., Tudor-Tiron, A. (2013), New corporate reporting trends. Analysis on the evolution of integrated reporting, annals of the University of Oradea, Economic Science Series, Vol. 22, No. 1, 1221–1228.

Druckman, P. (2014), Integrated reporting: A new governance tool, The Corporate Board, Vol. May/June, 6–10.

Dumay, J., Bernardi, C., Guthrie, J, Demartini, P. (2016), Integrated reporting: A structured literature review, Accounting Forum, Vol. 40, No. 3, 166–185.

Dumay, J., Bernardi, C., Guthrie, J., La Torre, M. (2017), Barriers to implementing the international integrated reporting framework: A contemporary academic perspective, Meditari Accountancy Research, Vol. 25, No. 4, 461–480.

Dumay, J., Dai, T. (2017), Integrated thinking as a cultural control? Meditari Accountancy Research, Vol. 25, No. 4, 574–604.

Dyduch, J. (2015), Środowiskowe informacje finansowe w raportach rocznych spółek publicznych z sektora chemicznego, Prace Naukowe Uniwersytetu Ekonomicznego we Wrocławiu, No. 396, 28–38.

Dyduch, J., Krasodomska, J. (2017), Determinants of corporate social responsibility disclosure: An empirical study of Polish listed companies, Sustainability, Vol. 9, No. 11, 1–24.

Dziawgo, D. (2016), Znaczenie raportowania pozafinansowego w opinii indywidualnych inwestorów, Prace Naukowe Uniwersytetu Ekonomicznego we Wrocławiu, No. 436, 105–114.

Eccles, R., Klimenko, S. (2019), The investor revolution, Harvard Business Review, Vol. 97, No. 3, 106–116.

Eccles, R., Krzus, M. (2010a), Integrated reporting for a sustainable strategy, Financial Executive, Vol. March, 29–32.

Eccles, R., Krzus, M. (2010b), One Report: Integrated Reporting for a Sustainable Strategy, Wiley & Sons, Somerset, NJ.

Eccles, R., Krzus, M. (2014), Integrated Reporting Movement: Meaning, Momentum, Motives, and Materiality, Wiley, New York.

Eccles, R., Krzus, M., Ribot, S. (2014), The Integrated Reporting Movement: Meaning, Momentum, Motives, and Materiality, Wiley, Hoboken.

Eccles, R., Krzus, M., Ribot, S. (2014b), The Sustainable Value Matrix in The Integrated Reporting Movement: Meaning, Momentum, Motives, and Materiality, John Wiley & Sons, Inc, New York.

Eccles, R., Krzus, M., Ribot, S. (2015), Model of best practice in integrated reporting, Journal of Applied Corporate Finance, Vol. 27, No. 2, 103–115.

Eccles, R., Krzus, M., Serafeim, G. (2011), Market Interest in Nonfinancial Information. Harvard Business School Working Paper, No. 12-018, http://www.audentia-gestion.fr/HARVARD/12-018.pdf (10.12.2022)

Eccles, R., Krzus, M., Tapscott, D. (2010), One Report: Integrated Reporting for a Sustainable Strategy, Wiley Publisher, 1st Edition.

Eccles, R., Saltzman, D. (2011), Achieving sustainability through integrated reporting, Stanford Social Innovation Review, Vol. 9, No. 3, 56–61.

Eccles, R., Serafeim, G. (2014), Corporate and Integrated Reporting: A Functional Perspective, "Harvard Business School Working Paper", No. 14-094, April 2014, http://papers.ssrn.com/sol3/papers.cfm?abstract_id=2388716 (14.04.2015)

EFQM. https://efqm.org/the-efqm-model/.

Elgers, P., Lo, M., Pfeiffer, R. (2001), Delayed security price adjustments to financial analysts' forecast of annual earnings, The Accounting Review, Vol. 76, No. 4, 613–632.

Epstein, M.J., Manzoni, J.F. (1997), The Balanced Scorecard and Tableau de Bord: A Global Perspective on Translating Strategy into Action, working paper in the INSTEAD Working Paper Series, https://flora.insead.edu/fichiersti_wp/inseadwp1997/97-82.pdf (20.08.2017)

Ernst & Young. (2011), Climate change and sustainability. How sustainability has expanded the CFO's role, http://www.ey.com/US/en/Services/Specialty-Services/Climate-Change-and-Sustainability-Services/How-sustainability-hasexpanded-the-CFOs-role

Ernst & Young. (2015), Tomorrow's investment rules 2.0 emerging risk and stranded assets have investors looking for more from nonfinancial reporting, https://www.seg.org.pl/storage/uploads/1626257472_tomorrows_investment_rules_2.0_ey.pdf

Fărcaş, T. (2015), The development of corporate reporting over time: From a traditional system to an integrated system, Audit Financiar, Vol. 13, No. 124, 106–113.
Feng, T., Cummings, L., Tweedie, D. (2017), Exploring integrated thinking in integrated reporting – an exploratory study in Australia, Journal of Intellectual Capital, Vol. 18, No. 2, 330–353.
Fiori, G., di Donato, F., Izzo, M. F. (2007), Corporate social responsibility and firms performance - an analysis on Italian listed companies, https://papers.ssrn.com/sol3/papers.cfm?abstract_id=1032851 (2.11.2017)
Flower, J. (2015), The international integrated reporting council: A story of failure, Critical Perspectives on Accounting, Vol. 27, No. March, 1–17.
Frías-Aceituno, J., Rodríguez-Ariza, L., García-Sanchez, I. (2013a), The role of the board in the dissemination of integrated corporate social reporting, Corporate Social Responsibility and Environmental Management, Vol. 20, No. 4, 219–233.
Frías-Aceituno, J., Rodríguez-Ariza, L., García-Sanchez, I. (2013b), Is integrated reporting determined by a country's legal system? An exploratory study, Journal of Cleaner Production, Vol. 44, No. April, 45–55.
Frías-Aceituno, J., Rodríguez-Ariza, L., García-Sanchez, I. (2014), Explanatory factors of integrated sustainability and financial reporting, Business Strategy and the Environment, Vol. 23, No. 1, 56–72.
Gad, J. (2013), Management board's report on the activities as a tool of corporate governance: The perspective of capital providers, supervisory boards, and other stakeholder, Modern Management Review, Vol. XXI, No. 23, 69–84.
Gad, J. (2015), Sprawozdanie z działalności we współczesnym modelu raportowania – praktyka sprawozdawcza spółek publicznych notowanych na GPW, Zarządzanie i Finanse, Wydawnictwo Uniwersytetu Gdańskiego, No. 1, 79–90.
García-Meca, E., Martinez, I. (2007), The use of intellectual capital information in investment decisions – an empirical study using analyst reports, International Journal of Accounting, Vol. 42, No. 1, 57–81.
García-Sánchez, I., Rodríguez-Ariza, L., Frías-Aceituno, J. (2013a), The cultural system and integrated reporting, International Business Review, Vol. 22, No. 5, 828–838.
Garstecki, D. (2015a), Raportowanie Zintegrowane w Teorii Oraz Praktyce Polskich Spółek, in: J. Krasodomska, K. Świetla (eds.), Współczesne Uwarunkowania Sprawozdawczości i Rewizji Finansowej, Uniwersytet Ekonomiczny w Krakowie, Kraków, 129–143.
Garstecki, D. (2015b), Zakres ujawnianych informacji finansowych w raporcie zintegrowanym wybranych przedsiębiorstw, Zeszyty Naukowe Uniwersytetu Szczecińskiego No. 873, Finanse, Rynki Finansowe, Ubezpieczenia No. 77, 503–512.
Gibassier, D., Rodrigue, M., Arjaliès, D. (2018), 'Integrated reporting is like God: No one has met him, but everybody talks about him': The power of myths in the adoption of management innovations, Accounting, Auditing and Accountability Journal, Vol. 31, No. 5, 1349–1380.
Godfrey, P. C., Merrill, C. B., Hansen, J. M. (2009), The relationship between corporate social responsibility and shareholder value: An empirical test of the risk management hypothesis, Strategic Management Journal, Vol. 30, No. 4, 425–445.
Gregorczyk, D. (2015), Raportowanie Zintegrowane w tworzeniu wspólnej wartości (CSV), Prace Naukowe Uniwersytetu Ekonomicznego we Wrocławiu No. 396, t. 2, 59–66.

Gregory, A., Tharyan, R., Whittaker, J. (2014), Corporate social responsibility and firm value: Disaggregating the effects on cash flow, risk and growth, Journal of Business Ethics, Vol. 124, No. 4, 633–657.

Grüning, M. (2002) Performance measurement system – Messung und Steuerung von Unterneh-mensleistung. Dissertation, Technische Universität Dresden.

Grüning, M., Grüning, M. (2002), Ansätze zum Performance Measurement. Performance-Measurement-Systeme: Messung und Steuerung von Unternehmensleistung, 21–65.

Gunarathne, N., Senaratne, S. (2017), Diffusion of integrated reporting in an emerging South Asian (SAARC) nation, Managerial Auditing Journal, Vol. 32, No. 4/5, 524–548.

Guthrie, J., Manes-Rossi, F., Levy Orelli, R. (2017), Integrated reporting and integrated thinking in Italian public sector organisations, Meditari Accountancy Research, Vol. 25, No. 4, 553–573.

Hąbek, P., Wolniak, R. (2015), Factors influencing the development of CSR reporting practices: Experts' versus preparers' points of view, Inzinerine Ekonomika-Engineering Economics, Vol. 26, No. 5, 560–570.

Haji, A., Anifowose, M. (2016), The trend of integrated reporting practice in South Africa: Ceremonial or substantive? Sustainability Accounting, Management and Policy Journal, Vol. 7, No. 2, 190–224.

Haller, Ch., van Staden, C. (2014), The value added statement - an appropriate instrument for integrated reporting, Accounting, Auditing and Accountability Journal, Vol. 27, No. 7, 1190–1216.

Hansen, F. (2001), Transparent Beauty, Part Two of a Series, data 06.01.2001, odczyt ze strony internetowej http://businessfinancemag.com, data odczytu 29.01.2009.

Healy, P.M., Palepu, K.G. (2001), Information asymmetry, corporate disclosure, and the capital markets: A review of the empirical disclosure literature, Journal of Accounting and Economics, Vol. 31, No. 1/3, 405–440.

Higgins, C., Stubbs, W., Love, T. (2014), Walking the talk(s): Organisational narratives of integrated reporting, Accounting, Auditing and Accountability Journal, Vol. 27, No. 7, 1090–1119.

Higgins, C., Stubbs, W., Tweedie, D., McCallum, G. (2019), Journey or toolbox? Integrated reporting and processes of organisational change, Accounting Auditing and Accountability Journal, Vol. 32, No. 6, 1662–1689.

Hoff, B., Wood, D., (2008), The use of non-financial information: What do investors want? Project Findings, Boston College Carroll School of Management.

IASB. (2010), Management Commentary, IFRS Practice Statement, International Accounting Standards Board, London.

IASB. (2011a), Przedmowa do wydania Międzynarodowych Standardów Sprawozdawczości Finansowej, Zakres i obowiązek stosowania Międzynarodowych Standardów Sprawozdawczości Finansowej MSSF, Vol. I, SKwP, IASB.

IASB. (2011b), Założenia koncepcyjne sprawozdawczości finansowej, in: Międzynarodowe Standardy Sprawozdawczości Finansowej MSSF, IFRS Foundation, Londyn.

ICAEW. (2010), New Reporting Models for Business. Information for Better Markets Initiative, Institute of Chartered Accountants in England and Wales, London.

IFRS. (2010), Staff Draft of Exposure Draft, IFRS X, Financial Statement Presentation, https://www.efrag.org/Assets/Download?assetUrl=%2Fsites%2Fwebpublishing%2FProject%20Documents%2F199%2FFSP%20ED_IASB%20staff%20draft%20July%202010.pdf&AspxAutoDetectCookieSupport=1

IIRC. (2011), Discussion paper towards integrated reporting – communicating value in the 21st century, http://integratedreporting.org/wp-content/uploads/2011/09/IR-Discussion-Paper-2011_spreads.pdf (20.08.2019)

IIRC. (2012), Pilot programme yearbook: Capturing the experiences of global businesses and investors, International Integrated Reporting Council, London, http://www.integratedreporting.org/wp-content/uploads/2012/10/THE-PILOT-PROGRAMME-2012-YEARBOOK.pdf (14.10.2020)

IIRC. (2013a), Business and investors explore the sustainability perspectives of integrated reporting, International Integrated Reporting Council, London, http://www.integratedreporting.org/wp-content/uploads/2013/12/IIRC-PP-Yearbook-2013_PDF4_PAGES.pdf (14.09.2021)

IIRC. (2013b), Business Model Background Paper for IR, March, https://integratedreporting.org/wp-content/uploads/2013/03/Business_Model.pdf (2.08.2019)

IIRC. (2013c), Consultation draft of the international integrated reporting framework, International Integrated Reporting Council, London, https://www.integratedreporting.org/wp-content/uploads/2013/03/Consultation-Draft-of-the-InternationalIR-Framework.pdf (14.09.2021)

IIRC. (2013d), The International <IR> Framework, https://www.integratedreporting.org/wp-content/uploads/2013/12/13-12-08-THE-INTERNATIONAL-IR-FRAMEWORK-2-1.pdf

IIRC. (2014), Creating value: Value to the board, International Integrated Reporting Council, London, https://www.integratedreporting.org/resource/creating-value-board/ (8.09.2021)

IIRC. (2015), Creating value integrated reporting and investor benefits, https://www.integratedreporting.org/wp-content/uploads/2015/12/Creating-Value-Integrated-Reporting-and-investor-benefits.pdf (19.11.2018)

IIRC. (2016), Creating value: The value of human capital reporting, International Integrated Reporting Council, London, https://www.integratedreporting.org/resource/creating-value-the-value-of-human-capital-reporting/ (8.09.2021)

IIRC. (2017a), Creating Value CFO Leadership in <IR>, International Integrated Reporting Council, London, https://www.integratedreporting.org/resource/creating-value-cfo-leadership-in-ir/ (8.09.2021)

IIRC. (2017b), The cyclical power of integrated thinking and reporting, https://www.integratedreporting.org/resource/creating-value-board/ (8.09.2021)

IIRC. (2021), The International <IR> Framework, https://integratedreporting.org/wp-content/uploads/2021/01/InternationalIntegratedReportingFramework.pdf (20.02.2021)

IIRC and Black Sun. (2012), Understanding transformation: Building the business case for integrated reporting, International Integrated Reporting Council, London, https://www.integratedreporting.org/resource/building-the-business-case-for-integrated-reporting/ (8.09.2021)

IIRC and Black Sun. (2014), Realizing the benefits: The impact of integrated reporting, International Integrated Reporting Council, London, https://www.integratedreporting.org/resource/realizing-the-benefits-the-impact-of-integrated-reporting/ (8.09.2021)

IIRC and Black Sun. (2015), The integrated reporting journey: The inside story, International Integrated Reporting Council, London, https://www.integratedreporting.org/resource/the-integrated-reporting-journey-the-inside-story-2/ (8.09.2021)

Ittner, C., Larcker, D., Randall, T. (2003), Performance implications of strategic performance measurement in financial service firms, Accounting, Organizations and Society, Vol. 28, No. 7–8, 715–741.

Ivković, Z., Jegadeesh, N. (2004), The timing and value of forecast and recommendation revisions, Journal of Financial Economics, Vol. 73, No. 3, 433–463.

Jensen, J., Berg, N. (2012), Determinants of traditional sustainability reporting versus integrated reporting: An intuitionalist approach, Business Strategy and the Environment, Vol. 21, No. 5, 299–316.

Jinga, G., Dumitru, M. (2015a), The change in management accounting from an institutional and contingency perspective: A case study for a Romanian company, International Journal of Social, Behavioral, Educational, Economic, Business and Industrial Engineering, Vol. 9, No. 6, 1913–1920.

Jinga, G., Dumitru, M. (2015b), The management accounting tools and the integrated reporting, SEA: Practical Application of Science, Vol. 3, No. 1, 45–49.

Kacała, J., Kołaczyk, E. (2013), Wdrażanie modelu doskonałości EFQM - determinanty, Zarządzanie i Finanse, Vol. 4, No. 2, 145–154.

Kaplan, R., Norton, D. (1992), The balanced scorecard: Measures that drive performance, Harvard Business Review, Vol. 70, No. 1, 71–79.

Kaplan, R., Norton, D. (1996), The Balanced Scorecard: Translating Strategy into Action, Harvard Business Review Press, Boston.

Kaplan, R., Norton, D. (1998), Using the Balanced Scorecard as a Strategic Management System, Harvard Business Review on Measuring Corporate Performance, Harvard Business School Press, Boston.

Kaplan, R., Norton, D. (2000), Having trouble with your strategy? Then map it, Harvard Business Review, Vol. September/October, 167–176.

Kaplan, R., Norton, D. (2004), The strategy map: Guide to aligning intangible assets, Strategy & Leadership, Vol. 32, No. 5, 10–17.

Kędzierska, I. (2012), Wybrane zagadnienia pomiaru dokonań, Zeszyty Naukowe Uniwersytetu Szczecińskiego No. 684 Finanse, Rynki Finansowe, Ubezpieczenia No. 45, 103–117.

Kent, P., Ung, K. (2003), Voluntary disclosure of forward-looking earnings information in Australia, Australian Journal of Management, Vol. 28, No. 3, 273–285.

Kiliç, M., Kuzey, C. (2018), Determinants of forward-looking disclosures in integrated reporting, Managerial Auditing Journal, Vol. 33, No. 1, 115–144.

Kippenberger, T. (1996), The performance pyramid, The Antidote, Vol. 1 No. 1, 10–11.

Kowalewski, M. (2015), Systemy Pomiaru Dokonań Przedsiębiorstwa, in: E. Nowak (ed.), Pomiar i Raportowanie Dokonań Przedsiębiorstwa, Wyd. CeDeWu.

KPMG (2011), Enhancing Management Commentary – Review of Practice.

Kranacher, M. (2011), Full disclosure: All investors need to know, CPA Journal, Vol. 81, No. 4, https://www.nysscpa.org/news/publications/the-cpa-journal/article-detail?ArticleID=10806#sthash.j4N63ELO.dpbs

Krasodomska, J. (2012), Zintegrowana sprawozdawczość spółek w 2020 roku, Zeszyty Teoretyczne Rachunkowości, Vol. 66, No. 122, 101–110.

Krasodomska, J. (2014), Informacje Niefinansowe w Sprawozdawczości Spółek, Wydawnictwo Uniwersytetu Ekonomicznego w Krakowie, Kraków.

Lai, A., Melloni, G., Stracchezzini, R. (2016), Corporate sustainable development: Is 'Integrated Reporting' a legitimation strategy? Business Strategy and the Environment, Vol. 25, No. 3, 165–177.

Lai, A., Melloni, G., Stacchezzini, R. (2018), Integrated reporting and narrative accountability: The role of preparers, Accounting, Auditing and Accountability Journal, Vol. 31, No. 5, 1381–1405. https://doi.org/10.1108/AAAJ-08-2016-2674

Lament, M. (2017), Raportowanie informacji niefinansowych w zakładach ubezpieczeń w polsce, Zeszyty Teoretyczne Rachunkowości, Vol. 2017, No. 91, 63–86.

Lang, M., Lundholm, R. (1996), Corporate disclosure policy and analyst behavior, Accounting Review, Vol. 71, No. 4, 467–492.

Lassini, U., Lionzo, A., Rossignoli, F. (2016), Does business model affect accounting choice? An empirical analysis of European listed companies, Journal of Management and Governance, Vol. 20, No. 2, 229–260.

Łęgowik-Świącik, S. (2018), Koncepcje Generowania Spirali Wartości w Modelach Biznesu, Wydawnictwo Wydziału Zarządzania Politechniki Częstochowskiej, Częstochowa.

Lev, B., Zarowin, P. (1999), The boundaries of financial reporting and how to extend them, Journal of Accounting Research, Vol. 37, No. 2, 353–385.

Li, B., Li, X. (2018), Research on the relationship between corporate social responsibility and financial performance based on grey correlation analysis: Taking the smartphone company as an example. Open Journal of Applied Sciences, Vol. 8, No. 9, 431–440. doi: 10.4236/ojapps.2018.89033

Lisi, I.E. (2018), Determinants and performance effects of social performance measurement systems, Journal of Business Ethics, Vol. 152, No. 1, 225–251.

Lohman, C., Fortuin, L., Wouters, M. (2004), Designing a performance measurement system: A case study, European Journal of Operational Research, Vol. 156, No. 2, 267–286.

Lueg, K., Lueg, R., Andersen, K., Dancianu, V. (2016), Integrated reporting with CSR practices: A pragmatic constructivist case study in a Danish cultural setting, Corporate Communications: An International Journal, Vol. 21, No. 1, 20–35.

Luo, X., Bhattacharya, C.B. (2006), Corporate social responsibility, customer satisfaction, and market value, Journal of Marketing, Vol. 70, No. 4, 1–18.

Luo, X., Wang, H., Raithel, S., Zheng, Q. (2014), Corporate social performance, analyst stock recommendations, and firm future returns, Strategic Management Journal, Vol. 36, No. 1, 123–136.

Macuda, M., Matuszak, Ł., Różańska, E. (2015), The concept of CSR in accounting theory And practice in Poland: An empirical study, Zeszyty Teoretyczne Rachunkowości, Vol. 84, No. 140, 115–137.

Maines, L., Bartov, E., Fairfield, P., Hirst, D., Iannaconi, P., Mallet, R., Schrand, C., Skinner, D., Vincent, L. (2002), Recommendations on disclosure of nonfinancial performance measures, Accounting Horizons, Vol. 16, No. 4, 353–362.

Malola, A., Maroun, W. (2019), The measurement and potential drivers of integrated report quality: Evidence from a pioneer in integrated reporting school of accountancy, South African Journal of Accounting Research, Vol. 33, No. 2, 114–144.

Marcinkowska, M. (2004), Raport roczny z działalności i wyników przedsiębiorstwa. Nowe tendencje w sprawozdawczości biznesowej, Oficyna Ekonomiczna, Kraków.

Maroun, W. (2017), Assuring the integrated report: Insights and recommendations from auditors and preparers, The British Accounting Review, Vol. 49, No. 3, 329–346.

Maroun, W., Atkins, J. (2015), The Challenges of Assuring Integrated Reports: Views from the South African Auditing Community, ACCA.

Maroun, W., Solomon, J. (2012), Integrated reporting: The influence of King III on social, ethical and environmental reporting, The Association of Chartered Certified Accountants, London, http://www.accaglobal.com/content/dam/acca/global/PDF-technical/integratedreporting/tech-tp-iirsa.pdf (18.05.2015)

Matuszak, Ł., Różańska, E. (2017), CSR disclosure in Polish-listed companies in the light of directive 2014/95/EU requirements: Empirical evidence, Sustainability, Vol. 9, No. 12, 2304.

Mazzotta, R., Bronzetti, G., Veltri, S. (2020), Are mandatory non-financial disclosures credible? Evidence from Italian listed companies, Corporate Social Responsibility and Environmental Management, Vol. 27, No. 4, 1535–3966.
McNally, M. A., Cerbone, D., Maroun, W. (2017), Exploring the challenges of preparing an integrated report, Meditari Accountancy Research, Vol. 25, No. 4, 481–504. https://doi.org/10.1108/MEDAR-10-2016-0085
McNally, M. A., Maroun, W. (2018), It is not always bad news: Illustrating the potential of integrated reporting using a case study in the eco-tourism industry, Accounting, Auditing and Accountability Journal, Vol. 31, No. 5, 1319–1348.
Melloni, G., Caglio, A., Perego, P. (2017), Saying more with less? Disclosure conciseness, completeness and balance in integrated reports, Journal of Accounting and Public Policy, Vol. 36, No. 3, 220–238.
Melloni, G., Stacchezzini, R., Lai, A. (2016), The tone of business model disclosure: An impression management analysis of the integrated reports, Journal of Management and Governance, Vol. 20, No. 2, 295–320.
Menicucci, E. (2013), The determinants of forward-looking information in management commentary: Evidence from Italian listed companies, International Business Research, Vol. 6, No. 5, 30–44.
MIA-ACCA. (2016), Integrated Reporting Survey, https://integratedreporting.org/wp-content/uploads/2016/09/MIA-ACCA-IR-survey-report_2016.pdf.pdf
Michalak, J. (2008), Pomiar Dokonań Od Wyniku Finansowego Do Balanced Scorecard, Difin, Warszawa, 458–459.
Michalak, J., Bek-Gaik, B., Karwowski, M (2018), Model Biznesu Jako Wyzwanie Dla Rachunkowości, Wydawnictwo Nieoczywiste, Warszawa.
Milne, M., Gray, R. (2013), W(h)ither ecology? The triple bottom line, the global reporting initiative, and corporate sustainability reporting, Journal of Business Ethics, Vol. 118, 13–29.
Mittal, R.K., Sinha, N., Singh, A. (2008), An analysis of linkage between economic value added and corporate social responsibility, Management Decision, Vol. 46, No. 9, 1437–1443.
Morros, J. (2016), The integrated reporting: A presentation of the current state of art. And aspects of integrated reporting that need further development, Intangible Capital, Vol. 12, No. 1, 336–356.
Murby, L., Gould, S. (2005), Effective Performance Management with the Balanced Scorecard. Technical Report, CIMA, INSEAD
National Accounting Standard No. 9 "Director's Report" (Official Journal of the Minister of Development and Finance of 2018, item 4, as amended), applicable to management reports covering the financial year commenced in 2014.
Neely, A., Adams, C., Crowe, P. (2001), The performance prism in practice, Measuring Business Excellence, Vol. 5, No. 2, 6–13.
Neely, A., Gregory, M., Platts, K. (1995), Performance measurement system design: A literature review and research agenda, International Journal of Operations and Production Management, Vol. 15, No. 4, 80–116.
Neely, A., Gregory, M., Platts, K. (2005), Performance measurement system design. A literature review and research agenda, International Journal of Operations and Production Management, Vol. 25, No. 12, 1228–1263.
Neely, A., Marr, B., Roos, G., Pike, S., Gupta, O. (2003), Towards the third generation of performance measurement, Controlling, Vol. 15, No. 3/4, 129–135.

Ngwakwe, C. (2008), Environmental responsibility and firm performance: Evidence from Nigeria, International Journal of Social, Human Science and Engineering, Vol. 2, No. 10, 6–13.

Niemiec, A. (ed.) (2016), System Pomiaru Dokonań w Przedsiębiorstwach, CeDeWu, Warszawa.

Niemiec, A. (2017), Istotność jako podstawowe kryterium selekcji kluczowych mierników dokonań (KPIs), 265–275.

Nita, B. (2014a), Koncepcje i uwarunkowania pomiaru i raportowania dokonań w przedsiębiorstwie, Economics and Management, No. 3, 38.

Nita, B. (2014b), Niefinansowy pomiar dokonań przedsiębiorstw produkcyjnych w teorii i w praktyce, Prace Naukowe Uniwersytetu Ekonomicznego We Wrocławiu, No. 335, 183–193.

Oliveira, J., Rodrigues, L. L., Craig, R. (2011), Risk-related disclosures by non-finance companies: Portuguese practices and disclosure characteristics, Managerial Auditing Journal, Vol. 26, No. 9, 817–839.

Orens, R., Lybaert, N. (2013), Disclosure of non-financial information: Relevant to financial analysts? Review of Business and Economic Literature, Vol. 58, No. 4, 375–405.

Orlitzky, M., Schmidt, F. L., Rynes, S. L. (2003), Corporate social and financial performance: A meta-analysis, Organisation Studies, Vol. 24, No. 3, 403–441. doi:10.1177/0170840603024003910

Osterwalder, A. (2004), The Business Model Ontology a Proposition in a Design Science Approach, Praca Dyplomowa, HEC, Lozanna.

Otley, D.T. (1999), Performance management: A framework for management control systems research, Management Accounting Research, Vol. 10, No. 4, 363–382.

Otola, I., Tylec, A. (2016), Społeczna odpowiedzialność biznesu a wyniki finansowe przedsiębiorstw, Zeszyty Naukowe Politechniki Częstochowskiej, Zarządzanie, Vol. 24, No. 1, 81–89.

Parmenter, D. (2015), Key Performance Indicators. Developing, Implementing and Using Winning KPIs, Wiley, New Jersey.

Pawłowski, M., Wąsowska, A. (2012), Pomiar społecznej odpowiedzialności biznesu w polskich warunkach - propozycja metodologiczna, Przegląd Organizacji, No. 1, 18–20.

Perego, P., Kennedy, S., Whiteman, G. (2016), A lot of icing but little cake? Taking integrated reporting forward, Journal of Cleaner Production, Vol. 136, No. Part A, 53–64.

Peršić, M., Halmi, L. (2017), Non-financial information and integrated reporting in the hospitality industry: Case study of Croatia, Copernican Journal of Finance and Accounting, Vol. 6, No. 3, 95–109.

PGNiG (2020), https://pgnig2020.pl/en/pgnig-group/value-creation-process/

Pierścionek, Z. (2011), Zarządzanie Strategiczne w Przedsiębiorstwie, Wydawnictwo Naukowe PWN, Warszawa.

Pistoni, A., Songini, L., Bavagnoli, F. (2018), Integrated reporting quality: An empirical analysis, Corporate Social Responsibility and Environmental Management, Vol. 25, No. 4, 489–507.

Pistoni, A., Songini, L., Perrone, O. (2016), The how and why of a firm's approach to CSR and sustainability: A case study of a large European company, Journal of Management and Governance, Vol. 20, No. 3, 655–685.

Pounder, B. (2012), Full disclosure vs. effective disclosure, Strategic Finance, Vol. 94, No. 2, 17–18.

Powell, T. C. (1995), Total quality management as competitive advantage: A review and empirical study, Strategic Management Journal, Vol. 16, No. 1, 15–27.

PricewaterhouseCoopers. (2007), Corporate reporting. Is it what investment professionals expect? http://www.pwc.com/gx/en/corporate-reporting/integrated-reporting/index.jhtml

Radley Yeldar. (2012), The value of extra-financial disclosure. What investors and analysts said, Accounting for Sustainability, Global Reporting Initiative, https://www.accountingforsustainability.org/en/knowledge-hub/reports/value-financial-disclosure.html

Rampersad, H. (2005), Total performance scorecard, Nanyang Business Review, Vol. 4, No. 1, 72–99.

Regulation of the Minister of Finance of March 29, 2018 on current and periodic information provided by security issuers on conditions under which information required by the legislation of a non-Member State may be recognized as equivalent (Journal of Laws 2018, item 757)

Remlein, M. (2016), Koszty i korzyści prezentowania dokonań przedsiębiorstwa społecznie odpowiedzialnego w zintegrowanym sprawozdaniu, Zeszyty Naukowe Politechniki Częstochowskiej Zarządzanie, Vol. 23, No. 2, 51–59.

Rensburg, R., Botha, E. (2014), Is integrated reporting the silver bullet of financial communication? A stakeholder perspective from South Africa, Public Relations Review, Vol. 40, No. 2, 144–152.

Robertson, F. A., Samy, M (2015), Factors affecting the diffusion of integrated reporting – A UK FTS 100 perspective, Sustainability Accounting, Management and Policy Journal, Vol. 6, No. 2, 190–223.

Roszkowska, P. (2011), Rewolucja w Raportowaniu Biznesowym. Interesariusze, Konkurencyjność, Społeczna Odpowiedzialność, Difin, Warszawa.

Samelak, J. (2013), Zintegrowane Sprawozdanie Przedsiębiorstwa Społecznie Odpowiedzialnego, Wydawnictwo Uniwersytetu Ekonomicznego w Poznaniu, Poznań.

Sierra-Garcia, A., Zorio-Grima, M., Garcia-Benau, I. (2013), Stakeholder engagement, corporate social responsibility and integrated reporting: An exploratory study, Corporate Social Responsibility and Environmental Management, Vol. 22, No. 5, 286–304.

Simpson, A. (2010), Analysts' use of non-financial information disclosures, Contemporary Accounting Research, Vol. 27, No. 1, 249–288.

Skowron-Grabowska, B. (2021), Łańcuchy Wartości w Zarządzaniu Organizacjami, Wyzwania innowacyjno-kryzysowe, Polskie Wydawnictwo Ekonomiczne S.A, Warszawa.

Śnieżek, E., Piłacik, J. (2016), Raportowanie informacji pozafinansowych o społecznej odpowiedzialności w lasach państwowych w świetle niektórych koncepcji teoretycznych, Studia Ekonomiczne. Zeszyty Naukowe Uniwersytetu Ekonomicznego w Katowicach, No. 284, 140–149.

Śnieżek, E., Wiatr, M. (2017), Refleksje na temat współczesnych form komunikacji z interesariuszami, Studia Ekonomiczne. Zeszyty Naukowe Uniwersytetu Ekonomicznego w Katowicach, No. 345, 114–126.

Sobańska, I. (2003), Wpływ MSR na integracje rachunkowości: Rachunkowość finansowa i rachunkowość zarządcza, Zeszyty Teoretyczne Rachunkowości, Vol. 13, No. 69, 247–255.

Sobczyk, M. (2013), Podstawy teoretyczne koncepcji zintegrowanego raportowania, Studia i Prace Kolegium Zarządzania i Finansów, Zeszyt Naukowy 130, Szkoła Główna Handlowa, 155–167.

Sobczyk, M. (2016), W poszukiwaniu wpływu dokonań CSR na wyniki finansowe (Searching the impact of corporate social performance on corporate financial performance), Prace Naukowe Uniwersytetu Ekonomicznego we Wrocławiu, No. 436, 261–269.

Sobczyk, M. (2017), Zakres pojęciowy terminu „informacja niefinansowa" jako źródło zróżnicowania ujawnień niefinansowych przedsiębiorstw, Finanse, Rynki Finansowe, Ubezpieczenia No. 4 (88) cz. 1 Rachunkowość w zarządzaniu jednostkami gospodarczymi, 395–401.

Steyn, M. (2014), Organisational benefits and implementation challenges of mandatory integrated reporting: Perspectives of senior executives at South African listed companies, Sustainability Accounting, Management and Policy Journal, Vol. 5, No. 4, 476–503.

Stubbs, W., Higgins, C. (2014), Integrated reporting and internal mechanisms of change, Accounting, Auditing and Accountability Journal, Vol. 27, No. 7, 1068–1089.

Suchman, M. C. (1995), Managing legitimacy: Strategic and institutional approaches, The Academy of Management Review, Vol. 20, No. 3, 571–610.

Świderska, G. K. (ed.) (2010), Controlling Kosztów i Rachunkowość Zarządcza, Difin, MAC Consulting.

Świderska, G. K., Bek-Gaik, B. (2016), Dokąd zmierza raportowanie biznesowe?, Studia Ekonomiczne No. 274, Zeszyty Naukowe Uniwersytetu Ekonomicznego w Katowicach, No. 274, 7–16.

Szadziewska, A. (2013), Rola rachunkowości w pomiarze efektywności działań CSR, Zrządzanie i Finanse, Vol. 4, No. 4, 257–277.

Szadziewska, A., Spigarska, E., Majerowska, E (2018), The disclosure of non-financial information by stock-exchange-listed companies in Poland, in the light of the changes introduced by the directive 2014/95/EU, Zeszyty Teoretyczne Rachunkowości, Vol. 99, No. 155, 65–95.

Tangen, S. (2004), Performance measurement: From philosophy to practice, International Journal of Productivity and Performance Management, Vol. 53, No. 8, 26–737.

Tang, Z., Hull, C.E., Rothenber, S. (2012), How corporate social responsibility engagement strategy moderates the CSR - financial performance relationship, Journal of Management Studies, Vol. 49, No. 7, 1274–1303.

Teixeira, A. (2004), Management commentary, Chartered Accounts Journal of New Zealand, Vol. 83, No. 6, 17–20.

Thomson, I. (2015), 'But does sustainability need capitalism or an integrated report' a commentary on 'The international integrated reporting council: A story of Failure' by flower, J, Critical Perspectives on Accounting, Vol. 27, No. March, 18–22.

Thomson Reuters, ASSET4 (2013), https://www.thomsonreuters.com/content/dam/openweb/documents/pdf/tr-com-financial/methodology/corporate-responsibility-ratings.pdf

Tweedie, D., Martinov-Bennie, N. (2015), Entitlements and time: Integrated reporting's double-edged agenda, Social and Environmental Accountability Journal, Vol. 35, No. 1, 49–61.

Urbaniec, M. (2015), Raportowanie CSR jako narzędzie doskonalenia działalności biznesowej, Prace Naukowe Uniwersytetu Ekonomicznego we Wrocławiu, No 378, 228–242.

Uyar, A., Kilic, M. (2012), Influence of corporate attributes on forward-looking information disclosure in publicly traded Turkish corporations, Procedia – Social and Behavioral Sciences, Vol. 62, 244–252.

van Bommel, K. (2014), Towards a legitimate compromise? Accounting, Auditing and Accountability Journal, Vol. 27, No. 7, 1157–1189.

Vance, S. C. (1975), Are socially responsible corporations good investment risks? Management Review, Vol. 64, No. 8, 18–24.

Velte, P., Stawinoga, M. (2016), Integrated reporting: The current state of empirical research, limitations and future research implications, Journal of Management Control, Vol. 28, No. 3, 275–320.

Veltri, S., Silvestri, A. (2015), The free state university integrated reporting: A critical consideration, Journal of Intellectual Capital, Vol. 16, No. 2, 443–462.

Vergauwen, P., Bollen, L., Oirbans, E. (2007), Intellectual capital disclosure and intangible value drivers: An empirical study, Management Decision, Vol. 45, No. 7, 1163–1180.

Vesty, G. M., Ren, C., Ji, S. (2018), Integrated reporting as a test of worth: A conversation with the chairman of an integrated reporting pilot organisation, Accounting, Auditing and Accountability Journal, Vol. 31, No. 5, 1406–1434.

Waddock, S. A., Graves, S. B. (1997), The corporate social performance - financial performance link, Strategic Management Journal, Vol. 18, No. 4, 303–319.

Walińska, E. (2012), Wynik całościowy w sprawozdaniu finansowym: jak go zrozumieć? Przegląd Organizacji, No. 12, 38–42.

Walińska, E. (2014), Doskonalenie sprawozdania finansowego jako narzędzia efektywnego nadzoru korporacyjnego, Studia Prawno-Ekonomiczne, Vol. 93, 351–365.

Walińska, E. (2015), Zintegrowany raport – Początek końca sprawozdania finansowego? Zeszyty Teoretyczne Rachunkowości, Vol. 82, No. 138, 151–165.

Walińska, E., Bek-Gaik, B., Gad, J., Rymkiewicz, B. (2015), Sprawozdawczość Przedsiębiorstwa Jako Narzędzie Komunikacji z Otoczeniem. Wymiar Finansowy i Niefinansowy, Wydawnictwo Uniwersytetu Łódzkiego, Łódź.

Walińska, E., Bek-Gaik, B., Gad, J. (2016), Sprawozdawczość finansowa i niefinansowa przedsiębiorstwa – w kierunku integracji, Wydawnictwo UŁ Łódź.

Walińska, E., Bek-Gaik, B., Gad, J. (2018), Informacje finansowe i niefinansowe w raporcie zintegrowanym – Praktyka spółek notowanych na giełdzie papierów wartościowych w warszawie, Zeszyty Teoretyczne Rachunkowości, Vol. 100, No. 156, 167–189.

Walińska, E., Gad, J. (2017), Kluczowe narzędzia raportowania korporacyjnego w praktyce polskiego rynku kapitałowego – Analiza przypadku, Zeszyty Teoretyczne Rachunkowości, Vol. 92, No. 148, 207–226.

Wang, H., Lu, W., Ye, M., Chau, K. W., Zhang, X. (2016), The curvilinear relationship between corporate social performance and corporate financial performance: Evidence from the international construction industry, Journal of Cleaner Production, Vol. 137, 1313–1322.

Waśniewski, P. (2015), Pomiar dokonań w małych i średnich przedsiębiorstwach w Polsce, Prace Naukowe Uniwersytetu Ekonomicznego we Wrocławiu, No. 389, 316–328.

Waśniewski, P. (2016), Kluczowe czynniki sukcesu jako podstawa pomiaru dokonań, Finanse, Rynki Finansowe, Ubezpieczenia, Vol. 2, No. 80, 163–176.

Wen, L. P., Kiew Heong, A. Y., Chee Hooi, S. L. (2017), Integrated reporting and financial performance: Evidence from Malaysia, Management and Accounting Review, Vol. 16, No. 2, 101–130.

Wettstein, T., Kueng, P. (2002), A maturity model for performance measurement systems, WIT Transactions on Information and Communication Technologies, Vol. 26, 113–122.

White, A. L. (1999), Sustainability and the accountable corporation, Environment, Vol. 41, No. 8 (October), 31–42.

White, A.L. (2005), New Wine, New Bottles: The Rise of Non-Financial Reporting, A Business Brief for Business for Social Responsibility by Allen L. White, http://www.globalreporting.org (15.10.2012).

WICI (2016), WICI Intangibles Reporting Framework Version 1.0 Consultation Draft, the World Intellectual Capital/Assets Initiative, https://www.wici-global.com/wirf/WICI_Intangibles_Reporting_Framework_v1.0.pdf

Wyatt, A. (2008), What financial and non-financial information on intangibles is value-relevant? A review of evidence, Accounting and Business Research, Vol. 38, No. 3, 217–256.

Yousef, E.A.M. 2020, The Association between Auditor Type and the Extent of Forward-Looking Disclosuresالعدد الثالث الجزء الثانى, Vol. 11, 872–904.

Żak, K. (2006), Nowe koncepcje systemu pomiaru dokonań przedsiębiorstwa, Studia Ekonomiczne Akademii Ekonomicznej w Katowicach, No. 37 Zarządzanie strategiczne w przedsiębiorstwie.

Zhou, S., Simnett, R., Green, W. (2017), Does integrated reporting matter to the capital market? Abucus, Vol. 53, No. 1, 94–132.

Zhou, S., Simnett, R., Hoang, H. (2019), Evaluating combined assurance as a new credibility enhancement technique-, Auditing: A Journal of Practice and Theory, Vol. 38, No. 2, 235–259.

Zyznarska-Dworczak, B. (2015), Wiarygodność raportowania zintegrowanego w świetle strategiczno-informacyjnego paradygmatu rachunkowości, Studia Oeconomica Posnaniensia, Vol. 3, No. 1, 191–204.

Index

Note: Page numbers in *italics* and **bold** refer to figures and bold, respectively.

FSC
www.fsc.org
MIX
Papier | Fördert gute Waldnutzung
FSC® C083411

Kolibri 360 GmbH
Ferdinand-Jühlke-Straße 7
99095 Erfurt, Deutschland
produktsicherheit@kolibri360.de